David's wc … seriously. It's time to "wake up, s … aight paths for our feet: "Therefore, … veak knees. 'Make level paths for y … t be disabled, but rather healed" … ately assessed where the church is today and where it will end up in most cases in the future—unless we as Christians begin to take seriously the call of God to be about our Father's business until he returns.

Jim Putman, Pastor and Author, *Real-Life Discipleship*

In this eye-opening book, *Resilient*, David Young articulates the spiritual battle that every Christ-following believer faces, and then constructs a very biblical, Christ-honoring response to that aggression. In exposing the reality Paul described in Ephesians 4:14–15, Young gives us practical help for living victoriously in our modern Babylon. It's a great read!

Jerry Harris, Teaching Pastor, The Crossings;
Publisher, *The Christian Standard*

In this fantastic book, David Young has given us a much-needed wake-up call warning us of the consequences of the secular progressive agenda in the United States. He powerfully illustrates the challenge with scriptures, history, science, facts, and stories. Even more importantly, he uses the Word of God to give us *very practical* instruction on how to respond with conviction, love, and wisdom as we fight this spiritual battle in the Jesus way.

Reese Neyland, Associate Director of Learning
Communities, Renew.org

In *Resilient,* David Young provides a clarion call to the church in America to stand firm in the face of growing hostility and opposition. Calls such as this sometimes offer a lot of heat, but very little light, appealing to emotion, fear, and nostalgia without much substance. Not so with this book. While engaging and extremely readable, it's also substantial. Loaded with both contemporary and historical examples, it clearly exposes the threats to Christians in North America and provides sound advice for standing firm as the people of God. Every pastor, every parent, and indeed every Christian, should read this book and take it to heart.

John Whittaker, DMin, Bible Teacher and
Creator of *The Listener's Commentary*

If you're a Bible-believing, God-fearing, Jesus-loving person who senses something horrific happening in our country but are nonetheless apprehensive about alarmist rhetoric and doomsday cynicism, David Young's *Resilient: Standing Firm in a Hostile World* is a breath of fresh air. It doesn't just document the crisis at hand with real-world specificity but it also: helps you cut through the cloud of confusion to diagnose the root problem; inspires you with a constant flow of gripping, true stories; and equips you with practical strategies to stand firm in this rising hostility—and to do so with a heart that is engulfed with love for King Jesus and his mission.

Jeff Duerler, Senior Pastor, Lifespring Community Church

David Young's latest book is a MUST read for every parent, grandparent, elder, preacher . . . every disciple of King Jesus. *Resilient* is written "to equip the flock of God to stand firm regardless of the cost" and "remind yourself that you follow a Savior who will not be defeated." David equipped me and encouraged me!

Rowlie Hutton, VP and Relationship Manager,
The Solomon Foundation

Resilient alerts us to the real adversary behind the threats that are increasingly surrounding us in North America. This book provides well-thought-out and tested practical advice on how to use the winning strategy that has been set in place by our Creator.

Tim Cook, Lead Planter 419 Ministries Canada;
Atlantic Canadian Regional Director, Renew.org

DAVID YOUNG

RESILIENT

Standing Firm in a Hostile World

A renew.org resource

RENEW.org

All emphases in Scripture quotations and other quotations are the author's.

ISBN (paperback) 978-1-959467-05-2
ISBN (Kindle) 978-1-959467-06-9
ISBN (ePub) 978-1-959467-07-6

Cover and interior design: Bryana Anderle at YouPublish (youpublish.com)

To Jeff and Susan

CONTENTS

FOREWORD

"I didn't know you were a far-right conspiracy theorist, John!" I had never been accused of this before, so I probed a little to understand where this woman was coming from. The year was 2020, and I had been asked to speak at a church about how swiftly the culture was changing. So what was the "conspiracy theory" I was peddling? I said that there is a cultural revolution against Western civilization, historic Christianity, and biological reality itself. For this revolution to take hold, secular progressives must indoctrinate our kids as early as possible, and part of this strategy is to teach children that being a boy or a girl is based on our subjective sense of self, not on objective reality.

A year and a half later, after schools opened up, this woman's eight-year-old came home from school with materials including the gender unicorn, which is a resource that teaches kids that gender is fluid and that sex is "assigned at birth." Parents all across the country are realizing that this is not a right-wing conspiracy theory—in fact, it's a progressive conspiracy to overthrow objective reality.

Yet many other Christians still seem to think that things aren't really all that different from how they have always been. Christ promised us that the world would hate us, so what's the big deal, right? Others conclude that the Western world is just going through a phase (like going goth in the 90s or growing a mullet in the 80s).

I believe that we are in the midst of a world-historical shift in the way humans view truth and reality. If you think that the current chaos is merely "business as usual," that will be dispelled within a few pages of this book.

David Young expertly lays out the state of things without alarmism or sensationalism. I agree with him that this is not foundationally a political battle, but a spiritual battle. As I write in my upcoming book, *Wimpy, Weak, and Woke*: "We are witnessing a war between gods. It's a winner-takes-all battle between the Living God and the false god of Man."[1] Progressivism pretends to promote tolerance and freedom, but it is surprisingly intolerant and anti-individual liberties for those who will not conform to its agenda. This philosophy aims to bring humanity into its own definitions of reality and perfection, starting by destroying the concept of God's created order. If Man is to become God, then he must kill the reflection of Christ on the earth. And where better to start than with what God said was "good"—namely, creational norms.

It has been difficult to find a book that presents us with practical answers for everyday people. Is it loving or unloving to use someone's preferred pronouns, or to attend a same-sex wedding? Should I refuse to work for a company that advocates for abortion? This is just to name a few dilemmas Christians face. Most Christians sincerely want to know how to please the Lord in these scenarios, but sadly, many pastors shy away from these incendiary topics. In contrast, Young has given us clear and bold answers to difficult questions such as these.

Importantly, this book is meant to spark conversations in small groups and discipling relationships. We need to be in relationship with each other as we wrestle with these dilemmas. Part of the reason we have been blindsided by progressivism is that many of us have not yet been forced to consider what Christ would have us do in order to live an uncompromising life that glorifies God in the face of hostility. You may not agree with all of Young's prescriptions. That's okay! I too have my caveats and nuances that need to be discussed within a trusted group of Jesus followers. But as we move forward together, let's agree to never compromise the Word of God—no matter what the culture demands, no matter the threat of losing our cred, our livelihoods, or even our freedom. And let us recognize that while we may be losing cultural applause, we have been given true *power* through the gift of the Holy Spirit (Acts 1:8): power to stand against the tide, power to say "no" to sin, power to love those who attack us, power to overcome the world. We are far from destitute. In fact, we have everything that we need to be resilient.

> "Be on your guard; stand firm in the faith; be courageous; be strong." (1 Corinthians 16:13)

— John L. Cooper, frontman of Skillet; author of *Awake and Alive to Truth*; host of *Cooper Stuff Podcast*

INTRODUCTION

Six months ago, the mother of one of the teens in my church sent me an email describing the difficulties her daughter faces in her public high school—even here in the conservative South. I'll paraphrase her comments:

> *Various organizations and online groups at our high school aggressively promote an LGBTQ agenda, and when my daughter has said "no" to these groups, she was labeled a hater and a bigot by many. She has even lost several friends over her views. All over the halls of her school are fliers and bulletins promoting LGBTQ propaganda; her friends pressure her to attend pride marches and parties; and some of her teachers talk frequently about their LGBTQ "heroes." One of her teachers has undergone a gender transition from male to female and insists that the students now call the teacher "Ms." Female school trips must accommodate males who identify as females, including rooming assignments for overnight trips. One of her friends started an online pro-life club, and she was viciously attacked online and in the halls for her position. The Christian Bible is frowned on, and at least once, a group was not allowed to post a Bible verse on a poster promoting an event at school. A teacher is not allowed to offer a Christian solution to various issues that students face, and students who are Christians face unending intimidation and marginalization.*

"How can my teenage daughter navigate such tremendous pressure and remain faithful to Jesus?" the mother asked me.

> Our world has become hostile to many of our Christian convictions.

That's why I am writing this book.

This book is written for the millions of Christians in North America who have suddenly discovered that our world has become hostile to many of our Christian convictions. This book is written for:

- Employees who are being pressured into supporting organizations that work against their values
- Christians whose churches or pastors appear to be drifting away from the gospel into progressive Christianity
- Parents and grandparents whose children or grandchildren are being indoctrinated by the culture with damaging sexual and gender ideologies
- Social media users who must avoid saying what they believe—or even simple facts—to avoid being scolded, censored, suspended, or canceled
- Persons who are criticized for embracing traditional values such as patriotism, rule of law, economic freedom, fairness, justice, and truth
- Supporters of pro-life positions who find themselves despised and maligned by those in the highest offices of the land
- Employees whose human resources departments seek to compel them to use certain forms of speech, such as the wrong pronouns
- Professionals whose licensing boards seek to compel them into adopting compromising beliefs
- Female athletes who must compete against males due to new rules within progressive athletic associations or misapplied Title IX regulations

- Christians who know they're being endlessly ridiculed, mocked, and condemned by Hollywood, many universities, the news media, and Washington elites
- Teenage Christians who feel alone in their Christian faith at school
- Crisis pregnancy centers and their workers whose organizations are vandalized by pro-abortion activists
- Christians whose family members are bullying them for not accommodating pagan values
- Leaders at Christian non-profits, Christian schools, and Christian ministries who suddenly find themselves facing hostile state regulations if they do not accommodate pagan values
- Christians who hesitate to post Bible verses on their social media for fear it may cost them a promotion at work or even their job itself
- Pastors, elders, and church leaders who feel they are fighting a tsunami of challenges and compromises among their members, and who are unclear about what to do
- The everyday Christian who knows that something has changed and knows it's not good

Many of you will welcome the strategies spelled out in this book, for you already know that you are facing the hostility of an aggressively non-Christian culture. You know that the world has changed. You know that, going forward, it will cost more to be a Christian in the US than it ever has.

YOU NEED THE STRATEGIES IN THIS BOOK

I've found a hunger among many Christians for this material. As I have spoken and written on this subject off and on for several years, I have noticed that though many hope my assessments are inaccurate, most know in their gut that something is wrong in America. I recently spoke about this topic in several sessions at a conference in Orlando. I noticed that throughout the event, the crowds at each of my sessions were growing larger and larger; some presentations were even standing room only. After the conference, many church leaders told me they were glad someone was finally speaking to the concerns so many Christians had.

I came home from that conference and did a series of sermons on the material. After the sermon series, people from all over the country who had listened to or watched the series online contacted me. A news program in Nashville even did a thirty-minute broadcast discussing my sermon series. Most of the feedback was encouraging. Many asked me to be put this material in a book, and one person even offered to pay for the editing costs to write it.

But I must be honest. Others, I mean other Christians, did not welcome the material. I have been surprised at the pushback I've experienced over this material these past couple of years. Shock. Denial. Equivocation. Even anger. Some are simply not tuned in to the hostility that Christians in North America are already facing, and so they just can't wrap their minds around this material. Others nostalgically believe that we are experiencing only a temporary insanity in America, and that our Constitution's First Amendment and our Christian heritage will protect us from genuine persecution. And some Christians have already switched sides in their hearts, embracing the tenets of progressivism, embarrassed by biblical Christianity, and only wearing the outer garbs of the faith.[2]

Appreciating the arguments of this book will be especially difficult for younger Christians because younger Americans do not have the advantage of seeing just how far the US has fallen away from a common, though unevenly practiced, Christian consensus. So younger Americans tend to be unaware of how much a Christian heritage has shaped the values we still hold dear in America—and how cutting off those roots will end in disaster for all Americans, not just for Christians.

Further, younger Americans have not been taught to value freedom—religious freedom, freedom of speech, free markets, free and rational thought, and the like. So many gravitate toward authoritarianism—seeking to curtail speech they don't like, canceling those with whom they disagree, railing against free markets and capitalism, bullying Christian non-profits and businesses into giving up our freedoms for the sake of secular ideology, and the like.

These younger Americans do not have the historical insight to understand where cultures that limit freedom of speech, religion, and association end up—the purges of Stalin, the National Socialists of Germany, Mao's forced starvation of millions of Chinese, the killing fields of Cambodia, the Stasi of East Germany, and others under callous and violent dictators. Instead, many young people today are beguiled by posters depicting Cuba's murderous Che striking a cool pose, promises of free stuff by socialist politicians, and the hope of a utopia efficiently managed by millions of bureaucrats on behalf of powerful overlords. Where "authoritarianism" once referred to large governments that brutally dictate every area of the individual's life, today in the hands of progressives, the term has been turned on its head to refer to limited governments that allow individuals the freedom to determine their own beliefs and their own lives. Many basic freedoms are now seen as vices for numerous Americans, while domineering and restrictive government is increasingly seen as a virtue. Younger Americans are on the precipice of massive cultural suicide but have no way to know it.

If you are a Gen Xer, a millennial, or a member of Gen Z, I encourage you to read about the authoritarian regimes I describe in the paragraph above—as well as about North Korea, Venezuela, and Communist Romania. And as you read, remember they all have one thing in common: each regime sought to control others to create heaven on earth, and the people they led (and lead today) ended up in earthly hell.

BUT WHY LISTEN TO ME?

You may have read this far and thought, *David's been watching too many conservative news channels!* Allow me to respond:

- I am no fan of sensationalism or of one-sided political pundits.
- I rarely listen to or watch public opinion programs—whether conservative or progressive.
- I oppose the reaction of many to politically militarize our faith to "take back America" for Jesus.
- I don't put my trust (nor do I recommend that you put your trust) in political solutions.
- I am just as concerned that we Christians don't overreact to these threats and become the worst version of ourselves as I am that we are being threatened by progressivism.
- I learned progressivism not from conservatives but from progressives.

My last two college degrees were from Vanderbilt University back in the 1990s. At that time, Vanderbilt was one of the most liberal universities in the world. Though a Bible-believing Christian myself, I heard the extreme, angry, manic, and even violent positions my liberal colleagues there held. I was shocked to see the rage of liberalism but was relieved to think that it was only the posture of a handful of restless graduate students and faculty members.

But since then, I've seen these positions go mainstream. Millions of ordinary Americans have become "liberals"—though now I think a better term would be "secular progressive" or simply "progressive." And I've seen the trajectory of progressivism. It is dark, angry, destructive, and, above all, totalitarian. It seeks to control everything—*everything*—and it won't stop until it conquers all competing belief systems, especially Bible-believing Christianity. The enemies of Christianity in America have

I've seen the trajectory of progressivism.

you in their crosshairs. And now that they control so many American institutions, you can bet that they are not about to back down. This is true even if you don't know it's true; if you don't want it to be true; or even if you've decided that Christians deserve the hostility we face.

I would say that my time at Vanderbilt began to prepare me to write this book. I confess I'm no expert in Western philosophy or history; in law or politics; in Darwin, Freud, or Marx; in post-modern thought; or in the inner workings of the progressive mind. I am just a Christian minister, though I've been at it for more than forty years.

But at Vanderbilt, I saw how progressivism produced anger, cynicism, a desire to tear down, and a willingness to force others to accept its claims or be punished. I was there when New Testament students (I was one of them) were warned not to refer to God as "he," even though the New Testament routinely does so. I was there when people were shunned for not saying the right things about sex and gender. I heard the demands of many faculty and students to boycott the movie *Red Dawn* because it presented a negative view of Marxism. I was there when many considered Lenin a hero and when the crimes of the Khmer Rouge were downplayed. It all seems so quaint now in comparison to the rage we see today. But in every case, it became obvious that progressivism would not be satisfied with any particular victory. Instead, progressivism is hell-bent on total conquest. The demands were *never* going to stop, and the beast was never going to be sated. Based on my time at Vanderbilt, I've seen where this movement is going today—and it doesn't end well.

I write as a Christian minister who lived among radical progressives. I write as a Christian minister who wants to equip the flock of God to stand firm regardless of the cost. I write as a believer in Jesus who is determined to stand firm, no matter what the world around me does. And I write as a Christian minister who has heard numerous examples of my own people being harassed, bullied, and censored by radical progressives. To take their stand and hold it, they need to be equipped.

Believe me, I've seen the hostility within my own circles. For example, one minister friend had a page removed from Facebook. His offense? He had celebrated with a woman who decided that being female—as God had created her—was a good thing. Another believer who works for a pharmacist was told he must fill prescriptions for abortion pills that terminate a pregnancy. If not, he would lose his job. In another instance, an insurance company told a church that it would probably not be able to provide liability insurance because the church's biblical views on gender would invite litigation. Another employer told an employee to support the pending Equality Act or be fired. The Equality Act expressly states that the Religious Freedom Restoration Act cannot protect Christians against heavy-handed sexual orientation and gender identity laws. When I was prepping for a speaking gig near Toronto, the host church advised me to be very careful in what I say about sexual sin because the Canadian government could punish the church if I were to say the wrong thing—even in a church!

What about the high school valedictorian told by the school administration to talk about anything except Jesus? Or the church near me that was booted off YouTube with no explanation given? Or the fourth grader who came home with an assignment to write a celebration card for a girl in her class who is transitioning to a boy—or receive a failing grade. Or the counselor who told me that the American Psychological Association's ethical guidelines now prevent even a Christian counselor from teaching what the Bible says about sex and gender. Or the ministry friend in Canada who ministers to Christians struggling with same-sex attraction in a nation that has now made it a crime to discourage homosexuality. What do they, and the thousands of others like them, do when confronted with this hostility to their faith? What do *you* do?

The issues in this book *will* demand your attention, even if you prefer they don't. Whether or not you wanted a war with progressivism, you have one, because progressivism has declared war on *you*. And because it stems from a spirit of godlessness, progressivism has no limits. Until Jesus returns, it will never be satisfied, it will never reach the bottom, it will never return to its senses, and it will never stop and say, "This is far enough." What began with "We shouldn't discriminate against persons who are same-sex attracted" is now at the stage of "Every school should have a drag queen." And this is just the beginning of the death spiral. It will get much, much worse.

So in this book, I hope to describe the nature of the hostility we Christians face in the West, especially in the United States. And then I want to articulate a battle plan for standing firm in the face of secular hostility.

IS THERE CHRISTIAN PERSECUTION IN AMERICA?

Before going any further, let me address a question you may have: Can we really say that Christians in America are being persecuted? Isn't persecution too big a word to describe the harassment that American Christians face? After all, aren't many American Christians flourishing, wealthy, employed in well-paying jobs, holding offices, publishing books, teaching at universities, and actively involved in government, business, and the community?

You'll need to decide for yourself if persecution is the right word. But it's important to acknowledge that persecution is an uneven thing. This has been true throughout Christian history. While any given regime may persecute the church, it may also allow individual Christians to flourish. In the second century AD, there were Christians in virtually every domain, even during times of persecution. Where Islamic nations have widely practiced *dhimmitude* (the deliberate suppression of Christians), these same nations have frequently had, at the very same time, Christians in prominent positions. When socialist Cuba was closing down churches and throwing Christians in prison, the country also had Christians serving in several of the nation's highest offices. Several high-ranking military officers in the Chinese army are evangelical Christians, despite the regime's increasing pressure and crackdown on Christian churches in many of the country's various provinces.

Before we explore how Christians in America are being mistreated, let's remind ourselves that Christians all over the globe face even more dire circumstances than we do. Based on research for Open Doors International's 2022 World Watch List ranking the fifty most dangerous countries for Christians, we know that persecution around the world is severe today:

- An average of thirteen Christians are murdered every single day because of their faith.
- One of every eight Christians faces high levels of persecution.
- Nearly four hundred Christians are martyred every month.
- 1,710 Christians are abducted every month.
- 4,448 churches are besieged every month.
- 4,277 Christians are detained or imprisoned without trial.
- In 2021, 4,761 Christians were murdered.
- That same year, 4,448 churches were attacked.[3]

We have not faced these levels of persecution as Christians in the US, though things are beginning to change. For decades, if not centuries, Christians in America enjoyed a de facto majority status. But we are quickly becoming a minority in America, and majority cultures frequently harass minorities. As progressivism assumes the majority role in America, we are beginning to find ourselves mistreated even here in America.

Though I am hesitant to use the word "persecution" when describing the hostility we Christians in North America face today, I do believe that what some have faced can rightly be called persecution. After all, the term "persecution" simply refers to mistreatment or hostility toward someone, especially for their beliefs. Christians across America are indeed facing both mistreatment and hostility. And with each passing day, the hostility grows. All signs indicate it will get worse. I could be wrong about what I think is on the horizon for the West, but I'm trying to be clear-minded and helpful, as I base what I've written on what has, in fact, *already happened.* If you're less inclined to see a storm of progressivism on the horizon, please stick with me because the principles we'll go through in this book will be relevant for you as you learn how to be a resilient follower of Jesus in a broken world—whatever forms the storms might take.

TAKE UP YOUR CROSS

Let's remind ourselves that as Christians, we were never promised an easy life. The apostle Paul warns of the exact opposite: "Everyone who wants to live a godly life in Christ Jesus will be persecuted, while evildoers and impostors will go from bad to worse, deceiving and being deceived" (2 Timothy 3:12–13). And Jesus says that following him will necessarily involve taking up a cross (Matthew 16:24). Many American Christians have had something of a vacation from hardship for the last two hundred-plus years. But that vacation is ending. We are no longer the home team in America. An aggressive progressivism has not only taken root but has also grown tall and bold, and it has targeted you and your family (present and future) because you follow Jesus.

We were never promised an easy life.

If you are a North American Christian, you have likely never had to learn how to stand in a hostile environment. But that's changing. You will need to make difficult choices, and you will get hurt. In a sense, though, this is good news. Without resistance, we grow flabby and weak. Aggressive progressivism—which is just another form of paganism—is bad for the US, but it will strengthen many Christians. You will become stronger. You will be blessed through your hardships. So pick up the mantle that Christians have worn for centuries.

And as we begin, remind yourself that you follow a Savior who will not be defeated. In spite of how things may appear, he alone is King of kings and Lord of lords. He will win, and he will reign.

We are not going to lose this battle because we follow a triumphant King. Because he is victorious, we are invincible.

Here's how to stand.

GOING THROUGH THIS BOOK AS A GROUP

The teachings found in this book are going to be helpful, but many of the topics are not commonly talked about in churches or between believers today. We believe that God wants us to help each other to be faithful disciples of Jesus, and we need to help each other process the issues presented. So we recommend that you consider joining together in a small group with other Christians to discuss and apply what will be taught.

Here are some helpful guidelines and a brief small group format agreement that may help you as you meet with other Christians or friends to go through this material. If you plan to use this book in a group, please do not skip this first step of getting a shared agreement on how you will function as a group. This agreement is a vital first step in forming a group that will provide you with a good experience as you seek to be faithful disciples of Jesus. We recommend that you print a copy or design your own version to be signed by each participant.

RECOMMENDED GROUP INTERACTION GUIDELINES

Confidentiality – Keeping personal information that is shared in the group confidential builds trust and shows value to the person.

Confidentiality can prevent gossip that values the story over the person; Jesus always valued the person above their story or their sin.

Don't Rescue and Don't Fix – When someone is sharing something deeply personal and/or painful, there can be a tendency to immediately jump in to try to make them feel better about themselves or the situation. Often, however, this compulsion to rescue will actually cause people to stop sharing and result in their not going as deep as they might have gone. Resist the temptation to rescue people with quick advice. Try to really listen to what people are sharing without trying to fix them. If they want your advice, they will ask for it. If it's appropriate, you may want to take time later to ask if you may offer some advice.

No Crosstalk – Be considerate of others as they are sharing. Don't have side conversations. Trust is built in the moments when everyone feels like they are being listened to and heard by the entire group. Treat others in the group as you would want to be treated.

Use Humor Responsibly – Fun is an essential part of small groups; however, when meeting in small group time, keep sarcastic comments, jokes, and laughter to a minimum to allow for an atmosphere of authenticity and vulnerability.

Give Everyone a Chance to Share – Be sensitive to the amount of time you share. Encourage everyone to participate in group discussions.

Use "I" Statements – We want to hear your personal thoughts and perspectives. Using "I" statements to answer discussion questions allows you to speak for yourself rather than generalizing by using terms such as "them," "the church," "us," or "we."

Fight for Relationship – Relationship reaches a whole new level when conflict is resolved in a healthy manner. When conflict or sin issues arise between group members, commit to fight for the relationship and discuss the struggle with the person you are in conflict with. It can also be a good idea to seek wise advice on how to fight for the relationship.

THE SMALL GROUP COVENANT

We want to base the group on our shared commitment. We will seek to agree on the following:

1. It is my desire to engage in this group and seek to grow in my understanding of Jesus and what it means to be his disciple while facing the challenges of our culture.
2. To help us enter fully into this group process, we will seek to uphold the following:
    - We will meet together every ______________________________.
    - We will start on time and end on time.
    - We will each read the assigned chapter(s) before our meeting.
    - We will uphold the group interaction guidelines (described above).

3. I commit to attending every meeting/gathering, to be there on time, and to have my preparation work done. I understand and agree that I will have to say no to important things to meet this commitment, and I am willing to do so.

    We will contact ______________________________________ in advance if something unforeseen happens and we simply cannot attend.

4. I commit to total confidentiality. What is said in the group stays in the group. I will not share with others what is said confidentially in the group without permission (even with my spouse).
5. I further commit that after twelve to eighteen months, I will prayerfully consider helping to launch a new group so that I actively engage in Jesus' disciple making commandment. And *if I sense that God is leading me*—I will start a group like this one myself.

Group Member's Name

Leader's Name

1

RECOGNIZE THE ADVERSARY

"Why do the nations say, 'Where is their God?' Our God is in heaven; he does whatever pleases him." (Psalm 115:2–3)

I am not trying to articulate a political position in this book. I want to tell you that upfront because almost every controversial topic today is somehow political. This book is not about politics. Instead, this book is about being faithful disciples of Jesus.

If we allow ourselves to indulge in excessive political engagement, we will take our eyes off our primary mission, which is to become mature disciples who make other disciples. Politics are important, but to Christians, politics are always secondary to our mission of living as faithful Christians who seek to bring the whole world to Jesus. But the good news is that, if we focus on our mission to make disciples, we will find ourselves changing politics, as well, when the hearts of millions are changed by Christ.

So rather than indulging in political theory, let's explore how we Christians can survive the increasing hostility in the Western world. Let me start by telling you about one of my friends.

He works as a manager for a large corporation that regularly supports pro-gay events such as "Pride" parades. The pressure at the corporation is immense. The HR department sends out pro-gay material several times per week to employees, and even the private social media accounts of corporate employees are scrutinized by the corporation to ensure they do not say the wrong things about LGBTQ issues. Several months ago, the manager's boss hinted that this June, during Pride month, all management would be expected to support the corporation's sponsorship of a Pride parade. The employee was facing a tough choice.

"All I want to do is to make widgets," he shared.

I have another friend who sells real estate. A faithful Christian, she placed a simple and small logo of the Christian fish in the bottom corner of her business cards . . . until her broker told her to remove it. "You cannot put a Christian symbol on your card," he told her. She pressed the issue, and the conversation went on for a few minutes. "Look," he finally said, "you can promote whatever you want, except you cannot promote the Christian faith. If you do, you're opening us up to a fair-housing discrimination lawsuit. It's plain and simple. It's where we are today."

My church serves numerous people in our community and abroad. One of the ministers in my church sometimes works in a homeless shelter. Some time back, he served a homeless woman who had a host of issues, including confusion over her gender. My minister friend spoke to her about the beauty of being what God created her to be. After some time, she joyfully embraced her womanhood and thanked the minister. The minister posted a short celebration of the story on Facebook. The next day, the post had been removed by the social media giant. No comments from Facebook. Just a cancellation of the reference.

Cancellation, coercion, harassment, and hostility. They're coming to your front door. They're already standing there, with a sledgehammer in hand.

If we are to stand in a hostile age, it's important to know at least a little bit about who the adversaries actually are. Although the American church faces many destructive forces, it's worth taking a moment here to explore the influential adversary behind so much of the hostility Christians are facing. Let's talk a little about progressivism.

UNDERSTAND PROGRESSIVISM

Across America, Christians are feeling the winds of change starting to blow against us. We now have multiple instances anyone can see:

- Amidst the COVID-19 pandemic in 2020, California's governor shut down thousands of churches and banned those who did meet from singing or chanting. At the same time, he allowed strip clubs and Hollywood film studios to remain open, active, and loud. For months, he actively encouraged massive protests with thousands of people taking to the streets even as they routinely violated every safety measure the governor had forced upon churches.
- When the Texas non-profit organization Christians Engaged filed for 501(c)(3) status in 2019, it took eighteen months for the Internal Revenue Service to respond. When it did, the IRS rejected their non-profit status, saying, "Bible teachings are typically affiliated with the [Republican] party and candidates. This disqualified you from exemption under the IRC Section 501(c)(3)."
- The University of Iowa kicked InterVarsity Christian Fellowship off its campus in the summer of 2018 after twenty-five years of ministry. Why? The Christian group refused to allow people who disagree with their Christian principles to serve as its leaders. At the same time, hundreds of other student organizations were allowed to remain on campus although they also required their leaders to support their particular beliefs. Thankfully, the federal

court has since ruled that this as a clear example of "viewpoint discrimination," and the university had to reverse its decision.[4]

- Dozens of black-clad Antifa militants carrying shields and weapons descended on an outdoor church service in Portland, Oregon, on August 7, 2021. Antifa members sprayed Christians and their children with bear repellent, lobbed flash bombs into the crowd, and trashed their church equipment. In video recordings of the assault, one Antifa member is heard shouting, "Where is your God now?" Portland police looked on and reportedly did nothing.
- The daughter of a Christian family came out as a lesbian in 2019 at a Christian university. When the parents gently tried to teach her what the Bible says, members of their own family accused the parents of being haters and threatened to cut off relations with them unless they accepted their daughter's new sexual orientation.
- At least fifty-six churches in Canada, as of July 30, 2021, have either been vandalized or set on fire. The Canadian government has been slow to respond, and the executive director of the British Columbia Civil Liberties Association (the oldest civil liberties group in Canada) tweeted a word of encouragement to the arsonists: "Burn it all down."
- In August 2019, the federal Office of Civil Rights of the US Department of Health & Human Services found that the University of Vermont Medical Center had violated a nurse's civil rights by trying to force her to "assist in an elective abortion procedure over the nurse's conscience-based objections." According to the nurse's testimony, she was asked to assist in a medical procedure and was only told it was an abortion when she arrived in the surgical room. Federal law has, at least up until recently, prohibited medical centers from forcing employees to perform abortions against their religious beliefs.

- When one member of the church I pastor, the North Boulevard Church, started college in 2021, one of his professors announced that he is gay and married to a man. "If anyone has a problem with that," he announced, "you can leave my class."

From where is all this opposition coming? What do each of these examples have in common?

The answer is *secular progressivism*, or more simply, *progressivism*. Many of the major institutions of America, millions of Americans, and especially the nation's elites have abandoned America's historic Christian consensus and adopted, instead, the ideology of progressivism as a form of civic religion.

So what is progressivism, who are progressives, and why have so many declared war on Christianity?

Progressivism is the ideology currently filling the space left behind by the retreat of Christianity in the West. It may acknowledge God, but it does not order the world around him or the tenets of the Christian faith. Rather, progressivism derives from a broad set of roots that, in one way or another, undermine Christianity.

Progressivism derives from a broad set of roots that undermine Christianity.

- *From the European Enlightenment,* progressivism came to distrust religious authority and to emphasize the individual human.
- *From the ideology of evolutionist Charles Darwin,* progressivism came to believe that we humans are all we have; there is no metaphysical meaning to life. So the only good life is the one that takes what it can get in this world.
- *From Karl Marx,* progressivism learned to divide people into social groups and pit them against each other—the so-called

oppressors against the so-called oppressed—agitating for a revolution intended to create a social utopia here on earth.

- *From postmodernism,* progressivism came to believe that there is no ultimate truth; there is only power disguised as claims to truth.
- *From Freud and the sexual revolution,* it came to define the human in terms of our sexual desires.
- *And Christianity?* Believe it or not, progressivism would not have been possible without Christianity because progressivism borrowed Christianity's moral imperative to fight for its convictions and much of our language, as well as the conviction that our path is the way, the truth, and the life.

Progressivism assumes the role that a majority religion typically serves—the role of helping to unite the nation around a set of values, ethics, ambitions, meanings, and goals. Progressivism believes, as does Christianity, that it charts the climax of history. But progressivism is practically godless, as it makes certain classes of humans the locus of moral authority. In this way, humans become their own gods, with the same fervent jealousy as the one true God.

As a result, progressivism functions as a religion in America. It is not neutral. Instead, it fights for what it believes. It has priests and prophets, institutions and holy places, dogma and rules, angels and demons, ethics and morality, and an eschatology that ends in an expected utopia—somewhere at the end of progress. All other religions, especially Christianity, stand in its way. Progressivism is as religious as a belief system can be, possessing a Puritan's fervor for right and wrong, a Catholic's commitment to dogma, a Mormon's obligation to proselytize, an evangelical's certainty in its rightness, and a mystic's vision of utopia.

Of course, these are historical and philosophical definitions of progressivism. However, there is really a deeper explanation of this ideology, which we'll explore in chapter 3. For now, I want to point out that progressivism is the religion of what Scripture calls the Antichrist ("whoever denies that Jesus is the Christ," according to 1 John 2:22). It is the religion for those who do not want to submit to King Jesus, but instead want to enthrone themselves as king over their kingdom. It is a religion of the dragon described in Revelation 12–13—a religion of disbelief, false gods, and demons. I know these are harsh assessments, but this is how the Bible describes any system that sets itself up against the one true God. Every ideology that rejects Jesus as king has come from the evil one, and it is nothing less than a tool in his hands designed to deceive the world and to wreck God's good creation. And this makes progressivism the enemy of the Christian faith. This is also why it tends toward totalitarianism. This is why there can be no truce between the church and the committed progressives. We are in the fight of our lives. Progressives know this. You should too.

And so we must understand this opponent in today's America and prepare ourselves to support other believers to stand against it.

Understanding the religious fervor of progressivism is important to grasping the argument of this book. Some will read this book and say that, in a pluralistic society, we Christians should be okay with progressivism's different belief system. America is, after all, a land where one is free to believe whatever one chooses, or to believe nothing at all.

But my argument is not that progressivism is merely *different* from Christianity—though that would merit its own book. My argument is that the followers of progressivism are *attacking* Christianity: that they're openly *hostile* toward the Christian faith, and that they're determined to silence the Christian faith. I am not arguing that LGBTQ advocates have no right to *disagree* with Christianity. I am arguing that certain LGBTQ advocates seek to *shut down* Christians. We do not merely find ourselves disagreeing with our progressive neighbors and seeking to persuade each other. They have been conditioned to see themselves at war with us, and it is a war they are determined to win.

DISTINGUISH BETWEEN PROGRESSIVISM AND CHRISTIANITY

Let me briefly name four areas where progressivism is antagonistic toward the Christian faith so you can understand what's truly motivating progressivism's war against Christianity.

Progressivism and Christianity have incompatible views of human nature.

Christians believe that humans were created in the image of God (Genesis 1:26). This fundamental conviction leads Christians to measure every human endeavor in terms of its relation to God—our morals, ethics, worth, purpose, destiny—everything. Christians view human nature in light of eternity. Progressivism may speak of human dignity, but the term is more sentimental than meaningful. If we weren't specially created by God in his image, then we are essentially no different from the beasts of the field—no matter how much sentiment and passion progressives bring to the term *dignity*.

Progressivism relocates the authority to discern truth and morality from God to certain classes of humans. Because of this, progressives practically become their own gods, and they must search for their own meaning. This search inevitably leads progressives to believe that pleasure—as defined by individual desire—is the greatest good of life. Anything that gets in the way of individual pleasure, of being "who you think you are," must be defined as evil and oppressive and then demolished. And by teaching holiness and righteousness, Christianity in America stands in the way of unbridled desire.

Take the example of abortion. There is no question of when human life begins. It begins at conception. Literally every single first-year biology student knows this. Because Christians believe that every human life bears the image of God, we believe that unborn babies must be nurtured and protected. Committed progressives, however, believe the greatest good is this-worldly pleasure. So progressives measure unborn babies in terms of whether or not people want them—whether they will limit our pleasure. If a mother or father believes their lives will be burdened by carrying a baby to term and then giving birth, progressives believe the babies should be killed. Because Christians stand against this appalling violence, progressives must make war on Christians. Our irreconcilable views of human nature demand war.

Progressivism and Christianity have incompatible views of human destiny.

The French mathematician and philosopher Blaise Pascal once observed that "man is neither angel nor beast, and unhappily whoever wants to act the angel, acts the beast." The Christian faith gets this. We know that humans were created in the image of God, but that we are deeply flawed by sin. Thus, for Christians, human flourishing will never be accomplished by mere human effort. Because of our deep-seated sinfulness, even with God's help, the world will never achieve anything like lasting progress. We will always be subject to futility, injustice, war, disease, and failure. We have stained the image of God in ourselves, so we are not capable of perfection with the world as it is. Although we are to "set an example by doing what is good" (Titus 2:7), perfection must wait as we wait for God to resurrect all things good at the return of Jesus.

Progressivism, however, sees humans as perfectible, through social engineering, therapy, affirmation, self-discovery, politics, law, or other means—including force. Ironically, however, this unrealistic assessment of humanity produces manic results, as it runs into the unmovable wall of reality. Regardless of how hard the progressive tries, equity is not achieved. No matter how many genders are invented, nature still gives us only two. No matter how many policies are enacted, there is still poverty, decay, and misery among vast numbers of people. These failures fuel the rage that frequently characterizes the movement. And they lead to the authoritarian impulse screaming to get out of progressives: *If we just had more power, we could force the world to be a better place.* Utopian thinking is bound to fail in massive ways. Massive failure produces rage. And rage needs a target. People may find a way to live without God, but they cannot live without a devil. So anything that appears to stand in the way of progressivism must be devilish—including Christianity.

The slogan inscribed on the wall of one Soviet gulag presents the progressive's creed well: "With an iron hand we will drive humanity to happiness!"[5]

Progressivism and Christianity have incompatible views of power and truth.

Christians believe there are such things as objective beauty, goodness, and truth. These principles are engrained in the very character of God and would exist even if humans did not. The Bible uses the term "truth" more than a hundred times. The Christian worldview is built on the conviction that truth both exists and is, at least partially, accessible to humans. Though concepts of truth have often been misused, Christians have helped create a world of systems and institutions grounded in the belief that, as Jesus says, "the truth will set you free" (John 8:32).

In this system, power is only a tool to lead humanity to truth. Governments exist, Paul reminds us, only to reward good behavior and punish the bad (Romans 13:1–6). Good government uses its power objectively and fairly to lead people toward true, virtuous, and beautiful lives.

But in progressivism the existence of objective truth has come under attack and is being replaced by raw claims to power. A fundamental tenet of postmodernism is the conviction that claims to truth are mere assertions of power. Truth has no real existence, progressives claim. Thus, for the progressive, truth is only a fiction; claims to truth are only valuable insofar as they bring about power. To quote one secular textbook asserting that reality is situational, "Truths only exist for this person in this predicament at this time in history."[6] Another says,

"There are no right or wrong arguments, only narratives or stories that are more or less relevant to the search for meaning."[7] The authors of these books purposely assert self-contradictory truth-claims like these to undermine truth, replacing it with raw assertions of power.

The existence of objective truth has come under attack.

This view of power over truth explains some of the bizarre exercises of progressivism. It explains why, in winter of 2021, the Oregon Department of Education considered supplying its schools with a mathematics toolkit designed to remove what its authors believe is a racial bias in math—not just in how math is taught, but in the actual objectivity of math itself. The toolkit explains: "The concept of mathematics being purely objective is unequivocally false, and teaching it is even much less so. Upholding the idea that there are always right and wrong answers perpetuates (sic) objectivity as well as fear of open conflict." Because the Christian belief that truth exists—even in something so sure as mathematics—stands in the way of ideology, progressives increasingly believe that such objectivity is not only wrong—it is evil.[8] This view explains why a CNN report in 2021 stated that, "It's not possible to know a person's gender identity at birth, and there is no consensus criteria for assigning sex at birth."[9] It is possible that editors at CNN do not know that every single one of the 26,000,000,000,000 cells in the body of a female baby has XX chromosomes. It is also possible that these editors have never seen under the diaper of a newborn. Either way, the anti-science, anti-truth position that such progressives are forced to take to advance their ideology reveals their ideological commitment. Truth is in the way of ideology.

Because Christians believe there exists such a thing as objective truth and that only the truth can set humans free, we stand in the way of progressivism. Thus, we must be targeted. Progressivism denies the reality of truth—claiming that objective truth does not exist. Of course, such a claim is self-contradictory, for the statement itself claims to be true. I like what English philosopher Roger Scruton said: "A writer who says that there are no truths, or that all truth is 'merely relative,' is asking you not to believe him. So don't."

Progressivism and Christianity have incompatible views of justice and equality.

Grounded in Judeo-Christian ethical systems, classical American theories of justice and equal treatment under the law are among the most profound judicial theories humanity has ever seen. Christian ethical systems argue that the government has the obligation to care for the poor and marginalized (which the Bible refers to as "righteousness"), as well as the obligation to be unbiased in the application of the law (which the Bible refers to as "impartiality"). We are to be both *righteous*, favoring the disadvantaged in the laws we establish, and *impartial*, favoring nobody in the application of our law.

This simple principle—good laws applied impartially—has produced some of the loftiest social results in human history, despite many imperfections. In fact, in many ways the great achievements in politics and jurisprudence that the world has seen are the results of this Christian theory of justice. After all, it was under Christian principles that such institutions as freedom of religion, speech, and assembly, the right to due process, the right to equal protection under the law, the rights of the people over those of the state, the right to equal access to public goods, and the like, have all flourished. Christians were the ones who led in the establishment of the modern concept of human rights, of just war theory, of various abolitionist movements, of the women's suffrage movement, of the Civil Rights movement, and of a hundred other institutions that have produced a better world.

Conversely, progressivism is currently rewriting classical theories of justice and equality using a variety of theories and terms. Ideological labels—when used by progressives—such as critical theory, intersectionality, social justice, and equity (instead of equality) all seek to undermine Christian and classical Western theories of justice and equality because progressivism, justice, and equality are pliable tools to be used in achieving power for various grievance groups.

But by rejecting righteous laws applied impartially, progressivism is creating a world of injustice and inequality—with no chance of righting itself. The Marxist assumptions of progressivism divide people into identity groups, then pit them against each other in a hopeless war for justice and equity. And the number and exotic nature of these groups continues to expand: blacks, whites, Latinx, men, women, cis, gays, lesbians, transgender persons, gender queers, trans-feminines, femme queens, pangenders, agenders, androgynes, two-spirits—the list never seems to end.

This Marxist assumption that everyone belongs either to an oppressed class or an oppressor class results in several serious and unjust consequences. First, it is wrong to suggest that our primary identity is a group identity. Both Scripture and nature teach us that we are far more complicated than "white," "black," "female," "hetero," or whatever. To assign people to a class based solely on their skin color, their gender, or their desires is to imprison people in a caste system that keeps humanity perennially divided, that wrongly assigns guilt to mere skin color, that provides not a shred of grace, that offers little truth, and that puts forth virtually no hope.

Second, it places blame for the world's ills only on a handful of people—those it deems the "oppressors." When the wildly popular race theorist Robin DiAngelo asserts that "white identity is inherently racist; white people do not exist outside the system of white supremacy,"[10] she ignores black racism, Asian racism, Middle Eastern racism, and the racism of a thousand people groups throughout history. Racism is not a function of "whiteness"; it is a function of fallen humanity. A few examples:

- The Burmese harass the Rohingyas.
- The Iranians discriminate against the Balochi.

- The Turks practice institutionalized racism against the Armenians.
- The mestizos of Bolivia look down on the Quechua.
- Anti-Semitism is common in Chile.
- The Pakistani people look down on the people of Bangladesh.
- The Bantu people of Congo mistreat the pygmies.
- Amhara elites of Ethiopia discriminate against the Afars.
- Race-based slavery is still practiced in Mauritania and Niger.
- Saudis often practice "tribe against tribe" discrimination.
- Ethnic Somalis stigmatize the Somali Bantu people, and on and on the list goes.

Demonizing one race under the pretense of justice and equality creates more injustice and inequality and conveniently ignores the intense injustice that others perpetrate—such as the racial genocide the Chinese government is currently committing against the Uyghurs as I write this paragraph.

Further, to conceive of humanity in terms of class warfare is to reduce or even eliminate personal responsibility and sin. Where Dr. Martin Luther King Jr. fought for a form of justice in which people would be judged by the content of their character, progressives today argue that character is of little importance. What matters is your class identity and how many claims to victimhood your class can make. When progressive author Ibram Kendi states that "racial discrimination is the sole cause of racial disparities in this country and in the world at large,"[11] he ignores the complexities of life and traps people into inescapable classes of people. As writer Rod Dreher dryly notes, "A white Pentecostal man living on disability in a trailer park is an oppressor; a black lesbian Ivy League professor is oppressed."

Now I am not making the argument that black Americans do not suffer injustice because of their race. They do. I want to be on record that I believe racial slights and injustices—especially against blacks—are both real and deeply embedded in America. I believe that

America still has a long way to go in restoring injustices against black Americans. But I also want to say that the solution to injustice and inequality is not a different form of injustice and inequality. The solution is, to quote Dr. King again, "to end any form of racial injustice and inequality."

Because Christians believe that people's character matters, that justice and fairness should be blind, and that the law should be statutorily righteous and procedurally impartial, we stand in the way of progressivism. Progressives have a different social agenda than Christians, so we must be attacked. It's really that simple.

RECOGNIZE THIS AS THE WAR THAT IT IS

Progressivism is an ideology functioning as a religion in America, and it has grown large enough that it believes now is the time to wage war against Christians. Whereas Christianity, rightly understood, sees a vast distinction between the role of the church and of the state, progressivism, which doesn't see itself as a religion, tends to make no distinction between its ideological claims and its political aims. As such, it seeks to do more than persuade or even convert you. You may not fully understand progressivism; who does? But whether or not you fully understand it, progressivism has declared war on you, and it is intent on silencing you, marginalizing you, bullying you, and forcing you to accept its tenets. As a Christian, you are in the way of progressivism. And you *will* be attacked.

In several important books, political and cultural author Rod Dreher describes in considerable detail how American progressivism follows the same playbooks as authoritarian regimes have in recent history, especially in Eastern Europe, the old Soviet Union, and China.[12] Dreher writes that American Christians will be facing the same forms of harassment, mistreatment, and even persecution that Christians in totalitarian regimes over the last century have encountered.

Dreher is right. Christians in the US are already facing hostility for our beliefs, and the trajectory of this hostility gives every appearance of worsening. I can say that my time spent with progressives over the decades leads me to believe that there is no real bottom to progressivism. More than a program to be implemented, it is a rage to be expressed against whatever its latest grievance is. That means, in my opinion, that things are going to get a whole lot worse for Christians in America. We can expect that progressivism will use the levers of government, business, education, and the media against us. Already in once so-called enlightened Western nations without a First Amendment, Christians are finding themselves arrested for simply stating Christian truths. It's coming to America, and there is no reason to think that progressives will not use any tool in their power to force Christians to give up our positions. Progressivism is totalitarian by nature.

> Progressivism is a rage to be expressed against whatever its latest grievance is.

In the next chapter, I will explore some of the strategies that progressivism is already using against Christians. But already here, based on how other totalitarian regimes have mistreated Christians, let me suggest just a few things likely coming your way. These may sound extreme, but you should know that versions of each of these strategies are already being implemented against Christians—here, in the West. Some of you will likely face these or similar hostilities:

- Expressing Christian positions on sex and gender will be treated as either a hate crime or mental illness. Children of principled Christians will be removed by the state under bogus pretexts such as "unfit parent" or "threats to the children."
- Your church will lose its tax-exempt status for refusing to accommodate progressive values. Opening a new church will

become increasingly difficult as public facilities become off-limits to Christian groups and as municipalities level property restrictions against Christians.

- Refusing to support Marxist-inspired organizations, Pride events, or the like will get you unceremoniously fired from your job.
- Activists will target your business, your home, and your church, and left-leaning politicians will pass legislation making it harder to be a simple Christian.
- Simple and common words will be redefined to turn them against you.
- Your medical practice will be ordered to perform procedures that you know to be damaging and wrong—mastectomies on children or abortions on pregnant women. Refusal to perform such procedures will cost you your job and your license.
- You will be ordered to use pronouns that you know to be false, or lose your teaching license. Your children will also be ordered to use the wrong pronouns at school; if they don't, they will be failed.
- You will find your bank accounts at risk, as well as difficulties in securing loans and mortgages, if you post Christian messages on social media, as US financial institutions greatly increase their use of "social scores" (so-called "Environmental Social Governance" policies). Your viewpoints will soon become part of your credit score and will be used against you if you are a Christian.
- Finding yourself in trouble with the law will become more complicated, as your Christian faith will automatically move you to "hate group" status, where penalties will be much stiffer.
- Schools across the country will paganize your children, teaching them that your values are harmful and wrong, then hide from you how they are undermining your parental responsibilities. Seeking redress from such educational abuse will be considered sedition.

- Christian universities will lose accreditation for teaching Christian positions. Graduates of those schools will be unable to work in their given professions.
- False accusations will be raised against you to discredit you or cost you your job. In a world where progressivism actively seeks to undermine due process and traditional liberal rights, the mere accusation will be sufficient to ruin you and place a curse over your head.
- Attorneys will be disbarred for refusing to go along with progressive principles. At some point, there will be few practicing Christian attorneys or judges, but a lot of anti-Christian jurists.
- You will be silenced at your own church, called a hater, told you are divisive, or simply thrown out—at church!—for standing for Christian principles. Alternately, if your church stands for biblical principles, your congregation may lose its property as your denomination goes progressive.
- You will be surveilled as an extremist. Your social media accounts will be monitored. Your purchasing history will be monitored. Even your travel will be monitored and curtailed because of your Christian positions.

So this is war, and you, dear Christian, need to see it for what it is. You will not be allowed to remain faithfully Christian without a fight. You will not be able to express Christian positions in public without threats and punishments. You will not be allowed to raise your children free from propaganda. You must learn to expect the "wiles of the devil," as Paul calls them (Ephesians 6:11): ridicule, speech codes, licensing restrictions, censorship, penalties, immense social pressure, marginalization, etc. Progressivism is totalitarian, and the sooner you realize this, the sooner you can begin to develop strategies for living faithfully to Jesus in a hostile culture.

You may not have asked for a war with the West, but you got one, like it or not.

STAND FIRM

In a lot of ways, the Christian faith in America has been on a long vacation from hostility. Until recently, even with all our faults in the US, the US generally provided a safe context for living out faithfully Christian lives.

The vacation is now over, and it's time to rejoin historic Christianity—which has often been mistreated through the centuries. Indeed, it is worth noting again that religious freedom is but a blip on the radar for Christians. Persecution has more often been the lot of Christians. To be Christian, in most places and throughout much of history, has been to be a mistreated minority. The British essayist G. K. Chesterton once quipped, "Jesus promises his disciples three things—that they would be completely fearless, and absurdly happy, and in constant trouble." Chesterton was right.

When reassuring the persecuted church in the ancient city of Philadelphia, Jesus mentions "the hour of trial that is going to come on the whole world to test the inhabitants of the earth" (Revelation 3:10). Until very recently, North American Christians have largely been spared this trial. But that's changing as Christians become the minority and those aligned with the secular spirit of the age claim majority status.

Now is the time to renew our commitment to Christ the King. Now is the time to clarify our positions and steel our resolve. Now is the time to "count it all joy" (James 1:2) when we are privileged to experience suffering for Christ, to pray for our enemies, and to bless those who persecute us. As Jesus says, now is the time to "hold on to what you have, so that no one will take your crown" (Revelation 3:10–11).

"In this world you will have trouble," Jesus promises. "But take heart! I have overcome the world" (John 16:33). We face a determined adversary, but we have a powerful Savior. Jesus is going to win. The most important and first step is to make up your mind, here and now, once and for all, that you will stand firm for Jesus. But first, let's get clarity on the threats we face, as we'll do in the next chapter.

Small Group Questions

1. Did you finish reading the chapter? If so, what stood out to you from the readings and why?
2. What does this chapter (in the first paragraphs) tell us about how the material in this book relates to politics—and why is that an important distinction to make?
3. According to this chapter, what are some of the major ideas associated with progressivism? How is progressivism like a religion?
4. What are some of the ways that progressivism is incompatible with Christianity, and why is it important to know these differences?
5. How do you feel about the contention in this chapter that we must recognize that the relationship between progressivism and Christianity is one of war? Explain why you feel the way you do.
6. Are there any situations that arise in this chapter where it would be helpful to role-play a conversation or a specific situation in order to help each other anticipate what we might face?
7. In light of the conversation we have had over this chapter, how can we pray for each other?

2

KNOW THE THREATS

"They will wage war against the Lamb, but the Lamb will triumph over them because he is Lord of lords and King of kings—and with him will be his called, chosen and faithful followers" (Revelation 17:14).

In early 2021 the California Department of Education proposed an ethnic studies model curriculum that addressed what one of its authors has called the evil of "theocide"—the arrival of Christianity on the shores of America.[13] This curriculum presumes that Christians wreck the otherwise peace-loving people of all other cultures. To address the "problem" of Christianity in California, the curriculum includes the worship of Aztec and Mayan gods through songs and chants, a mandate intended to change the loyalties of California's millions of school children away from Christianity, which is considered to be inherently colonialist, supremacist, and genocidal.

Videos surfaced showing school officials leading students in the worship of this idol. As with all ideologies, the ethnic studies curriculum must ignore reality: One of the idols children are required to worship *by name* is Tezcatlipoca—the god Aztecs served through human sacrifice and cannibalism. Historically, they killed and ate the many captives they acquired through colonialization, supremacist ideas, and genocide. I'm not exaggerating here. The curriculum literally required children to worship these idols. You can find the videos on YouTube. It is like a pep rally for the pagan gods, celebrating values directly opposed to Christianity. And it is all fueled by an embrace of progressivism.

What's going on here?

As I mentioned in the first chapter, a sea-change has occurred in America. Progressives have taken hold of the levers of many of America's most influential institutions. And since progressivism is an aggressive ideology incompatible with Christianity, it has declared war on Christians. We are enemy No. 1. *You* are the enemy. You need to understand this. This explains why, when American author Raymond Ibrahim's Facebook account posted a link to a documentary describing the beheading of Christians, Facebook locked his account. Reporting on Muslims massacring Christians violates Facebook's "community standards." It explains why Sensoy and DiAngelo tell us in their educational textbook, *Is Everyone Really Equal?*, that the oppressors of Muslims are Christians—in spite of the thousands of Christians who will be martyred at the hands of Muslims this year alone. They all share a common worldview: Christians are the world's enemies. We must be silenced.

To stand firm in a hostile environment, let's explore a few areas where the attacks against Christian principles are intense. Then we'll briefly discuss some of the strategies being used against Christians in America. This isn't fun stuff to read about, and it's even less fun to write about. But again, I have in mind those Christians who are already in the middle of these storms, and I can't abandon them by blissfully ignoring what they're facing.

PAY ATTENTION TO KEY AREAS OF HOSTILITY

Now that we've discussed progressivism, let's spell out several areas where progressivism is going after Christianity in the US.

Religious Freedom and Freedom of Conscience

Worldwide, Christians are the most marginalized, harassed, discriminated against, and persecuted people. Jesus Christ was persecuted, and Christianity was born into a world where both Jew and Roman would savage its adherents. But Christians, working with Enlightenment principles, developed the novel idea of religious freedom: that governments do not have the right to restrict religious activity and one's conscience.

In the United States, the Constitution enshrined this principle in the very first human right. Under the influence of the US, religious freedom is acknowledged today, though not always guaranteed and carried out, as a basic human right by the 193 nations in the United Nations. But since progressivism requires the marginalization of Christianity to implement its vision, progressives are beginning to assault religious freedom in America. Consider just the following example:

In 1993, in response to threats against Native People's religious rites, the US Congress passed the Religious Freedom Restoration Act (RFRA) to strengthen the freedom to practice one's faith in America. The bill was sponsored by Democrats in both the House and the Senate, won near unanimous approval, and was signed into law by President Bill Clinton. An Illinois state version of the RFRA was passed in 1998, with Senator Barak Obama voting for it. But as president, Obama's administration was ambivalent about the RFRA and in response to the administration's ambivalence, various states passed their own versions of the bill.

In 2015, Indiana also sought to pass a state version of the RFRA. But lots had changed since 1993. Since that year, progressivism had achieved a degree of critical mass in the nation's halls of power. Because progressivism stands against many of the Christian faith's tenets, a firestorm broke out in 2015 in response to Indiana's efforts to pass a RFRA. Major corporations and sports teams threatened to withdraw business from the state. Apple's CEO Tim Cook got in on the act, even though Apple employs laborers in China's sweat shops.

Celebrities condemned Indiana and the idea of religious freedom, and governors of other states even threatened to ban official travel to Indiana. This time, the Democratic party opposed the bill—worded almost identically to the federal version they had sponsored only twelve years before. No less than Bill Clinton's own wife reviled Indiana's attempts to pass a RFRA.

What changed between 1993 and 2015? Progressivism's vision of America had degenerated during those years, while progressives had gained enormous power and influence. Now, progressives argue that religious freedom is largely a vice, not a virtue. To quote the US Commission on Civil Rights from 2016, "The phrases 'religious liberty' and 'religious freedom' will stand for nothing except hypocrisy so long as they remain code words for discrimination, intolerance, racism, sexism, homophobia, Islamophobia, Christian supremacy, or any form of intolerance."

> Progressives argue that religious freedom is largely a vice, not a virtue.

Your Christian organizations—schools, non-profits, ministries, maybe even churches—will be increasingly subjected to discriminatory laws designed to make you conform to progressive values. Where other organizations will be free to operate consistently with their values, you will not be. You will likely face lawsuits, civil penalties, and silencing for exercising your religious freedom. Here. In America.

Religious freedom and freedom of conscience are fundamental human rights, and would be so even if there were no religions. They are something of a canary in the coal mine—when religious freedoms are curtailed, other freedoms are sure to topple. But progressivism seeks to marginalize the voices of Christians. We've come a long way since President John F. Kennedy pointed out that, "The rights of man come not from the generosity of the state but from the hand of God."

Abortion and the Value of Human Life

Christian teaching holds to the inviolable sacredness of human life. Every human being is created in the image of God and, therefore, possesses the right to life. Indeed, without the right to life, there can be no other rights. But through abortion, the secular West practices a utilitarian view of human life. The hedonistic sexual ethics of progressivism demands that something be done with the natural consequence of sex: babies. Abortion in America is a *solution*. As progressives see it, the problem is *babies*.

And progressives are seeking to force Christians to accept and even underwrite abortion. Already in certain jurisdictions, Christian counseling and family services have been bullied into referring people to abortion providers such as Planned Parenthood. Hospitals are being threatened over their refusal to perform abortions. Christian pharmacists and doctors are under the same threat, and if progressives get their way, they will lose federal dollars and even their licenses for refusing to do what they believe to be a great evil—kill babies. If you are an OB-GYN, progressives will try to force you to perform abortions on threat of law, a civil lawsuit, or both. It is only a matter of time.

In certain jurisdictions, children are encouraged to get abortions even without parental consent—subjecting children to serious surgeries, often in lightly regulated clinics, risking their health, their mental well-being, and their lives—not to mention killing their babies. In many states, a sixteen-year-old cannot get her ears pierced without parental permission. But that same girl can have her baby killed in a federally funded clinic.

Further, using a variety of disingenuous arguments about poverty or health care, progressives are working to force every American to fund abortions through tax dollars. The same federal government that sought to force the Catholic nuns' organization Little Sisters of the Poor to provide contraceptive coverage to their employees will also attempt to force Christians to provide abortion. This is why progressives are currently seeking to repeal the Hyde Amendment—which currently prevents certain federal funds from going directly to abortion. And as the federal government takes over more and more of America's healthcare system, the corruption inherent in a utilitarian view of human nature will increasingly surface, including such things as forced euthanasia.[14]

Christians must stand for human life, even when progressives exact a cost for such a stand. Abortion is an indefensible form of evil, and bullying Christians into providing abortions is a cynical and indefensible injustice. But it's coming your way.

Gender, Sex, and Family

None of the bullying that Christians face in America today is as intense as the treatment we receive for our views of gender, sex, and family. Christians believe in the simple biological fact of two genders, a fact that is taught in every biology class in America. We believe in the natural order of heterosexual relationships designed to produce healthy children. And we believe in the norm of one man and one woman in a committed married relationship.

Progressivism sees sex, gender, and marriage as malleable, to be shaped by the lusts and desires of any given person. Because sex is such an important part of secular values, progressivism simply cannot tolerate any disagreement in the areas of sex, gender, and marriage. Christian positions must be censored, and Christians must be silenced.

This means faithful Christians face serious challenges when we stand for what the Scriptures and natural law reveal about sex, gender, and marriage. Try to post a statement on social media criticizing America's sexual ethic, and you'll likely find the post removed. If not, you'll find yourself called every possible name and/or shamed, threatened, or fired. Try to explain the Christian position on sex and gender at work, and you might find yourself unemployed. Enter a career path in health care, and you'll find yourself in a mire of secular sexual mandates that force you to calculate your every move. Progressivism intends to bully the rest of the world into accepting it, affirming it, and even underwriting its own sexual ethics. Christian universities are forced to play the gender game or be sued and even lose their federal funding.

Examples are now in the thousands in America, but here's just one, again from California:

When Southern California Christian Pastor James Domen left behind a homosexual lifestyle to become a Christian, eventually becoming a pastor, his church began to post videos advocating Christian views of sex and family. But Vimeo cancelled his account, saying that his content amounted to "conversion therapy," violating Vimeo's rules against videos that "harass, incite hatred, or include discriminatory or defamatory speech." Domen sued, but he lost his case.[15]

This is shocking in light of progressivism's fluid view of sex and gender—where anyone can wake up at any moment and declare they have changed genders. In the world of progressivism, everyone is expected to acknowledge such a declaration, in spite of the utter lack of objective evidence. In California, failure to acknowledge a person's announced change can, in certain circumstances, land you in jail. And isn't it just a little bit of a betrayal of the truthfulness of progressivism's sex and gender theories when we now have dozens of so-called genders and orientations—fifty-eight and counting, according to one website? [16] Just consider one website that depicts the flags of progressivism's many genders: there is the 6-Striped LGBTQ+Q+ Pride Flag, the Original LGBTQ+Q+ Pride Flag, Transgender Pride Flag, Bisexual Pride Flag, Lesbian Pride Flag, Polysexual Pride Flag, Asexual Pride Flag, Demisexual Pride Flag, Pansexual Pride Flag, Philly Pride Flag, Intersex Pride Flag, QPOC Pride Flag, Genderqueer Pride Flag, Progress Pride Flag, Nonbinary Pride Flag, Bear Pride Flag, and the Straight Ally Pride Flag.[17] Given such a state of gender affairs among progressives, it is totalitarian to suggest that when a fourteen-year-old girl announces herself to be pangender or neutrois or two-spirit or male, she must be celebrated and showered with federal dollars,[18] but when a thirty-six-year-old man, Pastor James Domen, recognizes his natural orientation under the influence of Christian principles, he must be silenced.

In subsequent chapters, I will address America's hedonist sexual ethics and progressivism's determination to force you to adapt to them. Here, it is enough to say that nothing in today's North America riles progressives like Christian teachings on sexual holiness. And you won't be allowed to remain neutral on this subject.

PREPARE FOR INCREASING LEVELS OF HARASSMENT

Like all other dominant groups that seek to force minorities into accepting their agenda, progressivism is already using a variety of powerful social and legal tools to force Christians to fall in line with progressivism. Here are a few of the strategies you can expect progressives to use against you:

Expect propaganda and disinformation

For progressivism to work, the treasures of Western thought in general—and that of Christian thought in particular—must be discredited, and those who hold to these treasures must be silenced. So we Christians can expect an increasing amount of propaganda against biblical views of life, of truth, of justice, of religious freedom, and of sex and family. It's already a flood. The storm will only get worse.

History is constantly being rewritten by progressivism, disciplines are being retooled, new narratives are being created, and even the meanings of words are being changed. The promotion of same-sex activity is euphemistically referred to under banners such as "love is love." Same-sex marriage is called "marriage equality." Abortion is called "women's reproductive rights." Even simple words such as "they," "he," and "she" must undergo constant revisions, with new terms being added annually: zie, sie, zim, em, zir, hir, eirself, etc. Criminals are now sometimes called "justice-involved persons."[19] Planned Parenthood has begun using the term "folks with a vulva" rather than "women." The American Medical Association has begun to argue that sex should be removed as a legal designation on birth certificates so that people can choose their own sex. When hearings for Supreme Court Justice Amy Coney Barrett were conducted in the US Senate, she used the phrase "sexual preference." Despite the fact that many progressives routinely use the term, one progressive senator instructed Justice Barrett that the term is offensive. That very same day, an online dictionary changed the definition of the term to include a statement that its use is offensive.[20]

The term "science" can come to mean whatever it needs to mean for the progressive cause. So when Christians sought to gather to worship God during the pandemic, "the science" was against it. When protestors gathered by the tens of thousands in massive crowds of protest at the very same time, "the science" was in favor of it—with even the Centers for Disease Control and Prevention offering its scientific support of massive protests during a pandemic.

The term "science" can come to mean whatever it needs to mean.

Economic theories are subject to enormous amounts of propaganda. When progressivism promotes Marxism, it consistently fails to connect the nightmares of the Union of Soviet *Socialist* Republics with socialism, or the monstrous evils of German National *Socialism* (the Nazi party), or Mao's murderous "Great Leap Forward"—which resulted in tens of millions of deaths. With progressivism, you wouldn't know that the killing fields of Cambodia were socialist, the giant prison that is North Korea is socialist, the state-sponsored racism of Castro's Cuba was socialist, or that the shipwreck of the nation of Venezuela is socialist. The propaganda won't allow the truth. The same is true of progressivism's kid-gloves treatment of Islam, which is treated as a victimized religion, in spite of massive Muslim extremist behavior worldwide. Truth must be suppressed so that the ideology can be promoted.

In George Orwell's dystopic *1984,* a "Ministry of Truth" spends its time rewriting facts to align them with the dominant myth. In the US, progressives are pouring forth propaganda to prop up their narrative. We Christians may not be able to stop the propaganda. But as one survivor of the Soviet Union's socialist nightmare, Alexander Solzhenitsyn, urges: we *can* be the one people who choose to live not by lies.[21]

Expect scorn and shame

For the progressive narrative to dominate, other narratives must not get a hearing. This is a relatively new phenomenon in American progressivism and signals the end of the so-called period of "tolerance," "inclusiveness," and "dialogue." It shouldn't surprise us, however. These calls were only temporary—a way of changing the minds of millions of Americans until critical mass could be achieved. Now that progressives are holding the most influential social levers of power, they have no more need for such things as tolerance, diversity of thought, or dialogue. So institutions such as American universities—where such slogans such as "diversity is our strength" were born—are now the most ideologically segregated institutions in America, and diversity of thought will get you thrown out of college and many schools.[22] Hatred is the new love.

This is why conservatives and Christian speakers are routinely harassed when attempting to speak at American universities. It is why Christian positions are no longer engaged; rather, Christians are simply dismissed with labels such as "bigots" and "haters." Your own children and grandchildren will be conditioned to call you terms like these if you don't accept the secular ideology. Christians are de-platformed—removed from media accounts for taking Christian stands. This is why such organizations as the very problematic Southern Poverty Law Center and the gay advocacy Human Rights Council have tremendous authority to determine who is and who is not a hate group. One call from either of these organizations will get your book removed from Amazon and banned from Target. Cases in point: Restored Hope Network Executive Director Anne Paulk and pastoral counselor Joe Dallas both saw their books removed from Amazon for upsetting the progressives, as did attorney David Robinson and clinical psychologist Joseph Nicolosi. Meanwhile, books that glamorize sex between adults and their children are allowed to remain in the marketplace. As of early 2021, Amazon continued to sell the book, *Daddies & Brats: Taboo Erotic Collection*, whose description says that "Due to the explicit nature of these erotic short stories, it is simply impossible to summarize them without being totally inappropriate. But know they involve forbidden relationships that ALWAYS get out of hand."[23]

We Christians should not be ignorant of what's happening here. Progressives are already working on legislation that would legally censor "hate groups" altogether, removing free speech rights from Christians and those who disagree with secular ideology.

After the Supreme Court's decision to allow same-sex marriage across America in the Obergefell Case, Justice Samuel Alito warned that "those who cling to old beliefs will be able to whisper their thoughts in the recesses of their home but if they repeat those views in public, they will risk being labeled as bigots and treated as such by governments, employers, and schools." Alito's warning is coming true for Christians in secular America.

Expect discrimination

In 1996, the State of California passed Proposition 209, banning discrimination against people in public employment on the bases of race, sex, color, ethnicity, or national origin. The proposition signaled a determination to practice fairness and justice across the state in all it does. Not surprisingly to those who understand progressivism, in 2020 secular groups in California worked hard to pass another Proposition—Proposition 16—which constituted a *repeal* of Proposition 209 to allow open discrimination in California. The proposition didn't pass, but it did receive millions of votes. After centuries of discrimination, why would a state in the twenty-first century now be in favor of discrimination?

The answer is that progressives now believe some people should be given preferential treatment under the law. And this means, of course, that other people should be denied fairness and due process under the law.

It's a bad sign for Christians because it means that progressivism is comfortable marginalizing some people in favor of others. Given the disdain that progressives hold against Christians, this means we will see Christians and Christian institutions discriminated against in America for our faith. Several years ago, social researcher George Yancey conducted research on religious bias in academia and found that almost half of all academics are less willing to hire a candidate for an academic job if that person is a conservative Protestant. Further, his research shows that political and religious progressives possess vindictiveness and hostility toward conversative Christians. This comes as no surprise to Christians.[24]

This explains why Christian groups are being kicked off college campuses around the country. It explains why counselors now coach teens not to put Christian messages on their Facebook pages—they may forfeit admission into many colleges because of their faith. It explains why accreditation boards and professional organizations, such as the American Medical Association and the American Bar Association, have taken secular positions on such things as sex and gender and threaten to marginalize members who don't go along. It is why you—if you'll admit it to yourself—hesitate to say what you believe in public. You know you will be discriminated against if you speak too openly about your Christian beliefs.

In some regions of Muslim-majority Egypt, Christians have been denied so many job opportunities that the word "Christian" is now synonymous with "garbage collector."[25] Egypt today shows us how resilient we will need to be as America increasingly discriminates against Christians for their faith. We will need to make very difficult decisions about the schools we attend, the views we express, and the careers we choose. Progressives are already discriminating against Christians. It will get worse.

Expect lawsuits, fines, coercion, and possible imprisonment

Though being a Christian is not illegal in America, Christian behaviors are increasingly under threat of suits, fines, coercion, and possible imprisonment. I've already mentioned that in California in certain contexts it is a crime to refuse to call a person by their preferred pronoun, regardless of your religion. Christian colleges, ministries, and non-profits are already subject to fines and suits for failing to fall in line with secular principles. In Canada, which is historically a majority Christian nation and whose national anthem ends with the prayer that Canadians may remain "true and free," attempting to persuade a gay person to live by biblical principles is now a crime—punishable by up to five years in prison. In 2022, Finnish lawmaker Päivi Räsänen was placed on trial for tweeting several Bible verses about sexuality, including texts that condemn same-sex behavior. She stood threatened with up to six years in prison for merely speaking against the tenets of progressivism.

So far, America's First Amendment has protected Christians, but progressives are working 24/7 to get around religious protections. The Equality Act, passed by the House of Representatives in 2021, would amend the Civil Rights Act of 1964 to prohibit discrimination on the basis of sexual orientation and gender identity in a host of areas in America, including in public accommodations. The Act defines public accommodations very broadly to deny any organization that provides services or goods to the public the right to choose whom they employ or what kind of service they offer. The Act explicitly states that religious exemptions shall not be offered to Christians. And you can be sure that secular politicians will use the Act to punish Christians. Such punishment is already happening.

The most famous case is that of Jack Phillips, whose Masterpiece Bakery refused to place a pro-LGBTQ+ message on a cake for the wedding of a same-sex couple. It is worth noting that Phillips did not refuse to sell a wedding cake to the gay couple—he has sold many cakes to many LGBTQ persons. But Phillips was found guilty of unlawful discrimination because he refused to create an artistic message celebrating same-sex marriage. Other vendors have also been sued for similar reasons. Lorie Smith, the owner of a Christian graphics website, was also sued by the State of Colorado, which sought to compel her to create work celebrating gay weddings. The Tenth US Circuit Court of Appeals ruled in favor of the state—acknowledging that their ruling puts her religious rights at risk, that Smith doesn't discriminate against *anyone* (she only discriminates on which messages she'll compose), and even that other designers are legally allowed to discriminate based on their beliefs. But, the court argued, the double standard was allowable in her case, and the state could override her religious rights and compel her speech.

Because such cases can become conservative political talking points, they might seem distant for some Christians who wish not to get involved in political debates. But neither Phillips nor Smith started out looking to be at the center of political fights. They were just trying to follow Christ in their line of work, according to their convictions. As fellow Christians, we owe it to them not to be ashamed of them or indifferent to their predicament. In prison, Paul found it necessary to say regarding his own situation, "Do not be ashamed of the testimony about our Lord or of me his prisoner. Rather, join with me in suffering for the gospel, by the power of God" (2 Timothy 1:8).

> Join with me in suffering for the gospel.

In many countries around the world, there are laws strictly limiting the freedom of Christians to exercise their religion. Many Muslim countries have dhimmitude laws that restrict things Christians can say and do. In some of these countries, Christians are not even allowed to repair their church buildings. Police protection can be lacking, and mob action is a constant threat. Converting to Christianity from Islam can bring prison or even death. In Saudi Arabia, you cannot even carry a Bible in public. In North Korea, sometimes entire families are sentenced to labor camps simply because one member is a Christian. In China, landlords who allow house churches can be fined. Churches are pressured into teaching the tenets of communism and removing crosses. In other places around the world, surveillance of Christians and house churches is common—so much so that some of my church's congregations in the Global South must go through training on how to wipe clean one's phone to prevent authorities from tracking down one's Christian brothers and sisters.

So far, the United States is not like these nations. But as progressivism continues to grow in power and influence, we face the very real threat of financial, occupational, and even physical punishment.

DON'T BE SURPRISED

We shouldn't be surprised by hostility against Christians. Persecution has been a constant companion of the faith all the way back to Jesus.

> *If the world hates you, keep in mind that it hated me first. If you belonged to the world, it would love you as its own. As it is, you do not belong to the world, but I have chosen you out of the world. That is why the world hates you. Remember what I told you: "A servant is not greater than his master." If they persecuted me, they will persecute you also. (John 15:18–20)*

What *is* new is growing persecution of Christians in America. But it is here, it is real, and it doesn't appear to be going away. So we are left to wrestle with tough questions about how to live in a way that is faithful to Christ in an increasingly hostile culture. We find ourselves asking questions such as:

- What do I do when a family member tells me he or she is living in sexual sin and severs relations with me if I don't go along?
- What do I do when the workplace requires me to endorse values that go against my faith?
- How should I engage with businesses or brands whose leaders seem intent on attacking my beliefs?

Throughout the pages to follow, I will offer biblical answers to these questions and others like them to suggest practical guidance to the Christian who seeks to live in—but not of—this present world. Francis Schaeffer once posed the question, "How shall we then live?" That question is one every serious Christian is asking today. Fortunately, Christ did not leave us without an answer. And this is the time for American Christians to find that answer.

It starts by clarifying, once and for all, who we are in Christ. This is the subject for our next chapter.

Small Group Questions

1. Did you finish reading the chapter? If so, what stood out to you from the readings and why?
2. What is your reaction to the idea that Christian organizations will likely be subjected to discrimination laws in America? Explain your reaction.
3. How hard is it for you, personally, to uphold what Scripture teaches on abortion, gender, sex, and the family when in relationship with family or friends who disagree on these teachings? How do you handle it?
4. Were you aware of the high level of scorn and discrimination for Christians on college campuses

today? In your experience, is that different from in times past, and if so, in what ways is it different?

5. Review Jesus' teaching in John 15:18–20. In light of this teaching, how can we embrace persecution as a positive thing, and what is the most important thing for you to remember from this text?
6. Are there any situations that arise in this chapter where it would be helpful to role-play a conversation or a specific situation in order to help each other anticipate what we might face?
7. In light of the conversation we have had over this chapter, how can we pray for each other?

3

DECIDE, ONCE AND FOR ALL, WHO YOU ARE

"Be on your guard; stand firm in the faith; be courageous; be strong" (1 Corinthians 16:13).

"What if I can't, in good conscience, support him?"

A friend told me the story of the person who asked this incredibly brave question. At the time, my friend worked as an upper-level manager for a large tech-oriented American corporation, and he was sitting in a corporate meeting with a hundred other managers. The CEO, a well-liked and competent man, was advising the team that the company's future was in jeopardy due to fierce competition and antitrust regulations that were working against the company. There was a lump-in-the-throat silence in the room as the team contemplated the possibility of a restructuring, a buy-out, or even a bankruptcy.

The CEO gave a list of strategies the company was planning to deploy to remain solvent. In the complex world of corporate America, a connection with legislators and regulators can be a matter of life or death. The CEO announced that the company would be backing a man running for Congress—one who was friendly to the legislative needs of the company, but also was openly progressive on social issues. The CEO stated that he expected the managers in the room to support this candidate both in public and in private. It was a matter of corporate life and death.

A lone Christian raised his hand, which in itself was a violation of protocol in a meeting to announce a new direction (these kinds of meetings don't usually invite negotiation or dialogue). "This candidate supports abortion," the brave soul pointed out. "What if I can't, in good conscience, support him?"

There was a silence in the room louder than any gasp could ever be. Everyone craned their necks to see who had dared raise the challenge in such a grave meeting. The CEO seemed surprised, less by the content of the question, and more that someone challenged him: "Then you need to work somewhere else," he replied.

My friend never heard what happened to that Christian manager. Maybe he left. Maybe he was fired. Maybe he found a way to keep his job while dodging the issue. All my friend knew was that most of the other people he spoke to after the meeting were irritated by the man's question. They thought the needs of the company that employed thousands of people outweighed the ethical convictions of the lone man. One person even said, "He is living in another century."

If you had been in the room, what would you have said? One thing I know is that it is very likely that your own moment of decision will come just as it has for many Christians over the last two thousand years. In the Roman Empire, Christians were forced to choose between Christ and Caesar. When Islam swept the Middle East, North Africa, Turkey, and parts of Europe, Christians were often forced to convert to Islam or face severe punishment and subjugation. During the Middle Ages and the centuries following it, reformers and Protestants were frequently persecuted by Catholics (and, sometimes, the other way around). Entire wars were waged to suppress dissenting Christian communities. When Christian missionaries began traveling the world with the gospel in the nineteenth and twentieth centuries, some were killed for witnessing about Jesus in hostile cultures. In communist countries in the twentieth century, churches were closed down and Christians were marginalized, harassed, sent to labor camps, and killed.

Actual persecution against Christians because of our religion has been rare in North America. As I mentioned earlier, in many ways, we Christians in America have for the most part avoided hostility. But that appears to be changing. And you may well face your own moment of decision as our culture becomes increasingly hostile toward the faith.

So the question many have been forced to answer must be yours too. Christ or Caesar?

STAND FIRM ON YOUR BAPTISM

Years ago in the city of Jonesboro, Arkansas, two boys pulled the fire alarm at the Westside Middle School. As the students and their teachers exited the building, these boys began to shoot into the crowd from a slope across the parking lot, killing four students and a teacher. The thirty-two-year-old teacher was hit when she stepped in front of one of her sixth graders to save the student's life.

I've often thought about why that teacher would have given her life for the life of a student without hesitation. I can only imagine that this heroic teacher had already made the decision—years before—that she was responsible for the well-being of her students. When the moment of crisis struck, Shannon Wright, the sixth-grade teacher, simply acted on a decision she had made long before.

For the believer in Jesus Christ, baptism is the moment we declare to the world our intent to follow Jesus regardless of the cost. It starts with faith that Jesus is the one and only way, coupled with what the Bible calls repentance. We turn from the ways of the dominant culture and swear allegiance to Jesus. This is why baptism typically involves some form of confession: "I believe that Jesus Christ is the Son of God." In baptism we choose Christ over Caesar.

In baptism we choose Christ over Caesar.

Here's how Paul puts it: "We were therefore buried with him through baptism into death in order that, just as Christ was raised from the dead through the glory of the Father, we too may live a new life. For if *we have been united with him* in a death like his, we will certainly also be united with him in a resurrection like his" (Romans 6:4–5).

At your baptism, you didn't just get wet or simply express a sentiment. At your baptism, you declared to yourself, to your community, and, most importantly, to your God, that you would follow Jesus from this point forward. No matter what. Baptism is not a negotiation. It is not a dialogue. It is not a question. Baptism is a *confession.*

A "confession" is a statement of resolve. It is a declaration that you are all in and won't back down. *No matter what.* Your baptism has already answered the question of how you will respond if you are ever given the difficult choice: Christ or Caesar. You have *already* chosen Christ. When the metaphorical (or actual) bullets start flying, your choice has already been made.

You have *already* decided to stand on the teachings of Christ, which are not open for negotiation. You have *already* declared that you stand for life and will not support the killing of innocent babies. You have *already* stated that you will stand for truth when the unbeliever bullies you with propaganda. You have *already* stated your commitment to the family as God defines it. You have *already* affirmed the principles of religious freedom. You have *already* declared your belief in Jesus' teachings that any sexual practice other than that of one man and one woman in a committed married relationship is sinful. When you were baptized, you *already* made your decision about challenges such as these:

- If you are interviewing for a job and are advised that your Christianity may get in the way of the job expectations, you have *already* decided that you can't compromise your Christian principles. If it's truly an either-or, you'll find another job.
- If you find yourself facing an unexpected pregnancy, you will not consider abortion. Instead, you have *already* decided that you will make the situation right, love the baby, and stand for life.
- If your church begins to teach that the Scriptures are wrong when they disagree with secular principles, you have *already* decided that you will lovingly challenge your church's compromise. If your church refuses to listen, you have *already* decided that you will find another church.
- If you are taught gender theories in the university that run contrary to the teachings of Scripture, you have *already* decided that you will not accept them. If your grade is conditioned on the acceptance of such dishonesty, you have *already* decided to seek a waiver, accept a lower grade, or just withdraw from the class.
- If acquiring or maintaining a professional license necessitates that you affirm positions you know to be sinful, you have *already* decided to refuse the demand, to seek to redress the problem without compromising your commitment to Jesus, or to change careers.
- If you are in a group of people who start to make false or disparaging statements about Christ or his church, you have *already* decided not to join in. You have *already* decided that you will never slander Christ, but that you will always exalt him.
- If a social media mob rises in response to a news report, you have *already* decided to seek the truth and avoid acting on unfounded and distorted narratives. You have *already* decided to be a friend of the truth, not a captive to unfounded mob action.

- If your child decides to marry someone of the same sex, you have *already* decided to continue to love your child, but not to sponsor or host their wedding. You have *already* decided that you cannot celebrate or bless sin.

To falter in these areas sets you on a path to break your vow, renege on your promise, and betray your king. In biblical terminology, it puts you on a trajectory to committing apostasy. We need to remember Jesus' words in respect to apostasy: "No one who puts a hand to the plow and looks back is fit for service in the kingdom of God" (Luke 9:62). Peter instructed the first-century church to resist the evil one and to stand firm in the face of its persecution (1 Peter 5:8–9). We must do the same. We must resist evil and stand firm in our faith, resolving that we will be faithful to Jesus regardless of what happens.

GAIN STRENGTH FROM YOUR RESOLVE

When I was in junior high school, the coaches in my physical education class decided to teach us several dances. I had been taught by my church that dancing is sinful because it creates lustful situations. I doubt the church of my youth still teaches this (I really don't know), and I've since changed my own views on dancing. But back then, I had embraced the belief that Christians don't dance.

Up to that point, the question of whether I would dance had always been theoretical. Now suddenly and without warning, I was told I was going to dance. At first, I was afraid I would get in trouble with my parents if I danced.

I was embarrassed and afraid. And I was all alone. I pulled aside one of the coaches and asked if I could be excused from the exercise. The coach looked at me like I had just said I was from another planet and asked, "Why?"

I stumbled around for a moment and found I couldn't bring myself to say why. So she asked again. Finally, I explained that as a Christian, I believed it to be a sin to dance.

"We're all Christians in here," she replied. "Are you saying we are all wrong?" I replied that I wasn't trying to judge anyone else, but I simply couldn't do it. As she stared at me, I saw anger growing in her eyes. Then, to my utter humiliation, she announced to the seventy-five or so other kids that I was refusing to dance because I thought they were all sinners.

My peers stared at me with shock and, in the case of a few, disgust. Another coach called me over to the side. This coach was a member of my very own congregation. He put his hands on my shoulders and leaned over to put his face close to mine. "Can't you just give in this one time?" he asked. "Don't you see how they're all looking at you?" He wasn't angry. He was pleading. He was genuinely trying to help me and save me the embarrassment of the occasion.

But my motives changed when he asked me to compromise. Though my initial resistance stemmed from a fear of getting in trouble with my parents, I found my myself getting angry when feeling pressured to compromise. My heart steeled with conviction. "No," I said. "I'm not going to do it. And I'm not going to back down."

The coaches huddled up for a moment and then announced to the class that they would proceed with the dances, putting me in the corner of the gym and making me write endless pages of nonsense for as many days as the class danced. I started toward the corner when, to my surprise, a dozen other students raised their hands and asked if they could join me.

To be clear, what happened to me hardly qualifies as religious persecution, but I learned two important lessons that day. First, I learned that *when one person takes a stand, it gives others courage to stand.* For the rest of my schooling, people knew I was a Christian, and many would even come to me in times of need for a word of encouragement or biblical wisdom—even those who laughed at me that day.

The second lesson I learned was that *once you take a stand for what you believe is right, you get strength, resolve, and—oddly—peace.* After it dawned on me that the coaches were not going to back down, I, too, felt a strange sense of determination. I realized that it was time for me to get serious about my youthful faith. That decision gave me strength. At that moment, I knew who I was, I knew what I believed, and I knew where I stood. I found myself glad that I follow Jesus with nothing to hide and nothing to lose.

And since then, every time I have exercised resolve, it has made it easier to do so the next time. Throughout my years of ministry, I have been challenged a thousand times. I have faced off demons. I have been the subject of countless pages of rants online. I have been betrayed by some who were close to me. I have received death threats for stands I've taken and even been forced to go into hiding for my ministry. Every time opposition comes, I feel a sense of shock and often a sense of exhaustion quickly followed by a sense of peace. Every form of opposition simply increases my resolve in Christ.

REJOICE IN SUFFERING

> "Dear friends, do not be surprised at the fiery ordeal that has come on you to test you, as though something strange were happening to you. But rejoice inasmuch as you participate in the sufferings of Christ, so that you may be overjoyed when his glory is revealed." (1 Peter 4:12–13)

Peter's words are becoming increasingly relevant for Christians in America. Taking a courageous stand inspires others, brings peace, and, as Peter repeatedly saw in his life, opens doors for evangelizing even the enemies of the gospel. Roy is an Indian minister friend of mine who works in a massive city in the country. (I can't share the location for his safety.) On his arms, he bears the scars of his persecution from deflecting blows of a hundred beatings through the years by those who oppose his preaching—mostly Hindu extremists. Speaking to Roy, I'm reminded of the numerous Christians I've interviewed who have endured intense persecution like he has. They are all the most joyful and peaceful Christians I know. The glory of the Lord truly shines around them.

Roy told me of the great joy he has had in preaching the gospel, planting churches, and making disciples. At the time of our conversation, he had planted seventy-nine churches in and around his city. He has been arrested, beaten, threatened, and had family members kidnapped.

He has even been poisoned by a Hindu priest. Locals had warned Roy not to accept the priest's offer for dinner when Roy visited the village, but he couldn't resist the opportunity to preach the gospel to this village leader. After the two had a cordial supper, Roy went home. The very next day, the priest's wife suffered a massive hemorrhage. The desperate priest had heard that the prayers of Christians often saved lives, so he tracked down Roy and asked him to pray over his wife. Roy did. The hemorrhage healed. In a matter of days, the priest and his entire family professed faith in Christ and were baptized.

But there is more to the story. Only later did the priest reveal to Roy that he had poisoned Roy's food. When he found Roy the next day, he was shocked to discover that Roy was still alive. When he saw that Roy had no poisoning symptoms, the priest came to believe in Jesus—even before Roy's prayer healed his wife. That former Hindu priest became a Christian minister, planting numerous churches. Roy's faithfulness in the face of persecution convicted him.

And the incident steeled Roy's resolve. For those who stand on the reality of the gospel, there is great strength and joy. With each stand for the gospel, it gets easier. As James says, "Consider it pure joy, my brothers and sisters, whenever you face trials of many kinds, because you know that the testing of your faith produces perseverance. Let perseverance finish its work so that you may be mature and complete, not lacking anything" (James 1:2–4).

With each stand for the gospel, it gets easier.

The more you stand for Jesus, the more you'll know who you are, and the more you'll find the joy of Christian maturity. Opposition, resistance, and persecution are tools that God uses to refine us and make us whole. Peter puts it this way: "These [trials] have come so that the proven genuineness of your faith—of greater worth than gold, which perishes even though refined by fire—may result in praise, glory and honor when Jesus Christ is revealed" (1 Peter 1:7).

It may help to internalize some basic Christian resolutions that will serve as a compass each time you are faced with a new challenge. Commit these to memory, and then stand firmly on them when you are tested:

1. I will stand firm in Jesus and never deny him (1 Corinthians 16:13).
2. I will obey the Scriptures and never compromise them (Psalm 119:44).
3. I will be holy and never conform to the world (1 Thessalonians 4:7).
4. I will make disciples and never betray the gospel (Romans 1:16).
5. I will rescue sinners but never approve of sin (Galatians 6:1).
6. I will bless my enemies and never curse them (Matthew 5:44).
7. I will rejoice in my sufferings and never become bitter (1 Peter 4:16).
8. I will hope in Jesus and never hope in this world (Hebrews 10:23).

LIVE DEAD

Just before admonishing the Colossian Christians to avoid the cultural pressures of sexual sin, the Apostle Paul reminds us of a critical truth.

> Set your minds on things above, not on earthly things. For you died, and your life is now hidden with Christ in God. When Christ, who is your life, appears, then you also will appear with him in glory (Colossians 3:2–4).

In 1838, missionary James Calvert was sent to preach the gospel among the cannibals of the Fiji Islands, where he spent eighteen years preaching. On his way to the islands, reportedly the captain of his ship tried to dissuade him from the mission. "You will lose your life and the lives of those with you if you go among such savages," the captain said. Calvert gave a firm and confident reply: "We died before we came here."

Early in his life, Dr. Martin Luther King Jr. faced a crisis of courage. It was 1956, and he had just moved to Montgomery, Alabama, to lead the budding Civil Rights Movement. One night he received a phone call warning him that if he did not leave, his house would be blown up and his brains blown out. That night he wrestled with God in prayer, confessing his doubts, his fears, and his weaknesses. He was concerned for his family's life, and he also didn't want others to see his personal fears and become demoralized in the fight.

"And it seemed at that moment," he later remarked, "I could hear an inner voice saying to me, 'Martin Luther, stand up for righteousness, stand up for justice, stand up for truth and lo I will be with you even until the end of the world.' I heard the voice of Jesus saying to fight on. He promised never to leave me, never to leave me alone." Even after his house was blown up, this Christian evangelist went on to lead one of the greatest movements of righteousness the world has ever seen.[26]

Jesus promises us that following him will bring a cost. "Whoever wants to be my disciple must deny themselves and take up their cross daily and follow me. For whoever wants to save their life will lose it, but whoever loses their life for me will save it" (Luke 9:23–24). But he also promises he will be with us always, even to the end of the world (Matthew 28:20).

That's what we did when we were baptized; we died with him. Get that clear. Like James Calvert and many of the apostles before him said, you *already* died for Jesus. So whatever comes your way can be faced with confidence and joy. "For Christ's sake," the apostle

Paul says, "I delight in weaknesses, in insults, in hardships, in persecutions, in difficulties. For when I am weak, then I am strong" (2 Corinthians 12:10).

Compromise won't work, so refuse to do it. It is a form of unfaithfulness. Everybody loses when Christians compromise our witness. Deciding, once and for all, to stand with Jesus is the only hope you have. It is the only hope the world has, and it is the only hope your family has. Stand up for King Jesus. Refuse to back down.

Everybody loses when Christians compromise our witness.

When you feel you are not up to the task facing us, remind yourself that you already died in your baptism, having been raised with Christ to a new life (Romans 6:3–4). But you do not stand alone or by your own strength, for "the one who is in you is greater than the one who is in the world" (1 John 4:4).

The battle is spiritual, and you have the Holy Spirit of God. To this reality we now turn.

Small Group Questions

1. Did you finish reading the chapter? If so, what stood out to you from the readings and why?
2. Review Romans 6:3–4 and what it says about baptism. If you have been baptized, when you were baptized, did you see it as the declaration of obedience to Jesus that this chapter describes? Why or why not? If it did not, how can you claim that meaning now?
3. Can you remember situations (personally) where one person's courage to stand up for Jesus and his teachings helped others to also stand up? What happened?

4. Read 1 Peter 4:12–13. How do you naturally react to trials, and how easy or hard is it for you to follow this teaching? Explain.
5. What stands out to you about the eight "I will" statements in this chapter? How can these statements help you personally? Explain.
6. Are there any situations that arise in this chapter where it would be helpful to role-play a conversation or a specific situation in order to help each other anticipate what we might face?
7. In light of the conversation we have had over this chapter, how can we pray for each other?

4

GET SERIOUS ABOUT SPIRITUAL WARFARE

"For our struggle is not against flesh and blood, but against the rulers, against the authorities, against the powers of this dark world and against the spiritual forces of evil in the heavenly realms. Therefore put on the full armor of God, so that when the day of evil comes, you may be able to stand your ground, and after you have done everything, to stand" (Ephesians 6:12–13).

Grace and her husband Joseph are evangelists in Eastern India, where they have planted more than 140 churches, baptized hundreds of people, and seen the amazing power of God in the face of spiritual warfare. But evangelism in a Hindu country is tough work. The Hindu priests often thwart their efforts. It's not uncommon for church planters to be roughed up by Hindu extremist mobs and even the police. The government sometimes arrests Christians for the crime of trying to convert others to Jesus under anti-conversion laws.

India is home to numerous Christian martyrs—men and women who were simply trying to fulfill the mission of Jesus.

Our church has partnered with this couple in the gospel. Once, when Grace was visiting our church, we shared dinner in the house of a church member. That night, Grace told me that she and Joseph do not think of the opposition they face in political or cultural terms. Rather, she explained, they have come to see that the battle they face is spiritual—a war between the forces of good and the forces of evil. They are fighting against a demonic ideology, and the goal of the battle is to set their enemies free from the lies of the evil one.

Then she told a chilling story.

One of Grace's neighbors is from the upper caste and, as a Hindu, this woman somewhat arrogantly resisted Grace's efforts to share Jesus with her. But when the neighbor was diagnosed with tuberculosis, she turned to Grace for prayers. At first, the woman wouldn't come to Grace's house because Grace had also welcomed untouchables into her home. But eventually, the sick woman relented.

Rather than praying for the tuberculosis, however, Grace prayed that the woman would receive Jesus and Christian baptism. Suddenly, and without warning, a man's voice spoke through the sick woman loudly and defiantly: "I've been living peacefully in this woman for years and you are not going to drive me out!" Grace knew she was dealing with a demon. She continued to pray, calling on the name of Jesus and telling the demon he must leave the sick woman. After many hours, the demon left. The sick woman went home exhausted but breathing much better.

The next day, Grace's neighbor visited the doctor, who was shocked to see that the tuberculosis was completely gone. Blood tests confirmed it. Grace's best guess is that the demon had convinced the doctor the woman had tuberculosis to keep the doctor from discovering the demon.

The woman left the doctor's office, came to Grace's home, and was immediately baptized.

But that's not the end of the story. When the demon left the woman, it entered her brother. So Grace and the newly baptized woman went and prayed for him until the demon left him. He, too, was baptized. The demon moved from person to person—a total of eight times, with eight people being baptized as Grace and her team prayed against the demonic spirits.

When Grace told me the story, I commented to her that, with eight baptisms, this demon was a better evangelist than most of my church members!

So I have a question. Do you believe Grace's story with all its demons and its misdiagnosis?

Some of you will not, which raises the question, why not? We follow a Savior who regularly engaged in demonic warfare during his earthly ministry. We believe in Scriptures that presume the physical world is a mere projection of a much more real, powerful, and dangerous spiritual world. Our Scriptures are filled with references to the spiritual: God the Spirit, the Spirit of the Son, the Holy Spirit, cherubim, angels, archangels, seraphim, principalities, powers, Satan, demons, the Antichrist, the dragon, the beast, evil spirits, human spirits, and the like. Why would it surprise us to discover that all of these are real and that they are really doing something, making moves to expand their kingdom? Of all people, why would *Christians* find this spiritual reality hard to believe?

Why would *Christians* find this spiritual reality hard to believe?

The story of the loss of a spiritual worldview in the Christian West is a long one and too complicated for this book. But allow me to say that one of the downsides to the European Enlightenment was that the West came to believe that if we could describe *how* something worked, we could also come to know *why* it worked. But the two are totally different questions. We can explain *how* a frog jumps, for example. It's a matter of physics or chemistry or, if you like, biology. But we cannot explain *why* a frog jumps—why it exists in the first place, why it has the impulse to jump, what is going on in its mind, and, most importantly, what animates a frog in the first place. Why is a frog alive, and not just a lump of lifeless molecules? What is life, after all? What is breath?

These *why* questions are spiritual questions, which is why the term *spirit* in the Bible relates to terms for *breath* and even *life* itself. God formed Adam from the clay of the ground, and breathed in him the breath of life, and Adam became a living soul. The reason the entire universe exists is because of the spiritual. The reason the universe moves, holds together, and, above all, wants to live is because it is animated by spirits. This means that behind every physical phenomenon you experience—every single one!—there is a spirit at work, starting with God himself through Jesus Christ.

> For in [the Son] all things were created: things in heaven and on earth, visible and invisible, whether thrones or powers or rulers or authorities; all things have been created through him and for him. He is before all things, and in him all things hold together. (Colossians 1:16–17)

Paul's description of creation in Colossians 1 reveals that *everything* is spiritual: everything physical is influenced by something spiritual, has spiritual origins, and bears a spiritual purpose.

Of course, Americans use the term *spiritual*, but we typically mean something different than what the Bible means with the term (as well as what most of the world, throughout most of human history, means). When we say *spiritual*, Americans often merely mean *emotional*. When the Bible uses the term, however, it refers to the personal, real beings who are beyond physics but who interact with physics night and day, non-stop, in every corner of the universe. When the Bible uses the term, it is talking about angels and demons, the Holy Spirit and Satan, the archangels, and the beast. And the Bible makes it clear that these spiritual beings are even more real than the physical beings we see every day.

Why does all of this matter?

Because if we are to stand against the onslaught of hostility coming our way, we absolutely must understand that the battle we face is a spiritual one. We are not fighting against social media, licensing boards, HR departments, politicians, political parties, etc.—not ultimately, anyway. We are fighting against demons, principalities, and the powers of this dark world who are merely using physical authorities to seek to destroy us.

If we don't know who the real enemy is, we will fight all the wrong battles. The real enemies are Satan and his demons. The real battle is a spiritual battle.

RECOGNIZE THE ENEMY BEHIND THE ENEMY

The book of Revelation was written for Christians who were facing increasing amounts of persecution. In Western Asia Minor, the persecution was severe enough that there were already martyrs for the faith when John wrote down his visions in the book. The sources of the persecution were pretty much the same as ours: places of employment, family members, social networks of previous friends, the media that existed in those times—all of it under the auspices of the Roman government led by pagans who had come to hate Christians for their values, especially in the areas of sexuality, religious commitment, and the exclusivity of Christ. Rome was determined to silence Christians, even if it meant killing them all.

What's fascinating about Revelation is that the words "Rome" and "Roman" never appear in the book. It is true that Revelation 17:9 mentions the seven hills of Rome, but that's pretty much it. Instead, the book of Revelation teaches Christians about demons, Satan, compromised Christians, the beast, the dragon, Armageddon, heaven, hell, and all things spiritual. Indeed, Rome and the Romans are hardly mentioned in *any* of the letters written to suffering Christians in the New Testament. That's not because the New Testament writers were afraid of naming their persecutors. Rather, it's because the New Testament writers understood who their real enemy was: Satan, not Rome. Peter mentions Rome—under the spiritually bankrupt term "Babylon"—in 1 Peter 5:13, but only after warning the Christians a few verses before who the real enemy is:

> Be alert and of sober mind. Your enemy *the devil* prowls around like a roaring lion looking for someone to devour. Resist him, standing firm in the faith, because you know that the family of believers throughout the world is undergoing the same kind of sufferings. (1 Peter 5:8–9)

Rome's institutions and government were actively harassing and even persecuting Christians, but Peter kept the focus on the real enemy: Satan.

Revelation 12–13 demonstrates this spiritual worldview. Revelation 12 tells the story of a huge red dragon, who is almost certainly Satan in this text—and if not, is another kind of demon. In the story, the dragon tries to stop the work of Christ by attacking his mother while giving him birth, but is thwarted by God through the Archangel Michael. Enraged that he could not stop the work of Christ, the dragon turns his fury against the people of God, sending forth the evil beast of Revelation—who is almost certainly Rome and its institutions. Here is the text:

> Then the dragon was enraged at the woman and went off to wage war against the rest of her offspring—those who keep God's commands and hold fast their testimony about Jesus. The dragon stood on the shore of the sea. And I saw a beast coming out of the sea. It had ten horns and seven heads, with ten crowns on its horns, and on each head a blasphemous name. (Revelation 12:17–13:1)

The beast then persecutes Christians ferociously. And note how the beast seduces humanity: "People worshiped the dragon because he had given authority to the beast, and they also worshiped the beast" (Revelation 13:4). The persecution the Christians faced at the hands of Rome was motivated by people who had enslaved themselves to Satan. Rome was not really the problem. The problem was that the people of the Roman Empire were in bondage to Satan. They had believed Satan's lies. They shared in Satan's rage against righteousness. They had surrendered to Satan's power. Our real enemy is Satan. The battle will have tremendous political, cultural, and social dimensions to it, but at the end of the day, our battle is spiritual—not political, cultural, or social. Paul the apostle says it clearly: "For our struggle is not against flesh and blood, but against the rulers, against the authorities, against the powers of this dark world and against the spiritual forces of evil in the heavenly realms" (Ephesians 6:12).

At the end of the day, our battle is spiritual.

Understand this, and you'll be able to fight faithfully. Misunderstand this, and you'll squander all your ammunition on the wrong enemy: "get out the vote," "flip the courts," "retake the streets," and the like. These issues matter, of course, and I don't want to sound as though I am denying that. Politics get people killed. Culture can corrupt millions of people. Politics matter, and the culture wars are fought over very important issues. But bad politics and corrupt culture are *symptoms* of the real disease. And though symptoms must be treated, the real disease is the spiritual rebellion of humans against God, and the real enemy is Satan, who holds much of humanity in bondage. *We absolutely must understand this, or we'll lose the battle.*

So how does understanding the spiritual war behind our struggles change things?

It shifts our fight away from mere physical strategies toward spiritual strategies. It means that we fight, not merely with votes, tweets, coalitions, and the like. It means, rather, that we fight with truth, with the gospel, with hope, and above all with the love of Christ. We fight by making disciples of our opponents. When Grace's neighbor came to her, Grace understood that the neighbor's greatest need was not to be released from her politics or even from tuberculosis. Grace knew her neighbor's greatest need was to be released from the bondage of the evil one through the gospel of Jesus Christ. And once the neighbor was set free from the demon, the symptoms of her diseases—religious, social, and physical—all went away too.

UNDERSTAND SPIRITUAL BONDAGE

Our opponents are in bondage to the real enemy, Satan. So our battle plan is to set our opponents free from bondage. We don't fight *against* our opponents. We fight *for* them—for their souls and against the demons who have their souls in bondage.

To understand this better, remember that those who persecute us have been blinded by the evil one. Their motives have been shaped by their belief in his lies. As Satan has arrogantly and pridefully lifted himself up against the one true God, he has convinced our opponents to do the same. And their actions make sense to them because they follow the devil—"the ruler of the kingdom of the air, the spirit who is now at work in those who are disobedient" (Ephesians 2:2).

Because they are in bondage to the arrogant dragon and his demons, progressives will be compelled to persecute Christians. It is their obligation. Let that sink in. Progressivism, with its denial of the one true God, is of Satan, and its disciples are therefore in bondage. They are guilty of evil because they are blind. Look at what the apostle Paul wrote to the church of Corinth: "The god of this age has blinded the minds of unbelievers, so that they cannot see the light of the gospel that displays the glory of Christ, who is the image of God" (2 Corinthians 4:4).

Throughout his ministry, Jesus had to battle against demonic possession—demons actually taking control of people and possessing them. They still do this, of course, but much more commonly, demons today act through deceit. They lie, perverting every good and true gift from God into a curse and source of destruction. Deceit is the primary tool the evil one uses. When facing challenges from the Pharisees, Jesus said, "You belong to your father, the devil, and you want to carry out your father's desires. He was a murderer from the beginning, not holding to the truth, for there is no truth in him. When he lies, he speaks his native language, for he is a liar and the father of lies" (John 8:44).

We give the devil power over us when we believe his lies. The problem with our enemies is their acceptance of the evil one's lies. They are in bondage to deceit. Satan has convinced the world that either there is no God or, if God exists, he is primarily concerned with granting us our desires. Like he did in the Garden of Eden, Satan has convinced the world that they have the capacity to build their own paradise here on earth without God. He has schemed to persuade the world that there is no real truth, only power. He has swayed the world to believe that unborn babies are not human and come between the world and its desire for autonomy. He has brainwashed the world that achieving pleasure is the highest good and that sexual sin is a healthy expression of this pleasure. In every case, the evil one has convinced the world that we Christians stand in their way.

The devil lies. The world believes.

In this long passage, the apostle Paul describes how the world falls for such lies. It is a description that sounds as though it could have been written this morning in a national newspaper:

> For although they knew God, they neither glorified him as God nor gave thanks to him, but their thinking became futile and their foolish hearts were darkened. Although they claimed to be wise, they became fools and exchanged the glory of the immortal God for images made to look like a mortal human being and birds and animals and reptiles. Therefore God gave them over

> in the sinful desires of their hearts to sexual impurity for the degrading of their bodies with one another.
>
> They exchanged the truth about God for a lie and worshiped and served created things rather than the Creator—who is forever praised. Amen.
>
> Because of this, God gave them over to shameful lusts. Even their women exchanged natural sexual relations for unnatural ones. In the same way the men also abandoned natural relations with women and were inflamed with lust for one another. Men committed shameful acts with other men and received the due penalty for their error.
>
> Furthermore, just as they did not think it worthwhile to retain the knowledge of God, so God gave them over to a depraved mind, so that they do what ought not to be done. They have become filled with every kind of wickedness, evil, greed and depravity. They are full of envy, murder, strife, deceit and malice. They are gossips, slanderers, God-haters, insolent, arrogant and boastful; they invent ways of doing evil; they disobey their parents; they have no understanding, no fidelity, no love, no mercy. (Romans 1:21–31)

Unbelievers have the same access to God as do believers, but they neither glorified him as God, nor gave thanks to him. Rather, they darkened their hearts and exchanged the glory of God for their idols. They followed their sinful desires down the hole into ever-increasing decadence. As the prophet Jeremiah says, "Truth has perished; it has vanished from their lips" (Jeremiah 7:28).

Why does understanding this matter? Because we can easily waste our time fighting the wrong battles and using the wrong weapons. We could easily believe that we should fight against the dark powers of the world using worldly weapons. But we would fail. We can only fight the powers of this dark world with the power of the Spirit.

Recovering a robust relationship with the Holy Spirit is central to fighting the spiritual war in which we find ourselves. The Spirit equips us for the fight, working signs and wonders and powers, giving us power over the demonic, and eventually transforming us into the image of Christ.

I have written elsewhere about how the Holy Spirit does this.[27] Here, I will only say that a rich relationship with the Holy Spirit has always been central to standing strong in a hostile world. It is the Holy Spirit who will teach us what we need to survive this world (John 14:26). It is the Holy Spirit who will fill our hearts with the love of God for the fight (Romans 5:5). When we are unable to pray, it is the Holy Spirit who will groan on our behalf (Romans 8:26–27). It is the Holy Spirit who will give us the words we need when facing hostility (Matthew 10:20). It is the Holy Spirit who will help us put to death our own sin, which debilitates our fight (Romans 8:13). It is the Holy Spirit who will give strength to our inner being (Ephesians 3:16). It is the Holy Spirit who will give us the gifts we need for the fight (1 Corinthians 12:4). It is the Holy Spirit who will unite us with other believers so we can stand together (1 Corinthians 12:13). And it is the Holy Spirit who will raise us from the dead after the battle is over (Romans 8:11).

The battle is spiritual. Walk in the Spirit.

CULTIVATE THE ARMOR OF THE SPIRIT

What does this love look like? None other than the apostle Paul describes the spiritual equipment for the Christian (Ephesians 6:14–18):

Wrap truth around your waist. The foundation for our spiritual armor is our conviction that only the truth can set us free (John 8:32). This has been proven countless times in history. A million addicts have been set free after they found the courage to face the truth about their addictions in twelve-step programs across the globe. Marriages have been saved when one or both spouses started telling the truth to each other. Oppressive empires have been toppled after people finally stopped repeating lies and started telling the truth. We Christians "speak the truth in love" to those who are in bondage to the lies of the evil one. We expose the myths of progressivism so that we can set others free. To fight the spiritual battle, we cannot shy away from speaking the truth, and we cannot live by the lies of progressivism. Speak the truth and refuse to live by lies.

Put on the breastplate of righteousness. Living rightly ordered lives gives us integrity—a necessary ingredient in courage. After all, when we live in hypocrisy, we are constantly fearful of being exposed. A hypocrite living a double life will never have the fortitude to take a bold stand, lest others discover who they really are. For this reason, the integrity of living consistently with what we preach protects our internal workings. In addition, living rightly ordered lives demonstrates the beauty of the gospel to the world, even when we don't use words. In his first letter, the apostle Peter writes, "Live such good lives among the pagans that, though they accuse you of doing wrong, they may see your good deeds and glorify God on the day he visits us" (1 Peter 2:12). Christian honesty, goodness, generosity, and faithfulness will eventually give us courage to counter the endless slander the pagans hurl against us. Live a righteous life, and the light of Christ will shine into the darkness.

Put the gospel of peace on your feet. We are ambassadors of the good news of Jesus—we *go* with the gospel, as Jesus commissions us to do (Matthew 28:18–20). Even when we feel cornered by a hostile culture, as followers of Jesus, we refuse to stay quiet. As Christians, we play offense, not defense. We keep taking the gospel to the enemy. "As it is written: 'How beautiful are the feet of those who bring good news!'" (Romans 10:15). We will sometimes feel battered, stripped, and bullied from all fronts, but if we keep the proclamation of the gospel as our life's mission, we'll never find ourselves without a purpose in life. We can wake up every morning with a strategy, a mission, and a source of strength and joy. Make disciples of others, and they'll voluntarily give up their bondage to evil.

> Make disciples, and they'll voluntarily give up their bondage to evil.

Take up the shield of faith. Resisting hostility requires faith. Living in a hostile culture is not easy. We may find ourselves suffering through the enemy's destabilizing darts. To sustain us in the battle—to keep us focused and steady—we must walk by faith. We must trust that God is writing a bigger story than the one we're currently living. God has made enormous promises to us; Scripture shows us that some of these promises will only be realized through trials and suffering. God promises to work all things to our good (Romans 8:28); in faith we will realize that promise. God promises that no temptation will be stronger than we can endure (1 Corinthians 10:10–13); in faith we will realize that promise. God promises that he will give us the words we need when we face persecution (Matthew 10:19–20); in faith we will realize that promise. God promises that he will restore the lost fortunes of persecuted believers (Matthew 19:27–30); in faith we will realize that promise. God promises that those who are loyal to him will ultimately win (1 Corinthians 15:51–58); in faith we will realize that promise. Faith is the simple trust that says God's promises are bigger than the sufferings we currently face. Trust in God's power and his plans, and you will live fearlessly in the face of opposition.

Put on the helmet of salvation. The early church swept the Roman world for many reasons, but one of the greatest reasons was the hope it offered to a dysfunctional world. To women trapped in violent and oppressive marriages, the church offered the hope of a different kind of male. To slaves trapped in bondage, the church offered manumission. To widows and orphans living on the edge of survival, the church offered the hope of family. To people oppressed under autocratic regimes, the church offered the hope of a different kind of kingdom. In each case, the world was transformed by Christian hope. Such hope is like water to a thirsty soul—the human heart lives by hope. I believe that progressivism will eventually reveal its utter hopelessness and shame. The sexual revolution has destroyed millions of lives. The dishonesties of secular elites are becoming increasingly laughable. One day the blood of millions of aborted babies will shame Americans into repentance. The class warfare stoked by progressives in cynical powerplays will eventually exhaust itself. The ruined families, the millions of addicts, the homeless, the victims of crime, the confused children—one day they will be forced to search for something better, for a real and lasting hope. Stay the course. You have the hope of the world literally living within you. Bring hope to the world and watch how the demons run.

Deploy the sword of the Spirit—the Word of God. We do not have to figure out how to live all on our own; we have the written Word of God. For us it is a lamp, a compass, a source of peace and strength, and a faithful guide. But the Word of God is also a sword with which we "demolish arguments and every pretension that sets itself up against the knowledge of God, and we take captive every thought to make it obedient to Christ" (2 Corinthians 10:5). When we find ourselves forced or compelled to explain to the world what we believe, let the Word of God make our case. Scripture has the power to change hearts, including those of our opponents. There was never a time when we did not need the Word of God. But when hostility intensifies, as it has in North America right now, we desperately need to listen to and obey his Word. To fight our battles spiritually, we must commit to time in the Word every day of our lives. Feed on the Scriptures, and your strength will be unmatched by the world.

GET YOUR SPIRITUAL PRIORITIES RIGHT

One of my closest friends is a fellow pastor in town. A dozen years ago, Corey planted a church with a tiny handful of people. Today, his church has more than five thousand in attendance, and under his lead, his church has planted numerous other churches. Since starting his church, Corey has only preached verse by verse through the Bible. He is very serious about the Scriptures and unwilling to compromise them for anybody. He preaches strict holiness and speaks often about the absolute need for practicing the ethics of Scripture—including the Bible's sexual ethics.[28]

And yet Corey's church will have every kind of person in town attending any given weekend service: people who've had abortions, homeless people, former inmates, drug addicts, former prostitutes, people from broken homes, you name it. He may have the largest gathering of LGBTQ+ persons in town attending his church—he has many people at his church in same-sex relationships. So how does he preach such a firm message from the Bible and still draw such a non-churched crowd?

The answer is that Corey loves these people. And they know it. He is fighting sin—his own sin as well as the sin of others. But he is fighting sin using the weapons of the Spirit.

During the 2020 presidential elections, Corey and I were talking about what we should say to our churches. The elections were contentious, discouraging, and filled with fury. Both of our churches had people on either side of the election who wanted us to speak out against the evils of the other candidate. Corey and I were both frustrated by the pressure. Still in the middle of leading churches through a pandemic, we were also exhausted. Corey said something I won't forget.

"You know what really gets me?" he asked rhetorically. "It really gets me that some of my members will go out into the streets and yell all sorts of things against their political enemies, raising all kinds of heck. But these same people won't get off their rear ends and walk next door to disciple their own neighbor."

It's well said. We are fighting a spiritual battle, and our motive is love. We know the spiritual power of love. It has the power to dissolve a lie. Love has the power to change a heart. Love has the power to turn our tormenters into our brothers. The apostle Paul started out as a killer of Christians, but the love of Christ that Paul saw in the Christian Ananias turned Paul into the most influential Christian who has ever lived. Our battle is not against Republicans or Democrats. Our battle is against Satan. We love our enemies. We pray for those who persecute us. We bless those who curse us. And we seek to lead them to Jesus. We fight a spiritual battle. By loving our enemies, we can break through the lies they believe. Even the hardest opponent to the Christian faith may come to follow Jesus. We don't fight *against* our enemies. We fight *for* them.

And to do this, we must be people of prayer. And to that subject we now turn.

Small Group Questions

1. Did you finish reading the chapter? If so, what stood out to you from the readings and why?
2. Review Ephesians 6:12–13. What stands out to you from these verses and why?
3. Review 1 Peter 5:8–9. What stands out to you from these verses and why?
4. Some people have a background where there was a lot of teaching about spiritual warfare and others had backgrounds where there was hardly any teaching on it. If you are being transparent, is this material difficult or easy for you with your background? Explain.

5. This chapter teaches that a rich relationship with the Holy Spirit has always been central to standing strong in a hostile world. In what ways do you agree, and how can we each make that kind of relationship a reality?
6. Are there any situations that arise in this chapter where it would be helpful to role-play a conversation or a specific situation in order to help each other anticipate what we might face?
7. In light of the conversation we have had over this chapter, how can we pray for each other?

5

WATCH AND PRAY

"Watch and pray so that you will not fall into temptation. The spirit is willing, but the flesh is weak" (Mark 14:38).

A Middle Eastern friend who plants churches in Africa, the Middle East, and India recently told me about one of the Christians he has worked with in India. The hostile environment he lived in had made life difficult for this believer, and his rights had been severely restricted. Often, the man and his family only survived on handfuls of rice because they couldn't leave the house safely. Knowing that his family could be subject to mistreatment at any moment of any day, they kept a low profile. As a result, he spent much of his time simply in prayer. His neighbors knew he was a Christian, and they knew he spent a lot of time in prayer. His mantra was simple: "Watch and pray."

One day a neighbor knocked on his door. "I don't know you, but I hear you are a praying man," the neighbor said. "My son is sick. Would you come pray over him?"

"Sure," the Christian said. "Let me get my slippers on." He went and prayed for the boy then came home. A week later, the same man knocked at his door. "I want you to know that my son has been healed. My neighbor is in my house now. She is asking if you will come pray for her son."

"Sure," the Christian said. He went and prayed for the woman's son.

A few weeks later, there was another knock on the door. This time when the Christian opened the door, the entire neighborhood stood outside. The first man spoke again: "We know what you did for my son and for my neighbor's son. We are all wondering if you would tell us about this person Jesus?"

Within the month, the entire neighborhood had been baptized into Jesus. Such healing miracles are commonly reported among persecuted Christians around the world (especially in India)—while American Christians still debate whether or not miracles are possible. But when hostility toward Christians increases, if we will take to our knees and follow the lead of Jesus—watching and praying—we will begin to experience the power of God in extraordinary ways. The opposition may be fierce, but our resolve will be strong. The losses may be great, but the rewards will be greater. And the doors closed to us may be many, but the doors opened to us will be eternal.

As Paul wraps up his description of the spiritual armor necessary for following Jesus and living righteously in Ephesians 6, he instructs us to "pray in the Spirit on all occasions with all kinds of prayers and requests." Prayer is so central to the life of the Christian—in any culture, but especially in a hostile one—that it deserves its own chapter. Let's explore why watching and praying is so important to Christians facing hostility in North America.

LEARN TO WATCH

One can build an entire theology from Scripture on the concept of "watching." In the NIV translation, forms of the term "watch" appear more than a hundred times. Sometimes "watch" bears little theological gravity, as in Ruth 2:9, where Ruth is told to "watch the field where the men are harvesting." But often, the term "watch" carries heavy theological significance, such as when the Lord is said to "watch over" his people (e.g., Genesis 28:15; Psalm 121:7; Jeremiah 24:6). We are told to *watch* ourselves closely so that we: do not fall into disobedience (Deuteronomy 4:9); do not commit idolatry (Deuteronomy 4:15–16); prevent our tongues from speaking sinfully (Psalm 39:1); avoid false prophets, false teachers, and heresy (Matthew 7:15; Mark 8:15; Romans 16:17); avoid temptation and the devil's wiles (Matthew 26:41; Galatians 6:1; 1 Peter 5:8); avoid greed (Luke 12:15); and practice forgiveness (Luke 17:3).

What do all of these have in common?

In every case, "watching" means taking precautions against the attacks the evil one is launching against us as followers of Jesus. It means strengthening our resolve so that we will not fall into sin. It means actively anticipating the attacks of the evil one so that we are prepared when these attacks come.

> "Watching" means taking precautions against the attacks the evil one is launching.

Let me give you an example. Given the aggressiveness and increasing power of progressivism, you should *expect* to be challenged at your work. *Before* you're facing adversity, begin preparing for how to respond. I have a friend whose company's HR department has just issued a statement that all employees are to use the preferred pronouns of transgender persons. In chapter 9 below, I will address what I believe is the appropriate Christian response to pronoun questions, but my point right now is that we shouldn't be caught off guard when such policies are proposed and enacted. It's not hard to see where progressivism is going. It is not neutral, and it is not okay with Christians living consistent with Christian principles. You should go ahead and begin planning how you can respond when your company installs policies that require you to endorse transgender ideology. Will you simply go along? Will you find a way to remain hospitable without compromising the truth? Will you object even to the point of losing your job? Prepare yourself for what is coming your way so you are not caught off guard when it happens.

Here's another example. This one is drawn from the experience many have had in their own churches. Given the cultural influence that progressivism now has in America, you should prepare yourself for the possibility that your own church may begin to bend under progressivism's weight. Many churches have already exchanged the Bible's message of sin and salvation for progressivism's message of social policy and activism. You should expect that pastors and church leaders around you will begin to go silent on moral issues in order to avoid offending secular elites. You should expect pressures from various members to soften the non-negotiables of the Christian faith to present themselves to the world as nice people. Prepare for these subtle (and not subtle) compromises by praying for your church and its leaders, by encouraging a high view of Scripture, and by fortifying your own resolve. Jesus anticipates a falling away during times of hostility:

> At that time many will turn away from the faith and will betray and hate each other, and many false prophets will appear and deceive many people. Because of the increase of wickedness, the love of most will grow cold, but the one who stands firm to the end will be saved. (Matthew 24:10–13)

I recently spoke with a person from another state whose church has been committed to biblical teachings for decades. But over the last several years, they noticed that their minister had gone largely silent on sexual sin. Indeed, whenever this minister speaks of sexual sin, he almost exclusively advises the church not to practice "hate"—never mentioning what the Bible teaches about such sins. Last year, the church came out as affirming of same-sex behavior. My contact was shocked, but I was not. Once a church goes silent on major issues of morality and the faith, there is typically a form of decay developing underneath the public work of the church that will eventually rise to the surface. First, a church goes silent on sin. Then it conducts a "dialogue" about whether the sin is really a sin. The church soon decides that both positions are permissible within its teachings. And finally, the church begins to punish those who hold to biblical positions—calling biblical teachings "hate speech" and the like. We must be on guard, we must be watchful, for such decay. It's coming to a lot of churches near you.

But there is a second sense in which the Scriptures teach us to *watch*: watch for what God is doing. The ultimate example of this is to watch for the coming of Jesus at the end of this age: "Therefore keep watch, because you do not know on what day your Lord will come," Jesus says, in a text about persecution and the end of time (Matthew 24:42). But in addition to the end of time, we can watch for the presence of God in our daily lives (Psalm 59:9; Micah 7:7). We pray, he answers. Between our prayers and his answers, we watch, full of hope and anticipation.

This "watching" concept is important for thriving in a hostile environment—watching for the evil one's schemes and for Jesus at work in every circumstance. And in every circumstance, he will accomplish something for his glory. Watch for it, and you'll learn a sense of trust and joy.

Just one example.

Some years back, I was in one of the most difficult ministry seasons of my life. My church was struggling, and I had begun to wonder why I had gone into ministry in the first place. In the middle of this period of discouragement, a religion professor at a Christian college made a tacky remark to me about the failures of my congregation. I got mad. But then, I asked Jesus what he was going to do about it.

"Go away and pray about it," he said to me (in some sense—not audibly).

I did, and over the course of a weeklong prayer retreat, God put on my heart a vision for reviving the congregation. It was multi-faceted, but at the end of the day it focused on two things: making disciple making the main thing and planting disciple making churches. I had no idea how to do either successfully. Up to that point, ministry had prepared me for maintaining a church, but not for aggressively reaching a lost world. But I trusted that if it was God's will that we make disciples and plant churches, he would provide. I returned from the retreat and soon, my church began to embrace the vision, increasingly committing to these two initiatives.

For the next ten years, I had the time of my life. I was watching for Jesus to supply our needs, and he did—in ways I never could have expected. He brought us competent people who knew how to do both. He supplied us with millions and millions of dollars. He joined us to partners who were already planting churches and making disciples. I kept praying and watching. He kept showing up. And anticipating his work in a difficult situation sustained my hope and gave me great joy.

Since that time, my congregation has, in partnership with others, planted more than one thousand churches and baptized thousands of people. Jesus showed up. Watching for him sustained me when I was down, ridiculed, and unsure.

Many times over the years, I have thanked God for the tacky remark that professor made. Without it I may never have seen the miracles he brought through the faith of my congregation.

Watch!

MAKE PRAYER YOUR DAILY BREAD

Because watching is sometimes linked to praying in Scripture (e.g., 1 Peter 4:7), a significant part of living a prayer-filled life is watching our lives for the moral and biblical compromises we've talked about in this chapter. We should be praying against compromise. We should be praying that we learn how to practice, as Jesus does, both grace and truth. We must be praying for one another to have the strength to discern truth

> We should be praying against compromise.

in the midst of all the propaganda swirling around us. We must be praying that we can stand together in love and in unity, presenting the beautiful and authentic message of Christ. In short, we must be a people of prayer, and our churches must be houses of prayer.

But as a rule, North Americans have rather thin prayer lives, probably due to our pragmatic impulses as a people: we like to *do* more than we like to *wait*. Yet by neglecting the rich life that only waiting in daily prayer can cultivate, we can find ourselves empty, lonely, and groundless when we face opposition. So many persecuted Christians have learned to spend enormous amounts of time in prayer to survive in hostile cultures—like the Indian Christian I wrote about at the beginning of this chapter. Indeed, prayer becomes their daily bread. Communing with God nourishes their souls.

One amazing example of this nourishment comes, again, from my Middle Eastern friend. He told me about another persecuted Christian—a woman arrested in East Africa for evangelizing in a Muslim region of her country. Her punishment? She was placed in a shipping container with a small hole on top. The container was then buried with her in it . . . for seven years. You'd think the woman would go mad, but not according to my friend. He explains: "When Aamina was released, her face literally glowed. Yes. She had a glorious look in her eyes, and she was the happiest woman in town. When asked why she could be so full of joy given her imprisonment in such horrible conditions, she explained that she spent seven years in one non-stop prayer. It changed everything for her."

For the mistreated Christian, prayer becomes a secret source of strength, a hiding place, a refuge, and a comfort. Before things get tough, learn to make prayer your daily bread.

Here are some specific prayers you can pray when you face hostility for following Jesus:

Pray for grace and mercy in your time of need. God stands ready to give us grace when we most need it. "In my distress I called to the Lord; I cried to my God for help. From his temple he heard my voice; my cry came before him, into his ears" (Psalm 18:6). As hostility against us increases, grace and mercy from the world will decrease. But God delights in giving us grace and mercy: "Let us then approach God's throne of grace with confidence, so that we may receive mercy and find grace to help us in our time of need," the writer of Hebrews teaches (Hebrews 4:16).

The prayer of Jesus in the Garden of Gethsemane was, among other things, a prayer in search of mercy and grace. As the Son of God, Jesus was willing to accept God's will, but his human nature sweated drops of blood. In response to his anxiety, Luke tells us, God sent an angel to comfort him (Luke 22:43). Many of us have experienced such supernatural grace from God in times of extreme need.

When you face difficult decisions in a hostile world because of your faith, ask God for the grace to comfort you. When you experience loss—the loss of a privilege, a job, or a relationship—because of your faith in Jesus, ask God for grace. Scripture promises us that he will replace what we lose with something more valuable: himself. And we should remember that sometimes our weaknesses offer God a greater space for giving us his mercies. "My grace is sufficient for you, for my power is made perfect in weakness," the Lord explained to Paul in response to his requests to end his suffering (the "thorn in the flesh," 2 Corinthians 12:9).

Pray that you may not fall when tempted. Even in easy times, we find ourselves facing great temptation. But in times of trouble, the temptations can be crushing. If the opposition we face in the US increases, you will be tempted to ignore the truths of Scripture, to compromise your principles for feelings of security, and to sell out your principles to keep your family and friends. To avoid falling in times of temptation, we must pray regularly against it (Matthew 26:41). Do this specifically and by name: "Lord, do not let me play with the truth if my family drifts away," or, "Lord, do not let me yield to the pressure at work to say things I know aren't true." Praying over these temptations by name literally trains us to do the right thing if and when the actual moment comes. It acclimates us to righteousness.

Here's one specific temptation I've increasingly seen over the years: Christians who were faithfully committed to the Scriptures for years—until one of their adult children decided to marry someone of the same sex. Suddenly a mother and father who raised this child to love the Bible, who taught this child right from wrong, and who modeled God's intentions for marriage, begin to compromise their views to protect their relationship with their adult child. One couple who did this came to me, without provocation, to explain. "Our son has made it clear that if we don't accept his boyfriend, now his husband, we cannot have a relationship with him either. We know we used to believe this is wrong, and we still don't like it. But his husband is such a nice person, and God wants us to love everyone. So we no longer believe that same-sex activity is wrong. It's just love, after all."

Now, we should, of course, love everyone, and people actively sinning especially need our love so that we can help them escape their sins. And I would not advocate cutting off our children because they abandon Christian principles. There are many ways to maintain a relationship with family members whose values conflict with ours—we do it all the time. But we must never call what is wrong right simply to maintain a relationship. To do so robs everyone of what may be the only opportunity to hear the truth.

This decision may well be headed your way, assuming you're not already facing it. But remember that even though it will be painful, God will not allow you to be tempted beyond what you can bear (1 Corinthians 10:13). Treat everyone with love. Cultivate relationships that help lead others to Jesus. Show hospitality to those whose values and lifestyles are opposite yours. But pray specifically that your family and friends will not cave into a pagan sexual ethic; and pray specifically that, if they do, you will have the strength to say no to the sin, even if saying yes to the person—respectfully and lovingly, but also clearly.

Pray for boldness. When Peter and John were arrested by the Sanhedrin for healing in the name of Jesus, they were forced to spend the night in jail, put on trial, and threatened if they continued to preach the name of Jesus. Returning to their church, they gathered a crowd and prayed: "Lord, consider their threats and enable your servants to speak your word with great boldness. Stretch out your hand to heal and perform signs and wonders through the name of your holy servant Jesus" (Acts 4:29–30).

Persecution created boldness in the apostles. I have already mentioned an incident involving my junior high P.E. class. My punishment for refusing to do what I thought was wrong only emboldened me. In the same way, the apostles became bolder in the face of opposition—as they increasingly realized they were in a spiritual war, and there would be no truce. So they asked the Lord for even greater boldness. And in response, the Lord increased the signs and wonders among the believers: "After they prayed, the place where they were meeting was shaken. And they were all filled with the Holy Spirit and spoke the word of God boldly" (Acts 4:31).

Likewise, in a world that increasingly hates us and what we stand for, we must ask God for boldness—to stand for the truth, to bear the name of Jesus, and to show love, patience, and kindness to our enemies. Now this requires some discretion. Later in this book (chapter 10), I'll argue that there are times when we can dodge difficult situations or even remain silent. But such occasions should not dampen or inhibit our willingness to speak clearly when necessary. The pagan world is caught in a web of lies. Sometimes simply speaking the truth can change everything for them.

I know of a woman who had been thoroughly propagandized into the pro-abortion camp. She had adopted the typical narrative: abortion is "health care," unborn babies are "fetuses," and opponents of abortion are "anti-woman." Determined to change my mind after I condemned America's abortion industry, she met with me. She presented her case when I began to explain to her that, as a Christian, I simply could not condone killing babies. I described what a baby in the womb is, how other cultures have redefined people as other than human to justify abusing or killing them, and how the Christian faith loves everyone, including the unborn baby unwanted by its mother or father. At first, I saw a rage in the eyes of my conversationalist. Then I saw anguish. Then tears. It became obvious to me that she had never actually thought about what an abortion is. She had simply accepted the progressive propaganda.

Eventually, she became an avid pro-life advocate. All it took was someone taking the time to sit with her and lovingly present the truth. You will not always get these results. But if you are not bold enough to speak truth when you have the opportunity, how can anyone ever learn it?

Ask God to give you boldness, and he will.

Pray against the strongholds of the enemy. In 2 Corinthians 10:4–5, Paul teaches us that we have weapons capable of destroying the evil one's strongholds: Our weapons "have divine power to demolish strongholds. We demolish arguments and every pretension that sets itself up against the knowledge of God, and we take captive every thought to make it obedient to Christ."

What is a stronghold? The Old Testament uses the term "stronghold" dozens of times to describe a concentration of enemy power—a fort, a tower, a rally point. Often, God himself is called a "stronghold" for the believer—indicating that God can serve as a point of strength for those of us who cling to him. In the opposite way, the evil one can so infest an idea, a place, or a culture that such a place can be called a "stronghold." From such strongholds come enormous amounts of darkness and damage. We should pray against these. To borrow from an image Jesus uses, we should "bind the strong man" so that we can plunder his house—rescuing people from darkness.

I recently read a story about a pub in the Northwest that overtly presents itself as a stronghold of darkness. Even the name of the pub is a knock-off of Satan's name. The pub has training classes on witchcraft. It has "pagan nights." And its story came across my desk when the pub announced plans to host an eleven-year-old girl performing drag for adults in a drag queen story hour. Such blatant darkness is an indication of a stronghold. We can write against it (as I'm doing right now). We can post comments on it. We can lobby for legislative bodies to make such abuse of children a crime (and I'm for that). But as much as any of these things, we should pray that God would break down this stronghold and that the gospel will enter that pub. It's been done before. For example, after prayers and the faithful work of Christians, an abortion clinic in Miami was eventually shut down . . . and then turned into a Christian pregnancy center that has saved an estimated eighteen thousand unborn babies' lives.[29] Some prayed against the stronghold, and God answered.

Pray that God will open the heart of your enemies to the gospel. Jesus teaches us to pray for our enemies (Luke 6:27–28). But pray what? Obviously, Jesus doesn't want us praying that they continue in their rebellion. Rather, we should pray that God would open a door for the gospel in our enemies' lives. This is precisely what Paul asks the church in Colossae to do: "Devote yourselves to prayer, being watchful and thankful. And pray for us, too, that God may open a door for our message, so that we may proclaim the mystery of Christ, for which I am in chains" (Colossians 4:2–3). Paul not only asks the Christians in Colossae to pray for him; he asks them to pray that God will open doors for him so that he can win his opponents to the gospel.

Pray that God would open a door for the gospel.

This is the ultimate victory for the believer—and one to which I devote an entire chapter (chapter 12). For now I will simply affirm that we are to be praying that God will convict the hearts of those who oppose him so that they—like the apostle Paul, who started out a persecutor but ended up a missionary—can come to Jesus and bring many in their social networks with them. God can do this, and when we pray for it, he responds.

STANDING WITH JOY

Several years ago, I was talking to a man who has done extensive work evangelizing in China. The Chinese government has a mixed record on persecuting Christians, which it often assumes is a Western religion. When things are great in relations with the West, China generally allows Christians to live fairly ordinary lives. But when relations with the West are tense, China often cracks down on Christians, harassing them, penalizing them, and imprisoning some. And since President Xi Jinping has come into power, living as a Christian and being part of a church in China has become increasingly difficult and in some regions, dangerous.

My friend told me he was always surprised at who would and who would not renounce Jesus when a crackdown occurred. Often, he said, it was the gentlest, most quiet, and least assuming person—an older woman, or a middle-aged man—who would take the boldest stands and have the most joy. "After a while," my friend explained, "you learn to assess who will stand and who will fall by the kind of prayer life a person has. These little old ladies," to use his words, "and these empty nester men had spent enormous amounts of time in prayer—drawing close to God, rehearsing for trials and temptations, and preparing for the world to come. When hardship came, they were the ones who were ready and stood with joy."

Another friend of mine, Jerry Trousdale, once told me a story of prayer almost too impossible to believe, but I've seen it with my own eyes.[30]

Jerry did mission work in Sierra Leone in the early 1970s and had some success baptizing and planting churches. In 1976, he returned to the US to pursue a graduate degree in religion from Fuller Theological Seminary. He moved to Arcadia, California, and pastored a church there. At the same time, a group of ten women read the book *What Happens When Women Pray*, and they felt led to pray for, among other things, the gospel in Sierra Leone. They prayed against the strongholds in that country, especially Islam and animism.

This prayer ministry for Sierra Leone went on . . . for thirty-five years. Many of those praying for this West African nation knew next to nothing about how God might be answering those prayers. But they kept praying.

By the early 2000s, Jerry had teamed up with Shodankeh Johnson, a brilliant church leader from Sierra Leone, and they began to put into practice some of the disciple making, church planting strategies taught by David Watson, who himself had planted thousands of churches in Asia.

By the time Jerry joined my church in 2017, the movements that he, Shodankeh, and others had started had seen thousands of churches planted and tens of thousands of Muslims and animists baptized, including some from the most resistant people groups in the world. Indeed, I'm not exaggerating when I say that since this handful of women at the Arcadia Church of Christ started praying, more Muslims have been brought to Christ in the last fourteen years than in all the last fourteen centuries of history combined!

Jerry has been a leader for both Final Command Ministries and New Generations; Shodankeh leads New Harvest Ministries. Between these ministries and the works they have helped start, hundreds of thousands of people have now come to Jesus. Because strongholds—violent, deadly strongholds—have been broken down by the gospel. Because ten women decided to pray.

Prayer leads us to become like Christ, and this is crucial for his followers, for the worst thing we can do is compromise our faith to accommodate the world. So to this subject we now turn.

Small Group Questions

1. Did you finish reading the chapter? If so, what stood out to you from the readings and why?
2. Read Matthew 24:10–13. If we are going to be living in a time like the one described in these verses, what is the most important thing to remember and why?
3. This chapter teaches us that before we face adversity, we should begin preparing for how to respond. What is your reaction to that statement and why?
4. What are some ways we can help each other to prepare for the adversity this chapter describes?
5. What is the role prayer plays in preparing for adversity? How can we increase our practice of prayer as this chapter describes? What prayer advice has been most helpful to you? Explain.
6. Are there any situations that arise in this chapter where it would be helpful to role-play a conversation or a specific situation in order to help each other anticipate what we might face?
7. In light of the conversation we have had over this chapter, how can we pray for each other?

6

LIVE AS A NON-CONFORMIST

"Do not conform to the pattern of this world, but be transformed by the renewing of your mind. Then you will be able to test and approve what God's will is—his good, pleasing and perfect will" (Romans 12:2).

By 1938, J. Calvitt Clarke, a Presbyterian minister, had seen enough of the suffering of the children displaced by the Sino-Japanese Wars. A gifted fundraiser, Clarke decided to find American support for these children using a new model: child sponsorship. Each donor would be asked to sponsor an individual child (or more) at a set rate. The money would be used by local organizations to care for the children in China who were suffering. Calling his organization China's Children Fund, Clarke had enormous success raising funds for the children. By 1951, he decided to support children in other areas, so he changed the name of the organization to Christian Children's Fund (CCF).

CCF successfully supported children in numerous countries for years using Christian principles. Those of you who are older may remember the television commercials featuring actress Sally Struthers asking for support. CCF soon became one of the largest Christian ministries in the US.

Not long after Clarke founded CCF, another minister, Everett Swanson, saw similar devastation after the Korean War and wanted to help the children displaced in South Korea. Swanson decided to follow the model of CCF and founded Compassion International (CI), which also solicits sponsors for individual children in poverty or distress. Compassion International has also become one of the largest Christian ministries in the US.

But both organizations reached a fork in the road following the 1970s. As their ministries grew, each ministry had access to large donors who were interested in philanthropy but not in the Christian connection. Each found themselves tempted to abandon the Christian part of their ministries to broaden their donor base and, hence, the number of children they could serve.

As a result, CCF eventually decided to drop "Christian" from its name and adopt the name ChildFund—to make it easier to raise funds from trusts and corporations that wanted to avoid explicitly Christian work. It didn't take long, however, before the name change became a culture change. ChildFund still does good work, but it no longer considers itself distinctly Christian. Though it feeds and educates many children, the organization no longer leads them to the very Jesus who motivated the charity's work in the first place.

Meanwhile Compassion International's leadership faced the same choice: drop the Christian connections and increase their donor base, or keep the Christian connection and remain faithful to its mission. After intense soul-searching, Compassion decided that their only reason for helping children with health care, food, and education was the love of Christ. Compassion wanted to do more than help children navigate extreme poverty; they wanted to help children know Jesus. So Compassion decided to reinforce its Christian connection and strengthen its work through the local church wherever they serve. When the organization was encouraged by a marketing firm to drop the Christian connection, it reportedly responded, "No, not now, not ever."[31]

Why did ChildFund go one way and Compassion International the other?

GUARD AGAINST MISSION DRIFT

The answer is simple: mission drift.

By accommodating distinctly secular interests, ChildFund was able to raise huge amounts of money and greatly expand their work. But in the process, it lost the conviction that Christian principles are foundational. Such mission drift is everywhere in North American Christianity today. Ministries once founded to promote Christ and his work now often hide the Christ part, compromise the teachings of Scripture, and even work against Christian values. Businesses and charitable trusts once oriented toward Christian principles have often lost these values, sometimes funding institutions that even undermine the Christian faith. Many Christian schools and universities—including evangelical ones—are also quietly compromising their Christian convictions while still presenting themselves to potential students as "Christian."

And it's not just Christian non-profits, schools, and businesses. Many churches and entire denominations are also falling into deep compromise. Not all at once, mind you. Mission drift is, as the term implies, a gradual, often unintentional, process. It involves a thousand compromises with progressivism, until, one day, Christ is gone from the organization altogether.

If you are going to survive the assault now targeting you, you will have to recognize that compromise is defeat. The greatest enemy of all minority communities is not *opposition*. Rather, it is *compromise*. To assimilate to progressivism and its values is to lose your faith. What is faith anyway if it is not a commitment to doing things God's way instead of the world's ways? Compromise is a halfway house between

Christian faith and disbelief altogether. When you begin to compromise, you are already losing your faith.

> Compromise is a halfway house between Christian faith and disbelief altogether.

Let's briefly describe and respond to some of the areas where Christians find ourselves at highest risk.

NEVER COMPROMISE SCRIPTURE

As far as we know, God never literally picked up a pen and paper and wrote Scripture (although he did write the Ten Commandments on stone using his finger). This doesn't mean, however, that Scripture is not from God. Rather, as the apostle Paul boldly declares, "All Scripture is breathed out by God and profitable for teaching, for reproof, for correction, and for training in righteousness, that the man of God may be competent, equipped for every good work" (2 Timothy 3:16–17). Paul's term "breathed out by God" in this text is an explicit claim of inspiration. The Scriptures we have were literally breathed out by God, regardless of who was holding the pen. Peter describes how this worked: "Above all, you must understand that no prophecy of Scripture came about by the prophet's own interpretation of things. For prophecy never had its origin in the human will, but prophets, though human, spoke from God as they were carried along by the Holy Spirit" (2 Peter 1:20–21). The authors of the Scriptures were moved by the Holy Spirit as they wrote the very words of God.

This is consistent with what the Old Testament writers said about themselves. More than eight hundred times, the Old Testament uses the formulaic phrase: "The Lord says . . ." The phrase is intended to declare that the text contains the actual words of God. The phrase is used in the Torah—the bedrock of Judaism. It is used in the historical writings, which describe God's relationship to Israel. It is found in the poetic books of the Old Testament, which convey human reflections on God. And it is frequently used by the prophets, who believed they were declaring the actual words of God.

Because of this belief, the Old Testament can say of itself that it is "perfect, reviving the soul . . . sure, making wise the simple . . . right, rejoicing the heart . . . pure, enlightening the eyes . . . and true, and righteous altogether" (Psalm 19:7–9). It is why disobeying the Old Testament writings was a punishable offense in Israel—sometimes even by death. It explains why the psalmist wrote, "I meditate on your precepts and consider your ways. I delight in your decrees; I will not neglect your word" (Psalm 119:15–16).

Jesus and the apostles affirmed the inspiration and authority of the Old Testament, quoting from it and alluding to it more than three hundred times. Jesus declares that "until heaven and earth pass away, not an iota, not a dot, will pass from the Law until all is accomplished. Therefore, whoever relaxes one of the least of these commandments and teaches others to do the same will be called least in the kingdom of heaven, but whoever does them and teaches them will be called great in the kingdom of heaven" (Matthew 5:17–19). Jesus declares that Scripture cannot be broken (John 10:35), that the Old Testament is "the Word of God" (Mark 7:13), containing the "commandment of God" (Matthew 15:3). Paul writes that "the law is holy, and the commandment is holy and righteous and good . . . [and] spiritual" (Romans 7:12–14), that the entire Old Testament is about Christ (Romans 3:31; 8:3–4), and that Christians are the heirs of the Old Testament (1 Corinthians 10:11; Romans 15:4).

Further, Jesus promised his apostles that they would receive the Holy Spirit, who would guide *them*, as God had done with the Old Testament writers, in all truth (John 16:13), making the New Testament the inspired Word of God too. So Jesus says that people who obey his commands will obey the Scriptures too (John 15:20). Peter says that the first followers of Jesus "preached the gospel . . . by the Holy Spirit sent from heaven" (1 Peter 1:12). Peter calls Paul's writings Scripture (2 Peter 3:15–16), and Paul himself says that his writings are the Word of God (1 Thessalonians 2:13; Galatians 1:8–9; 1 Corinthians 14:37–38). And well they should be. Remember that Paul actually went to heaven, where he received a revelation directly from God (2 Corinthians 12:1–4). He performed signs, wonders, and powers to confirm his authority (Romans 15:18–19). The church itself is built on the foundation of the apostles and prophets (Ephesians 2:19–21), and the walls of heaven have the names of the Twelve Apostles inscribed on them (Revelation 21:14).

All of this means that to stand firm, we must stand on the sacred Scriptures as the very Word of God. Progressivism seeks to chip away at every conviction you have. If you are to clarify your convictions and prevent drift, you must spend real time in the Word of God, where you'll learn what questions matter the most and what answers are correct. We must make the Word of God the lamp for our feet, especially in troubled times. You must read it, meditate upon it, and obey it. Biblical ignorance invites compromise. Biblical respect produces strength. The psalmist declares, "I will speak of your statutes before kings and will not be put to shame, for I delight in your commands because I love them" (Psalm 119:46–47).

The Bible closes with these words: "I warn everyone who hears the words of the prophecy of this book: if anyone adds to them, God will add to him the plagues described in this book, and if anyone takes away from the words of the book of this prophecy, God will take away his share in the tree of life and in the holy city, which are described in this book" (Revelation 22:18–19). To stand firm, we must stand on the Word of God, and not on the platitudes of progressivism.

DO NOT PLAY WORD GAMES

I've already mentioned that propaganda and disinformation are among the primary tools of progressives in their assault against Christians. One way progressives do this is by redefining terms so as to render them toothless. We live in a world full of such propaganda, and we are susceptible to its effects. For this reason, we must be vigilant about guarding the fundamental meanings of words. Author George Orwell, who sought to expose the evils of twentieth-century Marxist regimes, said it well: "In a time of universal deceit, telling the truth is a revolutionary act."

I've already mentioned some of the terms being redefined in hostile America. The meanings of such basic terms as "gender," "male," "female," "man," "woman," "sex," "baby," "mother," "father," and others are in constant flux in America. Such obfuscation will inevitably beguile some of us Christians, making it necessary for us to repeatedly clarify these terms.

The Christian meaning of the term "love" is frequently perverted by progressives. In the Bible, love means putting the needs of others before your needs. Love seeks what is good for others. For this reason, true love cannot support sin and evil because sin and evil are never good for others. "Love . . . does not delight in evil," the apostle Paul says (1 Corinthians 13:6). God—who is the very definition of love—does not abide sin and evil; he will punish unrepentant sinners *for an eternity.*

For progressives and their Christian enablers, however, "love" means something like "accepting and affirming anything I say about myself"—and perhaps even enshrining it in law while punishing those who do not accept it. But this is propaganda used to normalize sin. As Christians, we must constantly remind the world that it is not loving to affirm sin in someone else's life, just as it is not loving to give cocaine to a drug addict.

For progressives, the virtue of "tolerance" is also perverted. Originally, tolerance meant "to tolerate," that is, to refuse to punish those who disagree. In progressivism, tolerance means to celebrate deviancy, or be punished by your school, social media companies, business, or government. In this meaning, "tolerance" is more a vice than a virtue, which is why the Bible frequently encourages us *not* to be tolerant (see Psalm 101:5, 1 Corinthians 5:1; Revelation 2:2, 20). Rather than tolerating sin, serious Christians practice redemption from sin, forgiveness, and restoration from sin. And they practice *patience* while helping people out of their sin.

We must also guard the special term "judge." Indulgent people are quick to point out that Jesus teaches against certain forms of judgment (Matthew 7:1–5). But those who are quick to say that we shouldn't judge often fail to point out that Jesus, in the very same sermon, warns us against false teachers and informs us that we will be able to identify sinners by their fruit: "Not everyone who says to me, 'Lord, Lord,' will enter the kingdom of heaven, but only the one who does the will of my Father who is in heaven" (Matthew 7:21). Jesus does not teach us to abstain from all forms of judging; he teaches us to refuse to be *hypocritical* in our judgments. "Judge for yourselves what is right," he says elsewhere. Though only God can pronounce final judgment on anyone, we Christians have the obligation to practice fair and biblical discernment, discretion, and judgment to remain holy. "Do you not know that the Lord's people will judge the world?" Paul asks (1 Corinthians 6:2).

Progressives seek to redefine many such terms to gaslight Christians. But we must stand firm on biblical terms and the Bible's definitions of each one.

Progressives seek to redefine many such terms to gaslight Christians.

Former Supreme Court Justice Antonin Scalia is perhaps best known for approaching laws using the principle of *textualism*: "When a court interprets a statute, the court's job is to read the statutory text and do what it says."[32] Justice Scalia tried to do what the Constitution actually *says* rather than play with words to do what he might *want*. In the same way, in an age of propaganda, Christians must do what the text says rather than play with words to do what we may want. We must be the guardians of the truth.

RESIST THE URGE TO CRITICIZE ONLY BIBLE-BELIEVING CHRISTIANS

In a world where compromise has created a large gray area among Christian believers, you cannot always tell where a person stands on important issues. But there is one significant indicator of what such "gray" Christians believe, even when they don't realize it: the specific direction they often aim their complaints.

Many believers reveal a compromising spirit, even while claiming to be Christians, when they complain only about other Christians. Embarrassed by biblical Christianity, these believers cannot find the stomach or the courage to criticize secular leaders, progressive Christian thought-shapers, advocates of unbiblical sexual ethics, Marxists with their destructive theories, etc. They are frequently embarrassed by biblical teachings. They downplay hard teachings of the Bible about such things as the justice of God and the exclusivity of Christ. They offer a steady stream of alternative readings of the Christian faith designed to soften its teachings about such things as sex and gender.

In other words, they *never* punch in the direction of progressivism. They *only* punch toward other Christian believers, especially Bible-believing Christians and evangelicals. They can never stop apologizing for the misadventures of other Christians. When progressives attack evangelical Christians, soft progressives rush to the microphones to apologize for evangelical beliefs. When progressivism misbehaves—which it does in numerous ways every day—it's crickets from these Christians. I call these believers "soft progressives"—Christians who claim apostolic Christianity but are desperate to fit in with the secular agenda.

These Christians allow progressivism to identify which issues are important, which definitions can be used, and which outcomes are acceptable. Whatever the issue, if progressivism is raging about it, they will take their eyes off biblical teachings about sin and salvation to join the secular conversation. Like a moth to the flame, the instinct of soft progressives—their natural reflex—is to flutter around progressivism wherever it is.

But if we are to stand firm in a hostile world, we must learn and accept that though Christians are guilty of innumerable foibles, stupidities, and sins, progressivism is from Satan. It is progressivism—not evangelicalism or other efforts at biblical Christianity—that threatens persecution against the faith in America. The temptation to see weaknesses on only one side reveals that you are probably *already* on the other side. It's a temptation we must avoid because it robs us of the ability to see the power and beauty of apostolic Christianity. We should, indeed, call out our brothers and sisters when they act wrongly. But faithful Christians recognize that progressivism is not merely a misreading or misapplication of the Christian faith. It is a hostile *rejection* of it. Soft progressivism always ends in unfaithfulness. We must be careful not to drift here.

REJECT THE COMPROMISE THAT IS PROGRESSIVE CHRISTIANITY

Thus far, we have dealt with progressivism in general, but here, let's take a moment to focus in on an influential subset of progressivism: progressive Christianity. I believe that progressive Christianity poses a massive threat to Christian faithfulness—so much so that I have written an entire book against progressive Christianity.[33] Since my thoughts on the subject are available in that book, here I only want to summarize the ways that progressive Christianity represents a drift from Christ that we must absolutely reject if we are to stand firm.

By its very definition, progressive Christianity is a compromise of the apostolic and historic faith to make Christianity fit in with secular progressivism. So it rewrites the Christian faith along the lines of whatever the latest secular and progressive theories are saying. To do this, progressive Christianity must practice the following:

1. Undermining Scripture. Progressive Christianity is desperate to *belong* in the world of elite, secular Westerners. The Christian Scriptures, however, stand in the way. For this reason, these progressives must constantly undermine the Bible to promote their ideology. So the Bible is constantly reinterpreted to align it with sentiment, as well as with select elements of science, pop psychology, and a variety of social theories. Biblical words are reshaped to mean the opposite of what they say. Various biblical authorities, such as the apostle Paul, are subjected to contorted interpretations or are marginalized, challenged, or simply dismissed. The Bible only matters insofar as it advances the cause of secular beliefs. Outside of progressive America, the Scriptures are generating a thousand disciple making movements that are literally changing the global South. People open their Bibles, read a text, obey it, and find true liberation. But you wouldn't know it from the way Western progressives approach Scriptures. The sword of the Spirit—the one thing that has the power to change the world—is sold for a pile of secular crumbs.[34]

Progressive New Testament scholar Luke Timothy Johnson illustrates this, while writing in approval of same-sex activity: "I think it important to state clearly that we do, in fact, reject the straightforward commands of Scripture, and appeal instead to another authority when we declare that same-sex unions can be holy and good. And what exactly is that authority? We appeal explicitly to the weight of our own experience . . ."[35] Such a hermeneutic is self-authenticating. Whatever I choose to experience becomes the authority through which I interpret my experience. With a faithless hermeneutic such as this, who needs unbelievers?

2. Downplaying the deity of Jesus. Because progressive Christianity seeks to unite humanity around its own utopic visions, claims to the divinity of Jesus get in the way. If Jesus is the Son of God, then he is not just one of many ways to God—he is the *only* way, and all other ways are wrong. This is why progressives tend to speak of

Jesus more as a role model or social activist—similar to Martin Luther King Jr., or Gandhi—than as the Son of God.

This rejection of Jesus as the Son of God explains why, for example, the Methodist school Shenandoah University in Winchester, Virginia, hired a Muslim chaplain for their Christian students in 2019. The Christian school explained to those who were shocked by the move that promoting a Muslim imam was a "Christian thing to do." Imagine a Muslim school in Egypt hiring a Christian pastor for its students, or a secular university in Southern California hiring a southern white male to lead its women's studies program. But progressive Christianity sees Muslims as a persecuted minority and Christians as the oppressors. So entire Christian denominations downplay the deity of Christ because this primary truth robs progressivism of one of its foundational beliefs: Christians are the problem, not the solution.

But the denial of Jesus as the divine Son of God results in no real reason to be Christian at all. This explains why every single American mainline Protestant denomination is in a free fall. If Jesus is not the Son of God, why waste your time on him? And since these denominations are functionally separating themselves from the Son of God, he is doing the same with them.

3. Rejecting the need for atonement and the justice of God. Progressive Christianity is largely a religion of white, elite Americans who have an optimistic view of human capacity and have experienced very little injustice or mistreatment in their lives. Furthermore, progressive Christians generally ignore Jesus' claim that sin is personal—not merely social—and that unforgiven individuals will face a day of judgment and condemnation at his return.

There are two side effects of this elitism. First, like secular progressives, most Christian progressives adopt a view of humanity that simply cannot accept the individual fallenness of humanity. This leads progressives to deny the need for atonement, arguing instead that Jesus simply died as a social justice martyr. This is reflected in the line famously passed around by progressive Christians that the doctrine of the atonement, were it true, would constitute a form of divine child abuse.[36]

Further, since most progressives have personally tended to be on the winning side of justice, they have very little sense of how much injustice exists in the world and why God would call himself a just God. This leads progressives to develop indulgent views of love, to deny any concept of the wrath of God, and to recoil at Jesus' teaching about hell. Progressive luminary Brian McLaren says that if hell is true, then the claims of the cross are false. He argues that, if hell is true, "God gets his way through coercion and violence and intimidation and domination just like every other kingdom does."[37] McLaren has created a god in McLaren's own image: sophisticated, open-minded, indulgent, urbane, and progressive. But this is not who God is.

Such progressive principles beguile believers into denying the atonement, the hope of a resurrected life, the seriousness of sin, and the notion of the wrath of God. Christian teachings like these (and more) stand in the way of progressivism's vision of America, which means progressive Christians must reject these teachings. But such a drift is nothing other than a total capitulation to progressivism itself. It is no Christianity at all.

4. Rewriting the mission of the church. The mission of the apostolic church has always been the proclamation of the good news that God has come in the person of Jesus Christ to redeem sinful humans and to prepare us for a resurrected life in a new creation. This is the meaning of the Great Commission—Jesus' last words in the Gospel of Matthew: "Go and make disciples of all nations." The apostolic church thus teaches individuals to deny their sinful desires, take up counter-cultural crosses, follow the way of Jesus, and take the good news to the nations.

In progressive Christianity, the church's mission is to support various social causes and public policy issues to achieve a better society here on earth—one where people are encouraged to follow their desires and become whatever *they* want to be.[38] Making disciples of

Jesus prepared for Christ's second coming is of little interest to progressive Christians, who instead devote their energies to issuing judgments about public policy.

A simple check of the websites of mainline denominations demonstrates this nationalist obsession with progressive public policy. On the day I'm writing this paragraph, the home page of the website for the Evangelical Lutheran Church of America (ELCA) features a call for diversity and repentance for racism, a celebration of women pastors, a proposed policy for gun control, a statement on gender justice, an article celebrating the ELCA's embrace of LGBTQIA+ persons, and the like. As far as I can see, the website is silent about the personal sins that Jesus lists in Mark 7:21–22: sexual immorality, theft, murder, adultery, greed, malice, deceit, lewdness, envy, slander, arrogance, and folly. The website for the Presbyterian Church USA (PCUSA) is similar, asking for donations toward its social justice projects, and on its "Social Issues" tab, offering left-leaning positions on abortion, gun violence, gender, capital punishment, and other social issues. Even the United Methodist Church (UMC), which still has many evangelicals in its flock, focuses its website on policy issues: race, illegal immigration, oppression, climate change, and others.

Of little concern on these websites are many of the issues addressed in the Scriptures. Drunkenness is on Jesus' list of sins, but alcohol and drug abuse, which wreck millions of lives in America, seem unworthy of the PCUSA's website. Greed is one of the big sins that Jesus condemns, but as far as I can tell, the massive and immoral debt the US government has racked up is not on any of these sites. These sites ignore the daily destruction and violence perpetrated by the left-wing Antifa movement. The collapse of freedom in Hong Kong by totalitarian China isn't mentioned. Jesus' concern with adultery and divorce is ignored. The martyrdom of Christians in socialist and Muslim states—a dozen per day every day of the year—is missing from these websites. The enslavement of black Africans by Muslim Arabs in Mauritania is not a problem either. The corruption of the Palestinian government and the terrorism of Hamas are missing from the PCUSA's website, but Israel's democracy is criticized.

Meanwhile, the Great Commission, which describes the real mission of the church, is subject to criticism by progressive Christians. Progressive Pastor Dawn Hutchings of Holy Cross Lutheran Church outside of Toronto goes so far as to state that Jesus' final words in the Gospel of Matthew are actually bad news: "The so-called 'Great Commission' is anything but the 'gospel,'" she declares. "Indeed, I have come to believe that this particular ending to the Gospel according to Matthew may be the source of the systemic racism which permeates, not just the Church, but also, all of the Western cultures and institutions which arose out of what history has dubbed the Holy Roman Empire."[39] A Christian pastor condemns the words of Jesus: this is the arrogant place where progressive Christianity stands.

Progressive Christianity distorts the meaning of the Christian faith and puts the well-being of millions of Christians at risk. We must have the courage and clarity to be faithful. We must not drift.

We must have the courage and clarity to be faithful.

DO NOT TRADE JESUS FOR ANYTHING

In February 2019, the United Methodist Church met in St. Louis to decide whether or not they would endorse same-sex activity. Many American UMC members argued that the church should give up on biblical sexuality and adopt pagan sexual values. African Methodists stood up in opposition, staunchly defending the Scriptures. Their boldness was exhilarating to those of us who want real Christianity. Here were men and women from one of the world's poorest continents confronting those with the prestige, money, and power of one of the world's largest denominations. Here were true believers speaking truth into power.

One African leader, Jerry P. Kulah, stood up in the middle of the deliberations and clearly stated the convictions of these African Christians: we will not capitulate to the decadence of American progressivism, he declared.

> Friends, please hear me, we Africans are not afraid of our sisters and brothers who identify as lesbian, gay, transgender, bi-sexual, questioning or queer. We love them and we hope the best for them, but we know of no compelling arguments for forsaking our church's understanding of Scripture and the teachings of the church universal. Please hear me when I say, as graciously as I can, we Africans are not children in need of western enlightenment when it comes to the church's sexual ethics. We do not need to hear a progressive US bishop lecture us about our need to grow up. Let me assure you, we Africans have had to engage in this debate for many years whether we liked it or not. We stand with the global church, not a culturally liberal church elite in the US. So if anyone is so naïve or condescending to think that we would sell our birthright in Jesus Christ for US dollars, they simply do not know us. Please understand me when I say that the vast majority of African United Methodists will never, ever trade Jesus and the truth of the Bible for money.[40]

Years ago, Dwight L. Baker pondered the question of how all of North Africa—once solidly Christian—so quickly converted to Islam when Muslims overran the region in the seventh and eighth centuries.[41] Of course, the threats and persecution against Christians by Muslims created enormous pressures to convert, but Baker rightly notes that this persecution cannot account for how a whole church vanished. His conclusion, after studying the history of the North African church, is that the North African Christians were not really convicted in their Christian faith at all when Islam arrived. They had multiple Christian rituals and sacraments, but no deep faith in

Jesus. They no longer had fresh experiences of the power and beauty of Christian truth and had thereby lost their sense of the living Christ. They had no real missionary impulse, so they were ill-equipped to persuade their own families to remain faithful to Jesus. And since many had come to focus on their own lives, they had no real heart for Jesus. So when Islam swept across their world, most people compromised, giving up their faith and plunging North Africa into centuries of Islamic rule.

Gene Habecker, President of Taylor University, articulates the resolve required to preserve your God-given mission against drift:

> You can't just assume that a mission will take care of itself. It will atrophy if you don't aggressively manage it in an ongoing way and continually reaffirm and integrate it into everything that you do over and over and over again. Mission management is never done, it's never done.[42]

Watch against drift and stand firm. In America, that includes redoubling your efforts to remain holy in a profane culture. We'll discuss that in the next chapter.

Small Group Questions

1. Did you finish reading the chapter? If so, what stood out to you from the readings and why?
2. Read Romans 12:1–2. What do these verses teach you about the nature of conformity? Would you describe yourself as naturally more of a conformist or a nonconformist?
3. How would you define mission drift in a church or Christian organization? How do we work against it?

4. Review what this chapter teaches about punching in the direction of progressivism or punching in the direction of Christianity. What are the dynamics that the chapter warns about and why are they important?
5. What are the four warning signs of progressivism in the church and why are they problematical?
6. Are there any situations that arise in this chapter where it would be helpful to role-play a conversation or a specific situation in order to help each other anticipate what we might face?
7. In light of the conversation we have had over this chapter, how can we pray for each other?

7

COMMIT TO HOLINESS

"Make every effort to live in peace with everyone and to be holy; without holiness no one will see the Lord" (Hebrews 12:14).

Somewhere around the beginning of the fifth century AD, pirates from what is now Ireland captured a sixteen-year-old boy in Roman Britain (or as we would say, England). They sold him into slavery back in Ireland, where he was forced to do the work of a shepherd under harsh treatment.

Conditions in Ireland at the time were unimaginably severe. Tribes were in a constant state of war, and the prevailing ethic for the Irish was that of the warrior. The measure of a man lay in how many others he had killed; honor was reserved for the man who had the most skulls in his collection. The music and art of the time often celebrated violence. Slaves were everywhere, usually captured in warring raids. They, along with women and girls, were treated as non-human property. Marriage often amounted to little more than rape, as warriors were permitted to have as many females as they liked and treat them however they liked. Religion was little more than a superstition, and human sacrifice was common, as Druids held a monopoly on all religious practices. Virtues that we take for granted—such as kindness, forgiveness, grace, tolerance, inclusivity, and the like—were vices in Ireland, and taken as signs of weakness that invited conquest. In a lot of ways, Ireland's ethical system was a war of all against all.

In such harsh conditions, this sixteen-year-old boy searched for a way to escape back to his family in England. A devout Christian with Christian parents, he made it a practice to pray one hundred times per day, every day, even in his dire circumstances. After six years of slavery, one day he heard a voice respond to his prayers. The divine voice informed him that a ship stood nearby, and if he made his way to the ship, it would take him home. Patricius, our young man, managed to slip away from the shepherd fields undetected and take the ship home, where his family exuberantly welcomed him.

But then something happened that would change the course of history.

In a series of dreams, Patricius began to receive a new round of divine visits. In one of those dreamy visits, an angel, looking like an Irishman, spoke directly to Patricius. "We beg you, Holy Boy," the angel cried, "come walk among us again."

The rest is history. Against all common sense and the advice of his community, Patricius, or as we know him, St. Patrick, returned to Ireland to evangelize the pagan country with the gospel. The many legends that surround Patrick—the shamrock, driving out the snakes, the walking stick, and other lore—reflect the holiness that the pagan Irish saw in Patrick.

Within his lifetime, much of Ireland came to Christ. The old pagan ethical system—with its violence, abuse, and cruelty—was so thoroughly overthrown by the gospel that, by the eighth century, Ireland contained some of the most educated, Christian, and virtuous people in the world, sending Christian missionaries as far away as Gaul (France today), Holland, Germany, Scandinavia, and, of course, England. Indeed, Ireland's Christian mission to England alone was world-changing, since the English-speaking world has sent more missionaries across the globe than virtually all other people groups *combined*. Today, the Irish are fond of saying "Ireland saved the world." It's flattery, but because of the world-changing evangelism the Irish conducted, it's not entirely flattery.

All because of one boy. All because of holiness consistently lived out in a godless place.

UNDERSTAND THE IMPORTANCE OF HOLINESS

The US is nothing like pre-Patrick Ireland, except in one sense: As Ireland lived by pagan values, so American progressives are also promoting pagan values in America, with predictably destructive results: poverty, homelessness, faithlessness, mental health crises, drug abuse, high incarceration rates, alcoholism, sexually transmitted infections and diseases, abortion, porn, and the like. It is worth noting that these ills are not *accidental* to progressivism. They are exactly the results that progressivism is designed to produce. When a man is encouraged by progressivism to have multiple hook-ups with a woman to whom he has made no commitment, and she is left with a baby she cannot support, that child grows up without the incalculable worth of a father's love. As a result, that child grows up with much higher risks of poverty, mental health issues, incarceration, violence, teen pregnancy, gang membership, drug abuse, etc. The hedonist sexual ethic of progressivism is perfectly designed—*willfully designed*—to achieve exactly these results.

If we are to stand firm in the face of opposition, we must stand with a different ethic: the ethic of holiness. Holiness will be the strength that allows Christians to say yes to real life and no to the paganism that increasingly plagues the world and opposes us.

> We must stand with a different ethic: the ethic of holiness.

Progressives understand that our holiness is a threat to their hedonism, and they are right. There can be no truce between ethics grounded in the holiness of God and ethics grounded in carnal pleasure. Christians have a holy view of life: Christ must permeate every area of our lives to be our Lord, both in private and in public. Because our holiness indicts progressivism's pleasure, progressivism intolerantly demands that we veil our faith in public. Christians understand that every human, including the unborn, bears the holy image of God. Progressives have a utilitarian view of life—human life has value only insofar as it produces pleasure. Christians' passion for protecting the unborn gets in the way of the hedonistic pleasures of progressives, so progressives are pushing to force all Americans to underwrite abortion through federal and state taxes. Christians have a holy view of sex: God created sex to join one man and one woman in a committed, monogamous marriage to produce safe and productive families where each child has the unique gifts a father and a mother can offer. Progressives view sex as only designed for pleasure, so uncommitted sex is celebrated, children are often abandoned by fathers (and sometimes, mothers), and Christians are scolded and bullied for not supporting unholy sexual sin.

There is, as author Kevin DeYoung says, a hole in America's holiness.[43]

So what is holiness and why does it matter? In the next two chapters, we'll look at how holiness affects our views of sex and gender—two areas where progressivism is especially bearing down on Christians. But before getting to those chapters, we need to explore what holiness means. Only then can we choose to live holy lives in all we do.

RIGHTLY DEFINE HOLINESS

The early twentieth-century religion philosopher Rudolf Otto famously defined holiness in terms of one's experience of "the numinous" (that which is completely different from the ordinary). Think of Moses's encounter with the other-worldly burning bush, which led him to take off his shoes. What Otto was suggesting is that right here, in the middle of what appears to be the ordinary world, lies the extraordinary—the connection of the physical with the spiritual. Sometimes that extraordinary breaks through the ordinary and presents itself, as Otto says, as a *mysterium tremendum et fascinans* ("a fearful and fascinating mystery").

To borrow a phrase from the apostle Paul's letter to the Colossian Christians, we can say that holiness describes the truth about creation's relationship to Christ: "All things have been created through him and for him. He is before all things, and in him all things hold together" (Colossians 1:16–17). This claim gives us a definition of holiness: Holiness is the divine dimension that exists in every single thing ever created. Holiness describes everything's divine origin ("through him"), everything's divine purpose ("for him"), everything's divine place in the universe ("before him"), and everything's divine construction ("holds together in him").

I'm not arguing that everything is divine. In a sense, only God is divine (depending on how we define that term). Only God is eternal, uncreated, unchanging, and not "made" of anything. Literally nothing else in the universe possesses these divine qualities. Nothing else is like God. Instead, literally everything else in the universe is created, temporal, malleable, and capable of not existing. God is "one of a kind," and neither depends on the creation nor can he in any way be reduced to the creation or anything within it. Only God is divine. Nothing else is.

But having said that, everything in the universe (except for evil—which is not really a "thing" so much as it is the corruption of a "thing") does have a divine origin and divine purpose. And it is this quality of "divine origin" and "divine purpose" that can be called "holiness."

Consider a couple examples:

- Holiness recognizes that *food* was created by God, given to us to strengthen our bodies so we could do God's will.

- Holiness recognizes that God bequeathed *art* to us for the purpose of worshiping God in truth and beauty.
- Holiness recognizes that God created *government*, instituted to promote good behavior and punish bad.
- Holiness recognizes the image of God in our *spouses*, who were given to us as provisions to help each person in the marriage become more like Jesus.
- Holiness recognizes that even such ordinary things as furniture, cars, houses, etc., were crafted by humans out of raw materials created by God and given to us so that we could rule God's creation with goodness.

Everything has a holy dimension. Everything comes from God, and everything is to be used for God. Christians know this, so we order everything to recognize and honor its holiness. This means that at the end of the day, holiness is an ethical system that rightly orders our interactions with all of creation. Holiness is an ethical system that recognizes what God has done in every single piece of creation and uses those pieces to honor and worship him.

Holiness is ordering life in ways that honor God in everything, every circumstance, and every space in the universe. It teaches us to prioritize our experiences so that everything's God-given origins are turned toward their God-given purposes. To sum it up, holiness is the Christian mandate for life, the basis for the Christian system, and our way of life. The apostle Peter puts it this way:

> As obedient children, do not conform to the evil desires you had when you lived in ignorance. But just as he who called you is holy, so be holy in all you do; for it is written: "Be holy, because I am holy" (1 Peter 1:14–16).

As an ethical system, holiness prioritizes life in the same way that God prioritizes life. This is not complicated, but in an unholy and profane world, it can be hard to perceive—much less to implement. Let's outline what holiness demands, in the order it demands it—so that we can order our lives in holiness and stand firm in a world whose ethical system is ordered around self, pride, and ultimately, pleasure.

Holiness teaches us:

- to love *God* first and to love him for his sake alone (and not for what we "get" out of it, although we know that loving God satisfies our heart's deepest need);
- to love *others* with the love of God second, also for God's sake (and not for what we "get" out of it, although loving others for the sake of God brings great joy);
- to love *ourselves* third as image bearers of God, but only for God's sake (and never for our own sake, although loving ourselves for the sake of God creates peace);
- and to refuse to love any *object* or *thing*, but only to *use* our stuff for the sake of the love of God (although using our stuff for the sake of God creates contentment).

These priorities, which define Christian holiness ethics, set us apart from secular ethics, which, of course, order everything around the pleasure of the self. Since progressivism is fueled by the king of the profane—the devil himself—progressivism simply cannot tolerate holiness. In the same way that demons recoil in horror and rage at the mention of Jesus' name, progressivism recoils at the holiness of Christians. After all, we are in a spiritual war.

LOVE GOD FOR THE SAKE OF GOD

God is "wholly other" than his creation. He is spiritual, and he is powerful and perfect beyond description. God's holiness is the sum total of this power and perfection: "'To whom will you compare me? Or who is my equal?' says the Holy One" (Isaiah 40:25). To approach God, then, is to experience awe and humility and even fear. As Hannah says in her song of thankfulness in 1 Samuel, "There is no one holy like the LORD; there is no one besides you; there is no Rock like our God" (1 Samuel 2:1–2). God is a holy God, and he expects us to treat him with reverence and awe. This is why his holiness is sometimes associated in Scripture with fire, terror, majesty, wrath, destruction, and judgment. His name is so holy that Jews wouldn't even say it. His face is so majestic that people believed they would die if they saw it. His decrees are so certain that to violate them is to provoke his anger. Worshiping anything other than this God will bring down his wrath. He is a jealous God because he alone is God. The God of the Bible is not to be trifled with. He is a holy God.

For this reason, the Bible often speaks of the appropriate response of humans to God as the "fear of the Lord." The phrase shouldn't be flattened simply to mean "being scared of God." It is a much richer term that means something like living fully aware that there is a God above all that we do, who is watching all that we do, and who will hold us accountable for all that we do. Losing the "fear of the Lord" is one of the greatest sins the West has committed, and we've seen its disastrous effects on the world. Living without "the fear of the Lord" leads us to assume that we can live however we want, with no accountability and no day of reckoning coming.

Aleksandr Solzhenitsyn, who managed to survive the gulags of the progressive Soviet Union and to write about their horrors, spoke of this loss of the fear of the Lord in his 1983 Templeton Prize Lecture, titled "Men Have Forgotten God." Arguing that World War I resulted in the collapse of a robust belief of God in Europe, Solzhenitsyn explained:

> The failings of human consciousness, deprived of its divine dimension, have been a determining factor in all the major crimes of this century. The first of these was World War I . . . that took place when Europe, bursting with health and abundance, fell into a rage of self-mutilation that could not but sap its strength for a century or more, and perhaps forever. The only possible explanation for this war is a mental eclipse among

> the leaders of Europe due to their lost awareness of a Supreme Power over them.[44]

We Christians must live fully aware that there is a God above, that he is watching over all of humanity, and that he will hold every single human accountable for what we do.

But fear of the Lord actually leads us not to dread, but to love. The justice of God is a good thing, not a bad thing. We love just judges. We love fair institutions. We admire good laws. In the same way, knowing who God is and how he judges leads us to love him above all else, for we know that we can trust him with his creation.

This is why the first and most eternal command for the Christian is to "love the Lord our God will all our heart, soul, mind, and strength" (Mark 12:30). We love God first, and this allows us to order everything else rightly in our lives. It allows us to face anything, to endure everything. We recognize the holiness of God, and everything else falls in place.

LOVE OTHERS FOR THE SAKE OF GOD

After he declared that loving God is the first command, Jesus explains that the second command is to love our neighbor as ourselves (Mark 12:31). We are, indeed, to love our neighbors second to God "as ourselves." But we must remember that while Christians love others "as ourselves," we do not love them "for ourselves." In other words, we love others, not because of what we get out of it, but rather, because they are made in the image of God.

Loving others out of the love of God is the root of all social ethics for Christians. We are gentle because of love. We are kind because of it. We practice grace, encouragement, support, forgiveness, patience, and all the other virtues because we recognize the image of God in every human. In this way, we seek to build up others in the image of God. This is why we vigorously oppose abortion: we don't measure the worth of an unborn human by whether or not they serve us; we measure their worth against the infinite worth of the image of God.

And this is why we oppose sin: we love people too much to support what's sinful and harmful in their lives. "Love does not delight in evil but rejoices with the truth" (1 Corinthians 13:6). This is why we love people too much to support them in such sexual sins as same-sex activity. It is why we love people too much to share in their lie about transgenderism. It is why we love people too much to encourage them to degrade themselves in porn. It is why we love people too much to bless casual sexual relations—where people use each other for personal pleasure, then leave the results to someone else to clean up. Christian love is true love. Just as it is not loving to offer whiskey to an alcoholic, it is not loving to encourage people to live in sin.

Instead, Christian love of others does the hard work of rescuing people from bondage. It does not affirm bondage, regardless of what anyone else says. Regardless of what *everyone* else says. Check out these Scripture passages:

> My brothers and sisters, if one of you should wander from the truth and someone should bring that person back, remember this: Whoever turns a sinner from the error of their way will save them from death and cover over a multitude of sins. (James 5:19–20)
>
> Opponents must be gently instructed, in the hope that God will grant them repentance leading them to a knowledge of the truth, and that they will come to their senses and escape from the trap of the devil, who has taken them captive to do his will. (2 Timothy 2:25–26)

Love seeks to rescue people from their sin so they can fully reflect the image of God.

LOVE YOURSELF FOR THE SAKE OF GOD

Jesus teaches us to love others "as ourselves," which presumes, of course, that loving oneself is a natural state of things. Because I was created in God's image, because I was given a mission from God, and because I am a child of God, I love myself—especially myself as God intends me to be. I love the free will God gave me. I love the Spirit who lives within me. I love the place where God put me. I love myself most when I worship the God who loves me.

Love of self, however, can be problematic, which is why Scripture qualifies it. The wrong kind of self-love is actually the primal sin of humanity. In the Bible, the self-love for the sake of the self is called "pride," and it is the source of all other sin. Self-love for the sake of the self requires that we turn our eyes from God, that we make our desires the lords of our lives, and that we become our own idol. This is what Jesus means when he says, "Anyone who loves their life will lose it, while anyone who hates their life in this world will keep it for eternal life" (John 12:25). To hate your life in this text means to hate loving yourself for your own sake.

Progressivism is built on the sinful side of self-love. It is all about finding your "authentic self"—which turns out to be whatever gives you pleasure—declaring it to the world, then forcing everyone else to promote it. Such self-love is the reason progressivism is so destructive. It quickly turns into a war of all against all.

But Christian ethics teach us to love ourselves for God's sake—to love ourselves for how we can serve God and others. This is why the ethics of the Christian faith teach us to practice humility, modesty, contentment, selflessness, etc. We are never to put ourselves in the place of God and never to love ourselves as though we have the inner power to direct ourselves. We find our peace and contentment when we submit to God's will, obey his Word, and love ourselves as his faithful children.

We find our peace and contentment when we submit to God's will.

BUT REFUSE TO LOVE YOUR STUFF

This is a big one and will require more discussion. Christians are taught, in a hundred ways, that we are not to love things and stuff—which the Bible frequently refers to as "the world." James states that friendship with the world makes you an enemy of God (James 4:4). John says,

> Do not love the world or anything in the world. If anyone loves the world, love for the Father is not in them. For everything in the world—the lust of the flesh, the lust of the eyes, and the pride of life—comes not from the Father but from the world. The world and its desires pass away . . . ." (1 John 2:15–17)

Loving the stuff of this world is what the apostle Paul calls "fleshly"—it is living for the purpose of satisfying our carnal pleasures. The accumulation of stuff, the desire for money, the attraction to luxuries—they are all the result of greed. Again, a form of the original sin of pride. And love of stuff cannot live in the same heart as the love of God. Paul contrasts those who live "in the flesh" with those who live "in the Spirit." The former are devoted to satisfying themselves: "The mind governed by the flesh is hostile to God; it does not submit to God's law, nor can it do so" (Romans 8:7). Note what Jesus says: "No one can serve two masters. Either you will hate the one and love the other, or you will be devoted to the one and despise the other. You cannot serve both God and money" (Matthew 6:24). And don't overlook how Jesus says this. He does not say that you *shouldn't* love both God and money. He says that you *cannot* love both God and money. It is not possible, because love of money robs us of the ability to love God.

We can use money, but we are never to love it. We were not created to love money. We were created to love God. Love of money is a form of unholiness that violates the image of God and the very fabric of the universe.

This is an important revelation for the persecuted church because if we love our possessions, if we are devoted to our luxuries, our pleasures, and our hobbies, we will falter at the moment when we must make a decision for Jesus. If you love your huge house, your fancy SUV, your retirement account, and your investments, then when your HR department gives you a choice to choose Jesus or choose compromise, you will hesitate, negotiate, and most likely, capitulate. If you love your pleasures and appetites, then when you are faced with the decision to promote a biblical sexual ethic or to compromise, you will likely change your beliefs to accept what the Bible condemns.

The rich young ruler came to Jesus evidently sincere in his desire to be part of the Jesus movement. After the young man asked how he could inherit eternal life, Jesus responded by citing some of the commandments. The ruler had kept these commands. Jesus then went further:

> "If you want to be perfect, go, sell your possessions and give to the poor, and you will have treasure in heaven. Then come, follow me." When the young man heard this, he went away sad, because he had great wealth. (Matthew 19:21–22)

If you have not already faced a similar situation, know that you and other Christians like you in the West will likely face more of them in the twenty-first century. Certain careers will become increasingly difficult for Christians to practice as progressives tighten restrictions designed to force us to compromise. For example, progressives will likely seek to require obstetrician-gynecologists to perform abortions or lose their licenses. What will OB-GYNs do when this day comes?

Corporate boards and HR departments will bully Christian employees into supporting LGBTQ+ activities and organizations or lose their jobs. What will Christians do when their insurance and retirement benefits are at stake in such scenarios?

Lawsuits will continue to be brought against Christians for refusing to bow before pagan values, perhaps costing real property. What will Christians do when unjust public accommodation rules are applied to our churches and nonprofits by government agencies, resulting in lawsuits? After all, there are dozens of bakeries in the vicinity of Jack Phillips's Masterpiece Bakery—but Phillips's bakery is repeatedly targeted by lawsuits because of his Christian beliefs (see the details in chapter 2 above). Litigants are not trying to get a wedding cake or gender transition cake; they are trying to destroy Jack Phillips.

You must decide whether you love the world or love God. You will not be allowed to remain neutral.

Decide now, before the moment of decision comes, that you can be content with much, but you can also be content with less, as the apostle Paul says of himself—sitting in prison for his faith (Philippians 4:10–13). After all, isn't it contentment that we hope we'll get from our wealth? We don't collect money because we like pictures of George Washington or Ben Franklin. We collect money because we believe it has the power to give us a degree of contentment. But isn't trusting in God the real source of contentment? Think of how many times you generously gave to someone else or practiced remarkable generosity. Didn't that bring you more contentment than hoarding your stuff? Only Jesus offers real contentment. A life lived for Jesus is a life free of worry about the things of this life:

> Therefore I tell you, do not worry about your life, what you will eat or drink; or about your body, what you will wear. Is not life more than food, and the body more than clothes? Look at the birds of the air; they do not sow or reap or store away in barns, and yet your heavenly Father feeds them. Are you not much more valuable than they? (Matthew 6:25–26)

God will provide what you need, even if you lose everything standing for him. Trust that God will be your provider. He will show himself strong on behalf of all those whose hearts are completely his, just as he has promised to do.

NAVIGATE YOUR HOLINESS IN A PROFANE WORLD

Let's go back to St. Patrick. When he returned to Ireland, the Irish saw a man living a holy life among and in front of pagans. It was seeing holiness in the midst of godlessness that eventually brought the Irish to their Lord. The same is true with you. You are to live a holy life—not hidden in a monastery, but right in front of even the pagans who harass you. Peter reminds us that our holiness has an influence on the world, even if we don't see it: "Live such good lives among the pagans that, though they accuse you of doing wrong, they may see your good deeds and glorify God on the day he visits us" (1 Peter 2:12).

But what Peter calls us to do, as well as the outcome, can be difficult. The world as it currently stands is under the influence of the evil one—so much so that he is sometimes described as the "god of this world" (2 Corinthians 4:4). Paul refers to him as "the ruler of the air, the spirit of disobedience at work among unbelievers" (Ephesians 2:1–3). To live faithfully for Jesus, we must work at removing our selfish love of the world. Jesus says anyone who wants to be his disciple must deny himself, take up his cross, and follow him (Luke 9:23). Following him will provoke the ire of the world (John 15:18–19). He teaches us that his kingdom is not of this world (John 18:36) and that it is our refusal to love the world (as it currently is) that will provoke its ire: "If you belonged to the world, it would love you as its own. As it is, you do not belong to the world, but I have chosen you out of the world. That is why the world hates you" (John 15:19).

So to be holy, we must separate ourselves from the acidic effects of the dominant culture around us, which teaches us every sort of disordered love: disinterest in the love of God, loving others for what we get out of them, loving ourselves for our own pleasure's sake, and loving our stuff. This does not mean that we withdraw from the world. The apostle Paul knows we must interact with unbelievers on a daily basis—in fact, we *should* interact with unbelievers since, after all, we have good news to share with them (1 Corinthians 9:22–23). But it does mean that we must "have nothing to do with the fruitless deeds of darkness" (Ephesians 5:11).

A critical step for living in the world without becoming corrupted by it is to maintain a strict diet when it comes to entertainment and media consumption. Much of the television and movie entertainment offered in America features content that reprograms the mind toward the unholy. Even secular America understands this enough to slap ratings on movies. Television is deeply sexualized in ways that dishonor Christian ethics. While Americans spend about one-third of their free time watching television, we are exposed to endless sexual content that is promiscuous, sensualized, and often degrading. The average teenager spends more time watching television than any other activity besides sleeping. Yet according to Teen Health and the Media:

> [T]wo out of every three shows on TV include sexual content . . . The most widely viewed shows—those airing in primetime on the major networks—are even more likely to include sexual content. Sexual intercourse is depicted or strongly implied in one of every ten shows on TV. Of those instances of sexual intercourse either depicted or strongly implied, only half occurred among couples who had an established relationship with one another. Ten percent involved couples who had just met.[45]

And this does not include the constant glamorization of greed, luxury, and crime, all of which subtly shapes our minds and makes us resistant to holiness. We become accustomed to unholiness, lose our shock of it, and begin to develop secret love affairs with it. Our addictions to our smartphones make things worse because much of what we experience on our digital devices simply fails to support our pursuit of holiness.

In contrast, the psalmist prays that God will "turn my eyes away from worthless things; preserve my life according to your word" (Psalm 119:37). The early church understood the absolute need to avoid godless entertainment. Historian Herbert Kane describes their concerns:

> In the early church Christians were encouraged to strictly separate themselves from the love of the world, so nothing was as scrupulously guarded as entertainment. The arena, the circus, and the theater were absolutely to be avoided by Christians, and no church member was permitted to be an actor or a gladiator or even to teach acting. This required public discipline and constant preaching.

Let me say it directly. If you regularly and uncritically feed on Christless entertainment, you will not be able to remain holy. You will assimilate. It is as simple as that.

The apostle Paul teaches us that we are to live by the Spirit—which means rightly ordering our lives around holiness. "For if you live according to the flesh, you will die; but if by the Spirit you put to death the misdeeds of the body, you will live. For those who are led by the Spirit of God are the children of God" (Romans 8:13–14). The world desperately needs to see the holiness of God in our lives, and we ourselves require holiness to see God. Holiness means rightly ordering the loves of our lives.

When we live holy lives, the world will resist—there is nothing the demonic hate more than holiness. But when we live in holiness, we find our place in creation. And the world sees the witness of the gospel before its very eyes.

> When we live in holiness, we find our place in creation.

STAND AGAINST THE WORLD FOR THE SAKE OF THE WORLD

In 1975, a group of nineteen concerned theologians and intellectuals from various Christian traditions met in Hartford, Connecticut, to remind the church to remain holy in the face of rising progressivism. They especially wanted to challenge Christians not to allow progressivism—or secularism, as they termed it—to shape our narrative. They published their statement in a booklet entitled *Against the World for the World.*

The title of that book describes the imperative for Christian holiness. Conforming to the world will not help it. Instead, conforming will cost the world the witness it desperately needs: holy witnesses. And it will cost us our holiness. The world will fight you, but it urgently needs your commitment to holiness as a witness of God's way in a disintegrating culture. It needs you to stand against the world, for the sake of the world.

Instead of conforming to the world, Christians understand that holiness is woven into the fabric of the universe, and we seek to live consistently with it. We love God for God's sake, love others for God's sake, love ourselves for God's sake, and we refuse to love our stuff. By discerning the holiness already in the creation, we find our place in God's creation, and we honor him.

To quote from the famous prayer ascribed by St. Patrick:

> Christ with me, Christ before me, Christ behind me,
> Christ in me, Christ beneath me, Christ above me,
> Christ on my right, Christ on my left,
> Christ when I lie down, Christ when I sit down,
> Christ in the heart of everyone who thinks of me,
> Christ in the mouth of everyone who speaks of me,
> Christ in the eye that sees me,
> Christ in the ear that hears me.

Small Group Questions

1. Did you finish reading the chapter? If so, what stood out to you from the readings and why?
2. Review 1 Peter 1:14–16. How would you define holiness, and how important is holiness in Scripture?
3. What kind of teachings on holiness have you experienced lately? Can you understand why many church leaders often neglect this topic? Explain.
4. What is the fear of the Lord, and how is that concept connected to holiness?
5. Review what this chapter teaches about self-love. What does it teach, and why is this concept important?
6. The chapter ends with St. Patrick's prayer. How can you use that prayer to encourage one another this week?
7. In light of the conversation we have had over this chapter, how can we pray for each other?

8

PROMOTE SEXUAL HOLINESS

"Marriage should be honored by all, and the marriage bed kept pure, for God will judge the adulterer and all the sexually immoral" (Hebrews 13:4).

Nadia Bolz-Weber is a foul-mouthed pastor who grew up in the very conservative fellowship of the churches of Christ, left them in her youth, experimented with various worldly lusts, then returned to the Lutheran church. In her sermons and her writings, Bolz-Weber promotes what the Bible calls immorality, delighting her audiences with vulgarity, sarcasm, and a steady barrage of ire against those who want to follow the Scriptures.

In 2019 Bolz-Weber published her book, *Shameless*, in which she advocates tearing down Christian sexual ethics and replacing them with what she calls "sexual flourishing," defined as whatever gives you pleasure, so long as you have consent.[46] To use her words about biblical sexual ethics, "Let's burn it the f*** down and start over." Believing that biblical sexual ethics are not only wrong but oppressive, she describes her own sexual experiences with a boyfriend as "an exfoliation of my entire spirit"—declaring afterward, like God did after creating Adam and Eve, that it was "good."

Bolz-Weber is not an obscure figure in the American world of Christianity. She is a rock star, a *New York Times* best-selling author, and a speaker in demand all over America—even at universities founded by Bible-believing Christians. She has more influence than I will ever have.

In her book, Bolz-Weber tells the story of a female member of her Lutheran congregation who resented what the Bible teaches about sexuality. The woman was angry that the Bible affirms sexual holiness—that sex is a gift from God to be enjoyed exclusively between one man and one woman in a committed married relationship. The woman wanted to be free from these teachings so she could pursue her own sexual ethic and still call herself a Christian.

And so, according to Bolz-Weber's approving narration, the woman tore out the pages of her Bible that condemned the woman's sexual sin and threw them into the fire. Then, realizing that biblical teachings on holiness are much bigger than the pages she had already burned, the woman tore out pages from the rest of the Bible too, except for the Gospels, burning these pages as well. The woman now felt free, according to Bolz-Weber, to follow her own desires and make her own definitions of the Christian religion.

Faithful Christians will, of course, be shocked by Bolz-Weber's rejection of Scripture, holiness, and two thousand years of Christian teaching. But they may well be more shocked at the reception Bolz-Weber has received from so many evangelicals. She is a coach for hundreds of thousands. An inspiration. A guru. Your Christian teens are probably reading her, and your Christian universities are using her books. Clearly, something has happened to the concept of holiness in America, and it's not good.

The first sexual revolution in the West occurred when Christianity reversed centuries of dysfunctional, deviant, and destructive sexual ethics and restored the natural order for the family—one man, one woman, in a committed married relationship. This revolution produced the foundations upon which Western civilization—with all its accomplishments—was built.

The second sexual revolution in the West occurred when secular America sought to undo this beautiful vision for the family to adopt a hedonistic sexual ethic, embracing disordered sexual identities and promoting loose and unstable collections of sexual arrangements and hookups for the purpose of carnal pleasure and personal gratification.[47] Though progressivism's new ethic has resulted in millions of sexually transmitted infections, AIDS, astronomical illegitimacy and divorce rates, abortion, a multi-billion dollar pornography industry, climbing rates of gender dysphoria, and the denial of a loving mother and father to millions of children who must spend the rest of their lives paying for the consequences of this pagan ethic, progressives believe that you must be forced to accept the ideology. You will not be allowed just to remain silent.

In his teaching about sexual ethics, the apostle Paul says,

> It is God's will that you should be sanctified: that you should avoid sexual immorality; that each of *you should learn to control your own body in a way that is holy and honorable*, not in passionate lust like the pagans, who do not know God; and that in this matter no one should wrong or take advantage of a brother or sister. (1 Thessalonians 4:3–6)

Because our sexual desires are so strong, they create all kinds of problems. This is especially the case in a culture that constantly promotes sexual sin. "It is bad to live in cities," Friedrich Nietzsche once famously said. "There are too many lecherous people." The West is now partly built on what twentieth-century German Catholic philosopher Josef Pieper calls "the stimulation of desires that men's cunning has devised." Christians did not make sexuality ground zero in the battle with the aggressive progressivism we face today. Sexual holiness *is* an important tenet of the Christian faith, but it would not be such a prominent issue for Christians if progressives did not make it so.

The promotion of sexual sin forces Christians to publicly and constantly defend the sexual ethics of Scripture in the face of destructive lusts. Progressives have made sex ground zero in the struggle between good and evil. The battle is now upon us, so we must understand the cost of sexual unholiness so that we can stand against it while demonstrating a better way.

> Progressives have made sex ground zero in the struggle.

LEARN WHY GOD'S INTENTIONS FOR SEX MATTER

From the beginning, God designed marriage as a natural covenant between one man and one woman, joined together for life. Each of us was created to live in one of two gendered forms, and these two genders were designed to complement one another. Gender complementarity is a beautiful part of the created order, reflecting the Trinitarian nature of God. As God the Father, God the Son, and God the Holy Spirit live in a loving union that produces life, so a man and a woman live in a complementarian union that also produces life. Indeed, it is worth remembering that every single human being on earth required the coming together of one man and one woman in such an intimate union. This is why we can call the biblical model of marriage "traditional marriage": it is reflected in Scripture, in history, in anthropology, and in nature.

Traditional marriage is brought up at the beginning of creation, where God is said to make humans "male and female" (Genesis 1:26). It is reflected in the Garden of Eden, where God brings forth woman from the side of man and joins them to create the wholeness of a family (Genesis 2:18–24). Throughout the Scriptures, we read stories that demonstrate heterosexual marriage, laws that regulate heterosexual marriage, poetry that celebrates heterosexual marriage, prophecies that denounce deviations from heterosexual marriage, and teachings that reinforce heterosexual marriage. Repeatedly, the Bible lauds traditional marriage and condemns deviations from it. Every time we read about sexual sin in the Scriptures, including lust, extra-marital sex, sexual assault, adultery, prostitution, same-sex activity, etc., we are being taught to uphold the natural and God-ordained norm of one man and one woman in a committed married relationship. In this way, every text that mentions sexual sin (or immorality, as it is often translated) is a condemnation against sexual deviations from the biblical design, including same-sex activity.

But it is not just the Bible that teaches us this. Throughout history and across the globe, natural law has taught us the inherent value of traditional marriage. Even when variations of traditional marriage have been practiced, the standard always eventually returns to traditional marriage.

This is because traditional marriage satisfies fundamental anthropological, psychological, and sociological needs we humans have. Traditional marriage stabilizes society, provides a safe and healthy environment for sex, and creates a family where humans can develop fully. This is why, until very recently, the US government promoted traditional marriage: good governments know that families are essential to the well-being of humans, and the US government believed, until secular progressivism, that only traditional marriage satisfies our needs.

Traditional marriage is designed to accomplish four things:

- Make persons whole through the principle of complementarity—providing each gender with the strengths of the other gender, uniting two different ways of relating to the world into one strong bond.
- Channel the human sex drive into committed relationships where sex can create a healthy bond between two individuals

who love each other, avoiding the wreck that hedonism makes of people's lives.
- Create a safe, loving, and healthy place where children can be brought into the world.
- Provide for families where children can be loved, cared for, and raised in healthy ways by two parents who give their children the unique gifts each gender offers.

Traditional marriage is a matter of holiness, since sexual morality is a subset of holiness. All of creation is woven together in a fabric of holiness, so any immoral action creates a tear in the fabric of the universe. For that reason, sexual sin is a form of injustice, ripping up a part of God's holy creation. Sex outside of marriage objectifies other humans and treats them as tools for our pleasure—a form of injustice against another. Casual sex frequently results in emotional pain, inflicting injustice upon ourselves and others simply for the sake of pleasure. When birth control is not practiced, sex frequently results in the creation of a human life—who is often destroyed in abortion or is robbed of committed parents in our hook-up culture.

Adultery perpetrates the destruction of the bonds of marriage, treating the innocent partner with grave injustice. Pornography objectifies persons, normally women, degrading them and de-humanizing them. Lust obscures love, distracting us from loving our neighbors as ourselves. In short, immorality is a form of injustice.

When a single act of sexual sin is committed, it results in injustice for somebody. But when an entire culture practices sexual sin, injustice blankets the land, and an entire civilization begins to crumble. This is what makes sexual sin so destructive. In North America, our sexual sin has created so many of our problems. America's hedonistic ethic is the greatest social injustice of our time. The results of this unholy ethic are now everywhere, and it is difficult to see how America can survive now that we have reached a tipping point of destruction unleashed by our sexual ethics.

The percentage of children living in single households is now around 35 percent. In cities like Cleveland and Detroit, the rate is more than 70 percent. In these homes, young boys are raised without the discipline and honor that only fathers can provide, so they grow up full of rage—rebels against a system that failed them. Having never received the full commitment of two parents, these young people often wander through life unable to sustain commitments. They can have difficulty keeping a job and frequently struggle to manage money. Sometimes they find companionship with other rebels, in gangs, where they collectively unleash their rage against the world that treated them so unjustly. Many young girls today spend their teen years looking for the love that no father ever gave them, becoming pregnant while still girls and propagating the broken system for the next generation.

As I already mentioned, this sexual ethic results in dramatic increases in drug and alcohol abuse, mental illness, suicide rates, STIs, crime, incarceration rates, pornography, child abuse, sexual assault and rape, poverty rates, and other social disfunctions. It greatly reduces academic performance in school and good mental health.[48]

And we must state very clearly that this social breakdown is not accidental, nor is it indicative of a lack of economic resources. The collapse of the family in America and the dysfunction it brings is the direct result of the ethical system built by secular progressivism, backed by progressive Christians, and codified in social systems across the West. These dysfunctions are the natural consequence of the sexual ethic that Bolz-Weber deliberately promotes. This destruction is *deliberate*—deliberately planned by progressivism.

In 2020, Mary Eberstadt published an article titled "Fury of the Fatherless" in which she rightly lays the blame for much of the disintegration of American life at the feet of a sexual ethic that cannot find the courage to speak up for those children born without committed parents—children abandoned by their fathers and raised by restless mothers and grandmothers, and who are often left with impoverished souls and living in economic poverty.[49] Progressivism has built a system where millions of children are now living in economic, emotional, relational, and spiritual poverty because this system encourages casual, uncommitted sex. Ask yourself why, in a nation with enough resources to feed the entire world, there are millions of children growing up in poverty. It is not because we don't have the resources. It is because our hedonism produces—encourages and even underwrites—the abandonment of children who grow up without the psychological, social, and material capital to live flourishing lives.

Unholiness has consequences, and pain and suffering are the natural consequences of sexual sin. In a brilliant explanation of the beauty of the Bible's sexual ethics, apologetics professor Sean McDowell asks us to imagine a world where everyone embraced a Christian sexual ethic. Listen to the good news we have to share:

> There would be no sexually transmitted diseases. No abortions. No brokenness from divorce. Every child would have a mother and a father and experience the love and acceptance each parent uniquely offers. There would be no rape, no sex abuse, no sex trafficking, pornography, and no need for a #MeToo campaign. There would be no sexual exploitation, no sexual abuse, no AIDS, chlamydia, herpes, HPV, or syphilis, no unwanted pregnancies, no pain from divorce, no deadbeat dads, no men who leave their wives for other women. No child would have to grow up in a home where a mom or dad merely abandoned them in order to "do it my way."[50]

In his popular book *Hillbilly Elegy*, author J. D. Vance describes his upbringing in a dysfunctional family created by this sexual ethic. Through hard work and a good education, Vance escaped the mental anguish such a world produces but has not forgotten the pain. Christians should understand the cost that hedonism has exacted on our children, which Vance calls adverse childhood experiences (ACE). He often had poor grades, depression, sleepless nights, stomach issues, and loneliness as he faced being sworn at, insulted, and humiliated by the adults who moved in and out of his mother's life. He grew up being pushed and grabbed, having things thrown at him, feeling a lack of support, living in the constant presence of alcohol and drugs, watching his mother being physically abused, and surrounded by attempts at suicide. These terrors inflicted on a child are the costs of progressivism's sexual ethics. These are the injustices of sexual sin. And this happens *millions* of times in America.[51]

But the problem is even worse because rather than working to restore the natural family of one man and one woman in a committed married relationship where children receive the unique benefits of both a father and a mother, progressives are continually looking for new ways to destroy the family by redefining marriage, redefining sex, even redefining biology to justify their hedonist ethic.

Heather Barwick is a wife and the mother of four children. Once a gay activist, she now opposes same-sex marriage. She was raised by a mother and her lesbian lover, and though she loves her mother, she recognizes that anything other than holiness ends in pain. "Same-sex marriage and parenting withhold either a mother or father from a child while telling him or her that it doesn't matter. That it's all the same," she says. "But it's not. A lot of us, a lot of your kids, are hurting. My father's absence created a huge hole in me, and I ached every day for a dad. I loved my mom's partner, but another mom could never have replaced the father I lost."[52]

Progressives are wrong to think that children will be fine without a father, or, of course, a mother. When same-sex male couples adopt children, they rob children of their mother. In her book *Being There*, Erica Komisar points out that research in psychology, neuroscience, and epigenetics all suggest what each of us should already know: mothers are biologically necessary for babies, something that nature itself teaches us, since it is written into the fabric of God's creation. But progressivism has always considered children a sort of inconvenience, and it is our children who bear the brunt of progressivism's sexual unholiness. The deliberate robbing of babies of a mother can easily stunt their development and leave them forever missing something nature itself demands. Progressivism commits a profound injustice against our children, and we will all pay the price.

We Christians have a message of good news about sex and marriage, and even in a hostile culture, we can and must promote our story.

EMBRACE THE CHRISTIAN RESPONSE TO LGBTQ QUESTIONS

None of us can escape the many SOGI (Sexual Orientation and Gender Identity) issues today because progressives are targeting Christians in these areas of sex and gender. But how are we to respond to them?

It is important not only that we personally commit to sexual holiness but also that we have clarity about basic Christian principles as they apply to LGBTQ+ and transgender issues. Let's explore how we can fully commit to holiness when confronted with these sexually charged issues.

But before we do, I want to offer a critique of the entire way the LGBTQ+ agenda is posed today. We are taught today that there are heterosexuals, bisexuals, homosexuals, and other "orientations." But what if none of these categories exist?

I believe that Christians lost part of the battle for sexual holiness when we agreed that a person who desires this or that sexual experience somehow belongs to a different biological or immutable category than a person who desires different sexual experiences. What if there is no such thing as "heterosexuals" or "homosexuals"?[53] Why should people be categorized by their desires? Caucasians are white because of their genetic makeup—they would be white even if they didn't know it. If you were to dig up a Caucasian body a hundred years from now, you would immediately say, "This is a Caucasian." But there is no genetic category of homosexuality or heterosexuality. People only speak of orientation based on what they desire. And we humans have all sorts of desires, but these don't create natural categories. Many people have had affairs. That doesn't create a "natural category" of persons who are ontologically different from those persons who haven't had affairs. It only proves that sometimes our desires can propel us to act in ways inconsistent with our best interests. Dig up the body of someone who practiced same-sex activity in their lifetime, and there is nothing that would tell you that they were "gay." It is a category that culture has made up.

So before going further into this discussion, I want to say that I reject the classification of people into ontological categories based on their desires—categories such as heterosexual and homosexual. For this reason, I am unwilling to classify men who have sex with men or women who have sex with women as natural classes of persons who deserve special treatment. Homosexuality, like heterosexuality, is not an immutable category analogous to race. We should treat people based on their actions, and not pretend persons belong to immutable categories simply because they have this or that desire. Let's look at specific ways we can respond to LGBTQ+ persons:

Love everyone and show extraordinary love to LGBTQ+ persons.

The Christian faith is premised on love: we love God above all, and we love our neighbors as ourselves. LGBTQ+ persons deserve love every bit as much as anyone, and in some cases, they may need it more than others. After all, there are tremendous pressures on many LGBTQ+ persons, and many feel a special pain from the Christian faith. Though acting on same-sex attraction is wrong like every other sexual sin, we must recognize that many LGBTQ+ persons did not choose to feel the way they feel. Many LGBTQ+ persons have carried their same-sex orientation or gender dissatisfaction all the way back to childhood. Most did not pick these feelings.

So whatever else Christians do, we must always start with love. Further, we must be careful to distinguish between an LGBTQ+ *person* and secular LGBTQ+ cultural and political *agenda*. They are not the same. So, though I adamantly oppose the secular sexual agenda, and I believe that acting on one's disordered sexual desires is sinful, I am deeply sympathetic with the LGBTQ+ person's sexual circumstances. After all, I too have sexual sin in my life. I have sometimes failed to live up to my own sexual standards. We are all sexual sinners in desperate need of grace, mercy, and healing.

> We must always start with love.

Affirm the beauty of God's designs for sex, gender, and family.

Make no mistake. I'm not saying we should accept sinful behavior. God designed sex, gender, and family in such a beautiful and healthy way that even nature itself confirms his design. Deviations from that design can be neither beautiful nor healthy; they are disordered or sinful or both. Disorders and sins can never be good, healthy, or right.

This is why Jesus teaches that heterosexual marriage is God's intent for humanity (Matthew 19:3–9). It is why traditional marriage serves as a sacred symbol for the relationship between Christ and the church (Ephesians 5:32). And it is why all cultures gravitate toward traditional marriage, regardless of what deviations may occur in those cultures.

God's intent is why governments recognize marriage. As the US Supreme Court rightly observed in Murphy v. Ramsey (1885), "The idea of the family, as consisting in and springing from the union for life of one man and one woman in the holy estate of matrimony" was "the sure foundation of all that is stable and noble in our civilization" and "the best guaranty of that reverent morality which is the source of all beneficent progress in social and political improvement."[54]

The US Conference of Catholic Bishops say that "a same-sex union contradicts the nature of marriage: It is not based on the natural complementarity of male and female; it cannot cooperate with God to create new life; and the natural purpose of sexual union cannot be achieved by a same-sex union. Persons in same-sex unions cannot enter into a true conjugal union. Therefore, it is wrong to equate their relationship to a marriage."[55]

Healthy traditional marriages are essential to the well-being of humans and civilizations. Same-sex marriage violates this public good. Assuming that same-sex marriage is merely an extension of the rights of marriage to a different class of persons is wrong. Same-sex marriage is not an expansion of a public good to a new group of individuals; it is a distortion of the very meaning of marriage that renders families incomplete and disordered. A society can stand the breakdown of some of its marriages. But when traditional marriage is increasingly undermined in any given society, a host of ills will necessarily follow. Linda Chavez, former executive director of the US Commission on Civil Rights, describes what we're facing as an "epidemic": "Historically, virtually all societies have condemned incest, adultery, and homosexuality because such practices, in distinctive ways, threaten the family. . . . Over the last twenty-five years, we have become increasingly tolerant of sexually permissive behavior. But that tolerance has had consequences. We face epidemics in sexually transmitted diseases, teenage pregnancies, abortions, illegitimacy, rape, and sexual abuse. Marriage rates are on the decline, and divorce is on the increase, especially among younger couples. The American family may not yet be an endangered species, but it is far from thriving."[56]

Acknowledge the sinfulness of same-sex activity.

Spin the globe and randomly place your finger on it. Wherever your finger lands, you can be sure the norm there has always been heterosexual marriage. This is why, in the 2015 Obergefell case legalizing same-sex marriage, Supreme Court Justice Samuel Alito observed that, until very recently, there had never been a nation or a culture that recognized marriage between two people of the same sex. Same-sex marriage cannot provide for complementarity. It cannot provide for procreation. It cannot give a child the unique love that only the combination of a father and a mother can offer. It is inherently disordered, as are all other sexual practices outside of traditional marriage.

The disordered character of same-sex activity is reflected in the increased number of health concerns in the LGBTQ+ community. A variety of research indicates that the gay and lesbian lifestyle increases health risks. Research from multiple studies shows that HIV infections are overwhelmingly higher among gay men but are virtually nonexistent among men who adhere to traditional marriage. Monkeypox is also almost exclusively a disease affecting gay men. Rates of other STI's, substance abuse, depression, alcohol abuse, and domestic violence are also higher among those practicing a gay or lesbian lifestyle. Simply do a search on "gay mortality rates," and you'll see all sorts of studies that suggest that practicing same-sex activity shortens the life expectancy of gay men.

Furthermore, all sexual sin creates victims. Sexual sin is a form of injustice; it betrays, mistreats, or defrauds somebody in the pursuit of gratification. Same-sex activity is no exception. For this reason, the Christian Scriptures explicitly condemn sexual sin, and sometimes name same-sex activity as particularly destructive:

- "Before they had gone to bed, all the men from every part of the city of Sodom—both young and old—surrounded the house. They called to Lot, 'Where are the men who came to you tonight? Bring them out to us so that we can have sex with them.' Lot went outside to meet them and shut the door behind him and said, 'No, my friends. Don't do this wicked thing'" (Genesis 19:4–7).
- "Do not have sexual relations with a man as one does with a woman; that is detestable" (Leviticus 18:22).

- "If a man has sexual relations with a man as one does with a woman, both of them have done what is detestable" (Leviticus 20:13).
- "While they were enjoying themselves, some of the wicked men of the city surrounded the house. Pounding on the door, they shouted to the old man who owned the house, 'Bring out the man who came to your house so we can have sex with him.' The owner of the house went outside and said to them, 'No, my friends, don't be so vile. Since this man is my guest, don't do this outrageous thing'" (Judges 19:22–23).
- "Because of this, God gave them over to shameful lusts. Even their women exchanged natural sexual relations for unnatural ones. In the same way the men also abandoned natural relations with women and were inflamed with lust for one another. Men committed shameful acts with other men, and received in themselves the due penalty for their error" (Romans 1:26–27).
- "Or do you not know that wrongdoers will not inherit the kingdom of God? Do not be deceived: Neither the sexually immoral nor idolaters nor adulterers nor men who have sex with men nor thieves nor the greedy nor drunkards nor slanderers nor swindlers will inherit the kingdom of God" (1 Corinthians 6:9–10).
- "We also know that the law is made not for the righteous but for lawbreakers and rebels, the ungodly and sinful, the unholy and irreligious, for those who kill their fathers or mothers, for murderers, for the sexually immoral, for those practicing homosexuality, for slave traders and liars and perjurers—and for whatever else is contrary to the sound doctrine" (1 Timothy 1:9–10).
- "[If God] condemned the cities of Sodom and Gomorrah by burning them to ashes, and made them an example of what is going to happen to the ungodly; and if he rescued Lot, a

righteous man, who was distressed by the depraved conduct of the lawless . . ." (2 Peter 2:6–7).

- "In a similar way, Sodom and Gomorrah and the surrounding towns gave themselves up to sexual immorality and perversion. They serve as an example of those who suffer the punishment of eternal fire" (Jude 7).

I am aware that many Christian revisionists have sought to undermine these texts by arguing such things as "the Bible doesn't mean what it says," or "the Bible didn't know about committed same-sex relationships as we do." But such claims are untrue, as many have faithfully pointed out.[57] The ancient world of the Bible knew virtually every conceivable form of sexuality and more marriage models than the modern West knows. Furthermore, the texts of the Scriptures are not ambiguous, as the detractors suggest. There is nothing ambiguous about this sentence: "If a man has sexual relations with a man as one does with a woman, both of them have done what is detestable" (Leviticus 20:13). The question is not, "What do the Scriptures teach?" but rather, "Why don't we want to obey the Scriptures?"

Further, I am aware that many Christians have argued that only a handful of Scriptures condemn same-sex activity, but these individuals are wrong. Since same-sex activity is considered immoral in the Bible, any time the Bible mentions the sin of immorality, it is also speaking against same-sex activity. Indeed, since biblical holiness includes treating our sexuality in ways consistent with the Christian teaching of "one man, one woman" in a committed married relationship, every time the Bible mentions holiness, it is also judging against same-sex activity. Homosexuality is condemned hundreds of times in the Bible.

So Christians must be both loving and firm in our resolve toward same-sex activity just as we are to be toward all sexual activity outside of marriage. We must recognize that it is not harmless but is disordered and that it undermines the most basic civilizing unit of the social order. It is a sin, and we must work to lead those who wrestle with this sin to Jesus. We should hold forth the lovely words that Paul offered to all of us sinners in a text that mentions same-sex activity: "And that is what some of you were. But you were washed, you were sanctified, you were justified in the name of the Lord Jesus Christ and by the Spirit of our God" (1 Corinthians 6:9–11).

As with all other sins, sexual sin is not unforgiveable, and we can escape the trap of any sin. That's why the gospel is *good* news.

> Sexual sin is not unforgiveable.

SHOW THE WORLD A BETTER WAY

At the age of sixteen, Joseph Sciambra went to see a local priest. As he tells his story, Sciambra wasn't really sure at the time why he decided, of all things, to talk to a priest. Though raised a Catholic, he had abandoned the Catholic faith. He had recently come out as gay, and he did so in the middle of the AIDS crisis. He was a lonely boy looking for some sort of direction. Explaining to the priest that God had made him gay, he waited for some guidance.

Rather than lovingly explaining to Joseph what the Scriptures teach, what natural law teaches, or what the church has taught for two thousand years, the priest affirmed to Joseph that God had made him gay. He advised Joseph to practice safe sex and to "act responsibly." That's it.

Two years later, Joseph moved to the Castro District of San Francisco, where he did not always practice safe sex or "act responsibly." As time went by, Joseph found himself going to another priest for advice. That priest gave him similar advice, encouraging Joseph to settle down with only one partner. The consent from two Christian leaders, in a sense, emboldened Joseph, but he knew something was wrong. "At sixteen, when I talked to that first priest, I had secretly wanted him to say something else," he writes. "I had wanted him to be strong—I had wanted him to rescue me from myself."

After years of living as a gay man, Joseph eventually returned to the Catholic faith of his childhood as a broken and humbled man. He had lost friends to AIDS and had seen—up front and personal—the cost of living an unchaste life.

And he now wonders: *Where was the church's truth when I needed it?* Joseph needed compassion and love. We all do. But he also needed truth. It is a sad world when those who believe the truths of God—truths about the utter need for the healing power of holiness—aren't bold enough to stand for the truth and share it.[58]

Nadia Bolz-Weber, the Lutheran pastor we talked about in the introduction to this chapter, should be teaching the world the beauty of holy living. Instead, she's lending God's name to one of the greatest injustices of our time. The world desperately needs *you* to stand firm even while it rushes headlong into the abyss. The world needs your faithful witness. And that is especially true when it comes to sexual holiness.

Small Group Questions

1. Did you finish reading the chapter? If so, what stood out to you from the readings and why?
2. Review Hebrews 13:4 and 1 Thessalonians 4:3–6. What do these passages teach, and how do most people in our culture feel about these teachings when they hear them? Explain.
3. Review Sean McDowell's summary of what would happen in a world that embraces and lives out the Christian sexual ethic. What is your reaction to his summary? How do you think your family and friends might react to it?
4. Read out loud the Scripture passages listed in this chapter discussing same-sex activity (the bullet-point list on pages 166–168).

5. As you reflect on the passages you read, is there good reason, based upon these passages, to think that Scripture is ambiguous on this topic? If you think the passages are clear, why is it that so many people are confused today? What kind of compassion should you feel or experience as you think about those impacted by the confusion?
6. How can we show the love of Christ to those who think that we are hateful because of our understanding of this chapter's topic?
7. In light of the conversation we have had over this chapter, how can we pray for each other?

9

GET CLARITY ABOUT THE TRANSGENDER MOVEMENT

"So God created mankind in his own image, in the image of God he created them; male and female he created them. . . . God saw all that he had made, and it was very good" (Genesis 1:27, 31).

After preaching a series of lessons about hostility toward Christians, I was contacted by a mother who does not live in my community but who had listened to my presentations. She was devastated, and her story will hurt your heart too. I have permission to share the story, but I'm altering it a bit to protect the identity of all involved.

It started a year ago when her eleven-year-old daughter blindsided the family by announcing that she was confused about her sexual orientation and gender.

Now before sharing the rest of the story, think about these questions: Why are eleven-year-old girls even troubled with such concerns? What kind of world sexualizes children at such an early age so thoroughly that they even know what sexual confusion and gender identity are?

Over the next several months, the young girl began to act like a boy. She changed her name and asked others to begin calling her "he/him." Her mother soon found out that several of her daughter's friends had also begun to identify as boys. They had been watching videos that encourage young girls—who face the natural insecurities of adolescence—to transition to boys. They had seen television programs and watched pop icons transition. They had been told they would find their true selves in transitioning, that they could overcome their insecurities, and that they would be welcomed and loved in their new trans community.

The girl's parents, who are devout Christians, tried to deal with the situation as best they could. They refused to call her by her chosen male name. They did not use "he" or "him" when speaking of her. They tried to help her see that she is beautiful just as God made her and that her gender is not an accident. But the girl responded in anger. She withdrew from them and soon lost interest in all her hobbies. She slipped into a deep depression and blamed her parents for it. She had been to counseling, but her parents were worried she was suicidal.

The family tried to manage the changes, but they had a hard time finding help. If they were in Canada, they might be prosecuted for trying to persuade the girl that she is a girl. In some municipalities in the US, city councils and state houses are debating similar laws.

The poor girl's parents have tried to be gentle and loving. They have done everything parents can do, but when they contacted me, they confessed that they could see no light at the end of the tunnel. The girl was miserable, and her family was living through a nightmare that, only a few years ago, was unthinkable.

Stories like this have been repeated hundreds of thousands of times over the last several years. Researchers estimate that there are more than a 1.3 million people over age thirteen in North America who identify as transgender.[59]

In the last few years, transgenderism has exploded in the US, and progressives have sometimes called transgenderism the civil rights issue of our era. Progressives are celebrating this disorder, and they are marshalling the language of "hate speech" and "conversion therapy" to stop people from questioning the new secular orthodoxy. This is odd coming from an ideology that repeatedly demands that the rest of us "believe science." Ask a progressive to define the word "woman." Then watch as they toss out anything that could be confused for science, or even reason or logic for that matter. The transgender movement is a bellwether of where progressivism is heading: the sexualizing of everything, including children, toward the pleasure ethic that lies behind much of what progressives say and believe—and the punishment of anyone who gets in the way of this ethic.

Very recently, the family I counseled has seen a great turn-around in their daughter. They pulled her out of public schools, homeschooled her, found a great Christian counselor, and poured love and truth into her. Fortunately, the girl has abandoned her transgender confusions and is becoming emotionally and spiritually whole, well, and happy again.

But we are facing a landslide of transgenderism, and it is not getting better. It's getting much, much worse. And progressives are promising to punish Christians who do not go along with the movement. So what is transgenderism and how should we Christians respond to it?[60]

UNDERSTAND GENDER DYSPHORIA

Until only recently, Americans linked one's gender to one's sex. A person's way of understanding themselves and of relating to the world (gender) was considered a product of the person's biology (sex). There are real genetic differences between men and women, including primary differences such as our chromosomes, reproductive systems, and secondary differences such as the shapes of our body, our dexterity, physical strength, the ways our brains work, etc. God created us with differences like these so that each gender could bring specific strengths to the world and the mutuality of marriage. For example, besides ovaries and a uterus, God also gave women broader hips than men to make carrying babies easier. Men were created with broader shoulders and a slight increase in physical strength to hunt for food and defend the family. These kinds of differences exist in virtually every species of mammals; the bodies of males and females are designed differently so that each can contribute to the whole.

In this model, *biological sex* is the actual genetic and bodily structure we received, and *gender* is how we express this sexual constitution. Gender springs from our bodies, which are physically pointed in certain directions. There is a teleology, or purpose, to our sex, and gender seeks to realize that.

There is a teleology, or purpose, to our sex.

We can draw a simple illustration from the antlers of the male deer. Because mating is often available only to the strongest buck, a large rack of antlers is a form of assurance that an individual buck can reproduce because it helps him fight off competing bucks. But carrying the large antlers of a mature male deer requires increased amounts of energy, which, in turn, requires more work to find food. For this reason, bucks must graze more often and farther afield than the does. The biological sex of the buck leads to the gendered pattern of grazing. The antlers are a matter of his sex, whereas the tendency to range farther afield and graze more often are expressions of his gender.

Sex and gender are not exactly the same, but the buck's gender springs from his sex and is a necessary function of it. Examples like this are literally *everywhere* in nature—so common that, until recently, very few people ever gave them much thought. As evolutionary psychologist Nigel Barber says in discussing the gender differences in animals, "Sex differences are real, biologically based, and here to stay."[61]

In recent years, however, we have begun to hear a relatively new term: "gender identity." Gender identity is the *feeling* someone has about their biological sex—the *feeling* that they are a male or female (or another gender, as some would argue). Evidently everybody has a gender identity, that is, a feeling that they are either this or that gender, typically masculine or feminine. But some individuals experience what's called *gender dysphoria*, the feeling that their sexual construction does not match their gender. Until very recently, gender dysphoria was considered a mental illness, and people were sometimes offered treatment designed to align their perception of themselves with their actual bodies.

We should not think that gender dysphoria is a chosen condition. Most persons experiencing gender dysphoria did not choose their condition, and many suffer immense pain because of it. Further, many people experiencing gender dysphoria are not transgender persons—they have not sought to change their gender or their body to resolve the problem. Many simply live with the pain, attempting to navigate the feeling as best they can. Others, especially children, grow out of gender dysphoria so long as it isn't agitated by the culture. We should remember that gender dysphoria is *not*, in Christian teaching, a sin—even though it is a *sign* of the disordered nature of fallen humanity, as are all other forms of dysphoria.

Where those suffering from gender dysphoria in the past sometimes sought treatment to align their feelings about gender with their actual bodies, many have now sought to align their bodies with their gender feelings in the last decade. They do this by changing how they act, the way they dress, how they speak of themselves, the pronouns they prefer, or their names. Some have even taken medications or undergone surgery designed to alter their bodies. Transgender persons seek to change either their gender identity or their bodies to resolve the tension between the two.

Transgender persons are those with gender dysphoria who act on it by presenting themselves to others as a gender inconsistent with their bodies. In recent years, transgender persons have come to expect others to honor their preferred identity, and their cause has been taken up by the political class, the news media, social media, Hollywood, corporate America, and others—in short, the entire secular establishment. Today, people in all areas of life are increasingly told they must recognize a person's chosen gender, or face censorship, bullying, firing, or, in extreme cases, fines and imprisonment.

It may be that the transgender movement presents one of the greatest risks of persecution against Christians in our time—as major North American institutions increasingly harass, censor, and punish those who disagree with the secular juggernaut of transgenderism.

APPRECIATE THE BEAUTY OF GENDER

Toward the end of this chapter, I will make some comments on how Christian parents can respond to their own children who may be gender-confused. Here, I want to address the question of transgenderism more generally. How do we respond to the sudden push in America to accept transgenderism? We must start by affirming the beauty of human gender.

Although sin has stained gender in the same way it has stained the rest of the world, gender remains a gift from God. Let's look at some ways Scripture affirms gender beauty:

- God created us male and female (Genesis 1:27) and brings together genders to form the oneness of marriage (Genesis 2:21–22).
- Gender is God's way of completing humanity: men, with all their unique strengths, and women, with all their unique strengths, join to complete one another and the community.
- Jesus affirms that we are created gendered and that our gender matters (Matthew 19:1–9).
- Paul distinguishes between our genders, pointing out the beauty of complementarity: each gender derives from the other and complements it (1 Corinthians 11:1–16).
- Certain roles in both the family and the church are gender-specific, again affirming complementarianism

(1 Corinthians 14:34–35; 1 Timothy 2:8–15). because of this, men and women are not to cross-dress or assume the other's gender (Deuteronomy 22:5; 1 Corinthians 11:1–16).
- The biblical truths about sex and gender are confirmed in real life, although sin has often stained God's gifts of sex and gender.

DO THE HARD WORK

Like our response to sexual identity issues, our Christian response to transgenderism must spring from love, expressing itself in kindness, gentleness, and a compassionate spirit. After all, many transgender people already suffer from the pain of gender dysphoria. They, like everyone else, need love.

But for the Christian, love is more than tolerance or kindness. Love means doing the hard work of helping others become the version of themselves that God has called them to be. Because we care about the well-being of everyone, including those who are transgender, we must help rescue people from their hurts, disorders, and sins. Leaving people in their brokenness is not love. It is laziness. We have a job to do: make disciples of all nations. This means that we are called to help everyone, including transgender persons, come to the truth of who they are in the eyes of God.

So we Christians must proclaim the beauty of God's designs for sex and gender, which necessarily involves presenting the truth. Only the truth can set people free. We must point out the hard truth that there really is no such thing as a male being born in a female body, even though there is such a thing as gender dysphoria. Regardless of how much a person may *feel* that they are the opposite sex, they simply are not. Feelings are both fleeting and unreliable. Feeling as though you are a different gender does not change your sex. A woman who fully believes that she is a man still has, in every single cell in her body, XX chromosomes. This is why gender dysphoria is called a *dysphoria*—a non-factual feeling about one's body. Feelings are not facts.

As the University Distinguished Service Professor of Psychiatry at Johns Hopkins Hospital, Paul McHugh, explains:

> [Gender dysphoria] belongs in the family of similarly disordered assumptions about the body, such as anorexia nervosa and body dysmorphic disorder. Its treatment should not be directed at the body as with surgery and hormones any more than one treats obesity-fearing anorexic patients with liposuction. The treatment should strive to correct the false, problematic nature of the assumption and to resolve the psychosocial conflicts provoking it. With youngsters, this is best done in family therapy.[62]

Gender dysphoria is a real condition. Feeling that one's identity does not match one's body is a true disorder. But claiming that one can become the opposite sex simply by announcing a new identity is profoundly *untrue.* One does not become a man or a woman merely by announcing it. To return to the illustration of deer, cutting off the antlers of a buck, limiting his range, and castrating him will not make him a doe, even if his ability to express his gender is now limited.

Dr. McHugh finds himself in the same odd place where Christians find ourselves today: having to explain basic reality to a culture that is desperate for what he calls a "meme" rather than a truth.

Further, taking chemicals to alter one's body to appear like the other sex is to admit that there is such a thing as the other sex: "woman" and "man" are real and natural categories. They are not mere social constructs. But transgenderism ultimately abolishes any meaningful way of talking about sex and gender. If someone can become a woman merely by saying they are a woman, what, then, does it mean to be a woman? Ask an advocate of transgenderism this simple question: "What is a woman?" The bizarre response you'll get demonstrates how unhinged from reality the ideology actually is.[63]

As an analogy, imagine if I, the descendent of English and Irish ancestors, declared myself to be black because that is how I feel about myself. Now some might wrongly say out of sympathy, "I'm good with that." But literally *everybody* would know the truth, even while affirming my racial dysphoria. *I am not black*, regardless of how I feel about it or how much I might want to be black. Further, if I were to lay claim to scholarships or grants designed for black students, I would be robbing true black people of what is rightly theirs. Merely claiming to be black doesn't make me, a white person, black. The truth is, I can *never* be black, even if I appropriated every single shred of black culture and painted my face black. Saying I am black does not magically make me black, regardless of how I feel. It's just not true. And if it were true, then the term *black* would cease to have any meaning in the same way that, if a boy can be a girl, the term "girl" has no meaning.

This reality explains why, again to quote Dr. McHugh, transgender persons generally do not find the happiness they seek when they transition to another gender.[64] The very real problem with gender dysphoria is not solved by fake impersonation of another gender.

Furthermore, the skyrocketing numbers of young people who have declared themselves to be transgender appears to indicate something other than true gender dysphoria. Until recently, very few people reported feelings of gender dysphoria. Today, whole groups of people report the problem. An entire cottage industry is springing up to supply persons, including children, with powerful drugs and surgeries with irreversible effects. As journalist Abigail Shrier shows in her book, *Irreversible Damage*, this sudden increase of transgenderism is the result of social pressure, aided by an entire industry seeking to further sexualize America and our children.

This explains why progressives abet transgenderism. They have decided that transgenderism is, as President Biden said, "the civil rights issue of our time." It presents a new boundary for progressives to destroy. This realization also explains why they approach the condition with a rage. They simply cannot abide anyone who wants to protect this boundary. So progressives increasingly promote transgenderism, even among children, often deliberately hiding from parents the pressure they create. By promoting transgenderism, progressives are perpetrating a morally criminal act: convincing girls that they are actually boys, then offering them drugs and mastectomies to "fix" their problem. No child should ever be told that he or she was born in the wrong body. To attempt to convince a child that they were born in the wrong body and then to chemically or surgically alter that child's body is a crime against humanity.

Christians must identify and point out the truth: Any culture that believes something, which it knows to be untrue, and then seeks to force others to *say* what they know is untrue breaks down the social bonds humans need to flourish. Forcing people to speak falsehoods is wrong and totalitarian. Lying is a form of bondage; cultural lies are destructive forms of bondage. You can see that propaganda brings with it very high costs.

Cultural lies are destructive forms of bondage.

But the untruthfulness of transgenderism creates another convoluted problem. Because a man who transitions to a woman is still a biological man, when he-she interacts sexually with another man, he commits a homosexual act. The same is true of a woman who may transition to a man and then have sexual relations with another woman. In both cases, homosexual sin is committed. Affirming transgenderism opens the door for same-sex activity, which is sinful.

For all these reasons, Christians must oppose transgenderism. It speaks untruths and it encourages same-sex activity. But we should not be under any illusions that we will be heard fairly in a culture that has already closed its eyes. As the leading American psychiatrist Paul McHugh warns, "Gird your loins if you would confront this matter. Hell hath no fury like a vested interest masquerading as a moral principle."[65]

RESPOND TO TRANSGENDER INDIVIDUALS WITH BOTH LOVE AND TRUTH

We Christians must be clear and firm in our statement about the transgender *movement*. But what about the transgender *persons* God brings into our lives? What does the church do with transgender people?

First, for those who are not transgender, but who still suffer from gender dysphoria, we should offer help and support. Because they often feel isolated and lonely, gender dysphoria can give rise to problems such as depression. The church must stand with people who experience gender dysphoria, offering them love and a safe place to live faithfully in Jesus.

Further, we should not construe gender to imply that someone must follow local gender *traditions* to be faithful to Jesus. Gender *customs* and *traditions* are not the same as gender, nor are they the same as biological sex. In Scotland, for example, a man might wear a skirt (a kilt) to a wedding. In a place like my home state of Tennessee, few men would ever consider doing such a thing. Yet neither is masculine or feminine; both are mere customs springing from the local culture.

Nevertheless, we must teach people to live consistently with the biological gender that God gave them. Living as a member of the opposite sex is disordered and untrue. And it opens the door for same-sex behavior. There are moral dimensions to transgenderism that the church must not neglect. It is loving to help transgender persons live consistent with their biological sex. It is unloving to encourage people to live dishonestly and, if someone is living as transgender, to participate in sexual sin.

When transgender people enter our lives—our family, our relationships, or our church—we should offer them kindness and a welcoming spirit. As followers of Jesus, we get the privilege of loving *everyone*.

And because we want to make disciples of all people, I recommend we do *not* start our relationship with transgender persons by disagreeing with them over their gender. Start with hospitality, inviting people into our lives, and then committing to helping them begin the same journey we all walk: living up to the standards of Jesus. Alcoholics Anonymous does not forbid alcoholics to come to its meetings—how ridiculous would that be! But at the same time, Alcoholics Anonymous does not suggest that being an alcoholic is okay, either. Instead, AA keeps its standards unflinchingly high while loving people enough to help them live up to those standards, even if it takes years to do.

It's the position we should all take toward all sin: love sinners well to help them attain the standards of the faith. We approach sexually disordered persons the same way we approach all people. We love them well to welcome them into our lives, and we love them too much to leave them in their lostness.

I have an acquaintance who transitioned from a man to a woman. He was not a Christian. But someone invited him to a women's Bible study group where he began to be discipled by the women. They did not argue over his gender. Rather, they welcomed him and loved him with the gospel. After some time, he decided he wanted to follow Jesus. At that point, they opened up with him about his transgenderism. Now having faith in Jesus, he decided to transition back to manhood. He was baptized and is today a faithful Christian. It was the love of Christians that attracted him to Jesus. It was their love that gave him the space he needed to learn to love the truth.[66]

Christians blend love and truth, and in doing so, we fulfill the last words of the book of James: "Whoever turns a sinner from the error of their way will save them from death and cover over a multitude of sins" (James 5:20).

LEARN HOW TO USE PRONOUNS

But what about the language of transgenderism? Should we accommodate transgender persons by using their preferred names and pronouns? The question is becoming increasingly urgent as many public institutions—schools, businesses, and government services—are telling employees they must use someone's pronoun of choice, regardless of religious beliefs. Before the courts struck it down, California's S.B. 219, the "LGBT Senior Bill of Rights," threatened fines and prison sentences in certain cases if someone does not use a person's preferred pronouns. Worse, progressive diversity trainers are beginning to urge such institutions not to allow employees to avoid pronouns altogether to circumvent the conflict. You will likely be told you *must* use pronouns, and you *must* use the compromising ones. It is a form of totalitarianism characteristic of today's progressivism.

First, we must remember what is at stake. As I mentioned earlier in this chapter, although transgender people should be treated with great compassion and grace, merely claiming to be another gender doesn't make it so. When we affirm what is patently false, we commit serious offenses. First, we tell lies when the world desperately needs to hear the truth. Telling a man that he is a woman keeps him in bondage to a false narrative. And when an entire culture forces people to believe what they know to be false, the social bonds we need to flourish collapse. People can live in the middle of lies, but not well.

Second, when we suggest that a man is a woman, we implicitly approve of same-sex activity. Because a man is not a woman, to present him as such is to give approval for him to have sex with another man.

Third, when we go along with the transgender narrative, even when we think we can say the words without meaning them, we risk falling for the lie ourselves. Call people by the wrong gender long enough, and you'll start to believe what you say—and your children will too. If we are not careful, we will create a world of compromise, and where there is compromise, there is soon capitulation.

And fourth, don't assume that the pronoun wars will end at "he/she." Already, people are inventing pronouns such as "demonself," "fae" (fairy), and even "god," and demanding that others use these pronouns. Will you go along when your university handbook tells you that you must call another student "god"? Progressivism has no bottom, so there is no way to predict how low it will go with pronouns. But you can be sure it won't stop at a simple truce with Christians.

At times, the issue can be complicated. Sometimes we may not know if a person is transgender or not. We may not know what a person's name signifies—for example, some transgender persons use their birth names. Furthermore, because we want to witness Jesus to everyone, including transgender persons, many of us will want to accommodate transgender people in our initial interactions to welcome them into our lives. For example, when transgender people show up at our churches, we don't want to insult them before we can even build a relationship with them.

As far as using a person's preferred names, remember that names don't have to be tied to gender. There may be no problem in calling a person a new name, depending on what it signifies. Perhaps you can find a middle ground that does not compromise your principles but does not lead to a fight.

When it comes to pronouns, however, because they are inherently tied to gender, your use of pronouns—whether you want it to or not—indicates your beliefs about one's gender. For this reason, with respect to pronouns, I believe we need to be moving away from using inappropriate pronouns and toward using proper ones. We may start our interactions with transgender persons by using whatever pronouns they request, especially as we want to invite people into our lives for the gospel. But at some point, you need to find ways to avoid using misleading pronouns—or avoid pronouns altogether. When you use a pronoun that affirms the wrong gender, you are likely encouraging the person you're addressing to sin. Further, if a weak brother or sister is around, or a child, you could easily mislead them into believing that God blesses transgenderism. And don't be naïve: if you continually say things that are not true, you'll begin to believe them yourself. "Take heed," Paul warns, "lest you fall" (1 Corinthians 10:12, KJV).

If you are being *ordered* to use the wrong pronouns in your workplace, look for ways to resist. Stand up to the bullies. If enough of us had stood up in times past, we wouldn't be where we are today. If enough of us tell the bullies of progressivism that they cannot, in fact, make us compromise our beliefs, they will back down. There are, after all, millions of Americans who claim to believe in the Scriptures. If we unite against others' demands that we live by lies and deception, we can find freedom.

FIND CLARITY IN YOUR OWN FAMILY

The transgender epidemic sweeping the West would be bad enough were it confined to adults. But it's not. Because progressivism sexualizes children, transgenderism is now an epidemic among children—fanned by social media, progressive politicians, professional organizations, HR departments, school counselors, sex and gender clinics, and above all, peers. False penises are now designed for elementary girls who wish to transition to boys. Chest binders are sold for girls as young as thirteen, and these binders have been known to destroy breast tissue and even crack ribs. Dangerous puberty blockers and powerful hormones (with effects that last a lifetime) are now being prescribed for children—sometimes without parental consent. Life-altering surgeries are given to fifteen-, sixteen- and seventeen-year-olds. Adult experts coach children in how to transition without their parents knowing, or how to threaten their parents into embracing their transgender identities. Threats of suicide or the loss of parental custody hang in the air for parents who do not go along with the transgender propaganda.

So what should you do if your child announces that he or she is gender-confused or transgender?

First, let me say this question is very complex, and I am not able to give a full response here. So I advise you to find good, Christian guides who can help you walk through what's likely to be a long and arduous journey. You should know that your child's public school will likely oppose you. Many in your family will oppose you. If your church is going progressive, it will oppose you. Your pediatrician may be against you. And your child will likely vociferously oppose you. You are likely to feel alone. Find good Christian support.

But a word of honesty here. You may soon find it difficult to get good Christian advice. Progressives are trying to make it illegal to help children avoid transgender impulses. In Canada, which has no First Amendment, it is now illegal to perform any practice, treatment, or service designed to change or repress a person's sexual orientation or gender identity. It appears likely that similar laws will be passed across the US, criminalizing the act of helping your people escape the transgender propaganda. Remember, progressivism is totalitarian and will not allow Christians to disagree with the sexualization of our children. Nevertheless, there are resources available for parents, and I've included a few in the resource page of this book.

Second, let me say that when a child expresses gender confusion or a transgender identity, realize that he or she is expressing very real and very painful feelings—loneliness, confusion, and fear. Transgenderism for your child is most likely an effort to resolve the intense swirl of hormones and social stress that makes adolescence so incredibly difficult for all children. Whatever else you do, recognize that your child is suffering, confused, and in a lot of pain. Empathize with their feelings. Strengthen your relationship with your child. Show compassion toward their pain. Though you are likely to be panicking inside, show strength, calm, and love toward your child. They did not choose the pain they feel, and it is not their fault that the transgender industry is lying to them. Rather than panicking, learn to ask questions like, "Help me understand what you're feeling." "Can you give me some time to think about this?" "Tell me about your pain, so I can love you well." Showing immense empathy is not the same as denying the facts. You can show empathy without affirming falsehoods.

Which leads me to my third thought. While we must show immense empathy toward our hurting children, we should not go along with things that simply are not true. Feelings are not facts, and feeling like you were born in the wrong body doesn't mean that you were. I'm not saying you should argue endlessly over your child's claims and changes—such as their new name or preferred pronouns. But it is fair to say to your child that though you deeply love them and plan to help them with their feelings, you believe that speaking lies to them ultimately does not help them. It is fair to tell your child that you cannot use their preferred pronouns, even while trying to identify common areas where you can still build connection. Telling your child that you care about their feelings but have no biological reason to affirm that their transition helps them overcome the magical thinking that accompanies adolescence. It helps them learn the difference between feelings and truth.

Feelings are not facts.

And remember that once a child starts down the transgender road, it is very likely they will end up taking radical steps before it's over—unholy sexual relationships, drugs, hormones, and even surgeries. It is possible that you will have to take radical steps. You may need to set boundaries in your child's friendships. You may need to change schools or even homeschool your child. You may well need to cancel your internet—since so much propaganda is coming online. In extreme cases, you might consider moving to a new location. The transgender epidemic is largely social—driven by other people and not by actual biology. For this reason, the Christian response to transgenderism will likely involve a new set of social relationships. Of course, this will not go well with your child, so I encourage you to be very strategic about whatever changes you make.

If your child is suffering from gender identity issues or is in the process of transitioning, you are likely in for a long, hard battle, but God is still good, and you will get through it. Pray for patience and wisdom. Look for allies who can support you, while you learn how to care for your child through their pain. Establish reasonable boundaries. Build the relationship, affirm your love, and disciple your child toward Christian truth, trusting that God is still in charge.

REBUILD AN ETHIC OF HOLINESS

Progressives have made it clear that they are willing to bully, harass, fine, fire, coerce, and even imprison Christians who do not go along with the transgender propaganda in America. They have made it clear they fully intend to indoctrinate your children, even if it means curtailing your rights as a parent. They are taking control of some of the most important institutions in America, and they will try to force you to get in line.

But it is worth remembering that sexual deviancy was a defining trait of the Roman Empire during the opening centuries of Christianity. Indeed, the church's unwillingness to accept Rome's sexual ethics along with its unwillingness to worship idols were the primary reasons Rome persecuted Christians. It was Rome's decadent sexual ethics that earned it the biblical name "whore of Babylon" (Revelation 17:5). And God's fury against Rome was largely due to its sexual sins, as he described Rome as "the great prostitute who corrupted the earth by her sexual sins" (Revelation 19:2).

But while Rome burned with its sexual debaucheries, Christians quietly built another world within the Empire. In this world, Rome's depravity was replaced by sexual holiness—by chastity, sexual purity, monogamous lifelong marriage, and strong families. Rome's institutionalized sexual abuse of both boys and girls, the violence that often accompanied sex, the frequency of rape against female and male slaves, the high divorce and abandonment rates, rampant same-sex activity, the mistreatment of women—all these were eventually diminished by the Christian ethic of sex and marriage. It is an amazing accomplishment: the church, through love and holiness, changed the world.

North America finds itself drifting toward the pagan ethics of ancient Rome. We are aspiring to be the new whore of Babylon. But we Christians can build a better world.

We did it once before. We can do it again.

Small Group Questions

1. Did you finish reading the chapter? If so, what stood out to you from the readings and why?
2. Let's take time to review the following three sections of Scripture:

    - God created us male and female (Genesis 1:27).
    - Men and women are not to cross-dress or assume the other's gender (Deuteronomy 22:5).
    - Jesus affirms that we are created gendered and that our gender matters (Matthew 19:4–6).

    What do these Scriptures teach about our maleness and femaleness, and how do these truths apply to the transgender conversation?
3. Read and discuss the comments by Paul McHugh of Johns Hopkins Hospital about transgenderism (page 180). What is your reaction to these comments?
4. This chapter's main recommendations are listed in the headings throughout the chapter. Pick one or two of these recommendations, and explain your reaction (e.g., agreeing/disagreeing, liking/disliking, etc.).
5. Are there any situations that arise in this chapter where it would be helpful to role-play a conversation or a specific situation in order to help each other anticipate what we might face?
6. In light of the conversation we have had over this chapter, how can we pray for each other?

10

BE WISE AS SNAKES, GENTLE AS DOVES

"I am sending you out like sheep among wolves. Therefore be as shrewd as snakes and as innocent as doves" (Matthew 10:16).

The Apocryphal Acts of John is a second-century work that purportedly tells stories about the apostle John's last years in Asia. Because the stories are most likely fiction, they tell us more about second-century Christian life than they tell us about John himself. Second-century Christians had to fight against paganism in such a way as to avoid getting the whole church killed.

One story is told about John's subtle form of protest against idolatry in the city of Ephesus. The Roman world was built around temples dedicated to a variety of pagan gods. Ephesus was no exception, and the city featured one of the marvels of the ancient world: the temple of Artemis, or as the Romans called the goddess, Diana. Ephesus was the seat of her worship, and the Ephesians were incredibly proud to be her patron city. According to Pliny the Elder, the temple measured 425 feet by 225 feet, with columns rising sixty feet in the air. It was nearly twice the size of the Parthenon in Athens.

The apostle Paul had learned the cost of dishonoring Artemis in the city of Ephesus. He almost lost his life in the theater there for crossing the union of idol makers (Acts 19:23–41). Dishonoring a local god was considered worse than being unpatriotic. This offense was thought to bring about a host of evils: pandemics, war, injustice, and the like.

According to the Acts of John, half a century after Paul's visit to Ephesus, the city was hosting a birthday party festival for Artemis. The apostle John knew he was expected to participate in the festival, as were all the citizens. But he refused to conform. So he went to the festivities, but rather than wearing white (symbolic of celebration), John put on all black—a serious insult to Artemis, but an act of integrity for the apostle. The people were furious.

The story is most likely a fable. It ends with John threatening to have the whole city destroyed and many people becoming Christians. But regardless of whether the story is historical or not, it demonstrates one of the great challenges that we Christians face when we live in the world but refuse to be of the world. How do we raise our families, go to work, engage in the marketplace, and practice our values in a world where we and our beliefs may not be welcome? How can we be good citizens of our communities without adopting their values? How can we remain faithful to Christ when so much of our culture is unfaithful?

The Apocryphal Acts of John reflect where Christians in the Roman Empire found themselves. They were exiles in their culture. They were a minority community in a hostile culture. As Peter says in 1 Peter 2, they were foreigners, and they knew they had to live by a different set of values. As Paul says, they had dual citizenship: they lived in the Empire, but their loyalties lay in heaven (Philippians 3:20).

Rather than curse their status, the early Christians embraced their exile. They found joy in living rightly-ordered lives in a disordered world. They would go to work among the pagans, but they would come home to their people, relax with their people, sing their own songs with their people, tell stories among their people, and celebrate the values of their people. The second-century "Epistle to Diognetus" includes a snippet of how this looked:

> [Christians] dwell in their own countries, but simply as sojourners. As citizens, they share in all things with others, and yet endure all things as if foreigners. Every foreign land is to them as their native country, and every land of their birth as a land of strangers. They marry, as do all [others]; they beget children; but they do not destroy their offspring. They have a common table, but not a common bed. They are in the flesh, but they do not live after the flesh. They pass their days on earth, but they are citizens of heaven. They obey the prescribed laws, and at the same time surpass the laws by their lives. They love all men, and are persecuted by all. They are unknown and condemned; they are put to death, and restored to life. They are poor, yet make many rich; they are in lack of all things, and yet abound in all; they are dishonoured, and yet in their very dishonour are glorified. They are evil spoken of, and yet are justified; they are reviled, and bless; they are insulted, and repay the insult with honour; they do good, yet are punished as evil-doers. When punished, they rejoice as if quickened into life; they are assailed by the Jews as foreigners, and are persecuted by the Greeks; yet those who hate them are unable to assign any reason for their hatred. To sum up all in one word—what the soul is in the body, Christians are in the world.[67]

Though the West was largely built upon Christian values, we now find ourselves in a place similar to Christians in the Roman Empire—foreigners in our own land. But the early church thrived as a community in exile and eventually changed the world. And we can too. But to do this, we will require what Jesus calls the wisdom of a snake and the gentleness of a dove (Matthew 10:16).

REFUSE TO ASSIMILATE

The greatest threat a minority community faces in a hostile culture is not persecution but assimilation. Assimilation threatens the distinct way of life for a minority community, the absorption of its values, and the loss of its children who begin to act like the majority culture around them. Assimilation is the greatest threat the people of God have *always* faced.

Assimilation is the greatest threat the people of God have *always* faced.

The cultural exile of the Black community in the Jim Crow South provides an excellent model for how all Christians must learn to survive in the increasingly hostile culture of the West. Black Americans living in the Jim Crow South could not remove themselves from the dominant culture around them. They had to live within it while maintaining their own heritage. They lived as exiles in their own country. They developed their own cuisine, their own customs, and their own rhythms. They might speak one way when interacting in public with whites, but when they got home, they had their own vernacular. They developed their own music—music that today is the envy of the world. They had their own stories, their own heroes, and their own institutions. Their churches were among the strongest in the world, and these churches often became the center of Black life. In a similar way, we Christians of all races must learn to live within the dominant culture without becoming like that culture.

There is no biblical mandate for Christians to pull out of the world. The apostle Paul explicitly states that we cannot isolate ourselves from the world. Teaching the church that it must remove from its fellowship those who live in unrepentant sin, Paul says, "I wrote to you in my letter not to associate with sexually immoral people—not at all meaning the people of this world who are immoral, or the greedy and swindlers, or idolaters. *In that case you would have to leave this world*" (1 Corinthians 5:9–10).

Paul's point is that we must practice holiness while still *in* the world. We must learn to *insulate* ourselves from cultural unholiness, but we must not *isolate* ourselves from a culture that needs our witness. We must fortify ourselves while remaining engaged in the world for the sake of the gospel. We must do this without compromising our Christian principles. But how do we do this?

BE A FAITHFUL PRESENCE

Christians have no warrant for withdrawing from the world. The opposite is true. We have a mandate to go *into* the world with the gospel, not to withdraw from the world (see Matthew 28:19–20). To withdraw from the world would be to rob the world of the gospel message that only Christians have. So we are right to live among our pagan neighbors, to have jobs among unbelievers, to interact with our faithless family members, and to engage our increasingly secular nation.

But we must do these things while maintaining faithfulness to Jesus. We must practice *faithful presence.* That is, we must be the people who, in the middle of faithless venues, display the virtues of Christ and witness a better way to the world.

Take the illustration of John the apostle above. The story gives us an example of how God has called us to live. John did not withdraw from the pagan city of Ephesus. Rather, according to the legend, John lived right in the middle of the city. He witnessed Christ to his neighbors, to the shopkeepers where he shopped, to the trade unions who controlled much of the city's economy, and to the politicians who protected the pagan interests of Rome in Ephesus. But as the story goes, John never compromised his faith to do this—which is why the legend says that he wore black to the city's pagan celebration. He was engaging his community but doing so in a way that signaled his unwillingness to compromise his Christian convictions. The story shows us how John lived as a faithful presence in the city of Ephesus, caring about his city, contributing to his city, witnessing to his city, but unwilling to compromise his faith to the city. Again, this is not likely historical, but it tells us how the early church survived persecution, and we can still learn from it.

We must learn to live in the same way we see here. Gone are the days when you could assume that everybody in your neighborhood, at your job, in your school, or in your social circles basically agreed with Christian principles. They don't. This is even true for so-called Christian institutions, many of which are deeply compromised. Instead, we can even assume that each of these social circles stand against some of our Christian beliefs. But rather than do the easy thing and withdraw from them, we need to learn to be a friend to others without compromising our convictions. How do we do this? The rest of this chapter gives some strategies for how to present a faithful witness in a pagan world, but before going further, I want to establish a few boundaries.

First, let me say that some institutions may be so corrupt that Christians should not associate with them. There will be some institutions for which there can be no faithful Christian witness because the institution itself promotes unchristian behavior. For example, Planned Parenthood. Christians should not work for or knowingly support the institution. It promotes great evil. There can be no faithful Christian presence working for Planned Parenthood. To work there *is* to promote evil.

For most of us, however, the lines between good and evil will be much less clear in any given institution. For example, can you work for a department store that sells clothing and appliances, etc., but also donates money to causes you disagree with? Can you hold mutual funds, some of whose investments support things you disagree with? Can you go to a Christian university whose administration compromises the Christian faith? The answer is yes, so long as (1) the primary work of the institution is not the promotion of evil and (2) you personally remain faithful, refusing to promote what is wrong.

I once worked on the assembly line of a fertilizer plant. Now if the plant where I worked had supported a "pride" parade (which, as far as I am aware, it did not), that would not lead me to quit my job on the line. I cannot control all of the decisions the plant's officers make. And in a global world, vast numbers of corporations and businesses support things I personally don't want to support. Rather, I would have continued on that assembly line, doing the best work I could for the glory of Christ.

But, and this is very important, I would *not* have allowed myself to serve as the company's liaison with the pride event. I would not have wanted my photo in the local papers celebrating the event. I would not have wanted to help plan an event that violates my allegiance to Christ. I would not have wanted to signal to other believers that I support such an event. So if I held a position at the plant where I was personally asked to actively support something that violated my faith, I would have sought some sort of new position in the plant, or I would have tried to deflect the responsibility, or, as a last resort, I would have quit my job. There is a difference between being in the world, with all its compromises, and personally being the point person for a compromise. The former is almost unavoidable; the latter is more than a faithful Christian can do.

Let me take the analogy even further. Imagine if my fertilizer plant were operating in Germany in 1942—there were many such plants in Germany during the war years. Imagine if the executives at my plant joined the Nazi party—which they almost certainly would have done because only Nazis were allowed to hold high positions in 1940s Germany. I would not have quit my job over that. After all, even such mundane groups as bicycle associations and chess clubs were forced to declare some sort of allegiance to the Nazi party. If, however, my plant, which worked with dangerous chemicals all day long, were suddenly asked by the government to produce Zyklon-B (the chemical used to massacre Jews in concentration camps), I would have had no choice but to quit my job. A line would have been crossed—the company moved from a plant that had to operate in a Nazi world to being a company that directly supported the killing of millions of people. That's a line a Christian cannot cross.

Second, let me say that "faithful presence" means one thing for adults, but it means something different for children or for Christians who aren't mature in their faith. Adults who are strong in the faith can enter into the pagan world's strongholds and stand clearly for Christ. But children and "immature" Christians should be much more cautious. I would avoid putting children into overtly pagan situations. Children typically do not have the moral or intellectual strength to avoid being corrupted by pagan values. Nor do immature Christians. The strong Christian who is not tempted by alcohol can enter a bar and evangelize. But to send children or recovering alcoholics into bars to evangelize is a form of insanity. Children and immature Christians must be protected from pagan influences until they are mature enough to enter into the world of progressivism with the gospel. Protect the weak from the world. Send out the strong.

And finally, when it comes to *social* settings (not work, school, or civic), let me say that we must be discerning in our "faithful presence." We should interact with unbelieving family members and friends. Do you have a gay uncle, parent, or child? Welcome them into your home and into your life! Show the grace of God! Be a true friend!

But, and again this is very important, if you have a Christian (not an unbeliever) in your circles who has *abandoned* Christian principles after baptism, your approach *must* change. The New Testament teaches that we must try to *rescue* believers who are abandoning the faith. We cannot accept their behavior, even if it means we must practice discipline. Even if it eventually means withholding levels of fellowship. I will return to this subject in chapter 11. Right now, I only want to note that the Christian is loving toward *all*, including the lost. That means welcoming them into your life *as is* to help them become what

God wants them to be. Toward the faithless Christian, that means practicing loving discipline for the purpose of restoring them to Jesus. This distinction is critical if we are to be faithful to Christ.

PRACTICE CHRISTIAN SUBVERSION

The apostle Peter addresses Christians living in a hostile culture as *exiles*. It is a fitting label: We live as a minority community expecting a different world but still in a world whose values are opposed to ours. We truly are exiles.

Exile communities must refuse to assimilate, but they must also survive. To do both requires a form of nuance that can easily be abused but which is biblical nonetheless. I'll call it the principle of Christian subversion. Exiles must sometimes conceal their true feelings and beliefs as they quietly and gently subvert the hostile culture around them.

This is what it means to be "wise as snakes and gentle as doves" (Matthew 10:16). This metaphor suggests that sometimes we must hide in the grass until we are ready to strike with the love of the gospel. And it suggests that while we are strategizing about how to bring the gospel into a hostile environment, we must reflect a gentle and smiling presence. In other words, in a hostile culture, we don't have to play all our cards at once. We can be subversive, gently playing along insofar as we don't sin, until we can fully subvert the hostile culture in which we live. We are as "sheep among wolves" who must "be on [our] guard" (Matthew 10:16–17). Every exile community must learn when to speak and when to be silent. Because we Christians are not only trying to survive but also trying to win over the dominant culture, we can and should strategically use the principles of quiet subversion.

We can and should strategically use the principles of quiet subversion.

Subversion involves knowing when to lie low and speaking truth at only the right moment. It involves going along with certain policies that we wish weren't in place (so long as we don't sin), while quietly overturning them from behind the scenes. It involves sometimes smiling when we hear untrue or unholy things, knowing that we don't have to state our opinions every time they are provoked.

Jesus himself practiced such subversion. Repeatedly in the Gospels, Jesus tells various individuals not to tell others who he is—even commanding demons not to identify him. There may be complex reasons for Jesus' refusal to identify himself, but one reason is that Jesus knew the officials would kill him if they heard him identify himself. Jesus' "messianic secret" was not kept in fear; it was strategic. Jesus was subverting the world and was careful about when and how he revealed his intentions.

The apostle Paul practiced a form of subversion as well. When he was on trial before the Sanhedrin, which was split between Pharisees who believed in the resurrection and Sadducees who did not, Paul shrewdly explained that he was a Pharisee who was on trial for believing in the resurrection (Acts 23:6). It was not untrue, but it was strategic. Paul's comment deliberately divided the Sanhedrin, thrusting them into gridlock, enabling him to move up the courts, eventually standing before Caesar himself. Paul was not afraid; he was subverting his persecutors and strategically dividing them for the sake of the gospel.

Even the birthing nurses of ancient Israel practiced a form of subversion. When Pharaoh ordered the murder of Israelite babies, the midwives quietly refused, explaining to Pharaoh that Jewish women were giving birth before the nurses could arrive (Exodus 1:17–20). Because these midwives are commended in the Scriptures, one can probably assume they were deliberately arriving late to each delivery. At any rate, they were subverting Pharaoh's commands to do evil.

Subversion invites us to interact with the world in some sort of public way, while allowing us to relax our demeanor privately around other believers. Several years ago, a short video clip circulated of then-President Obama greeting the players of the 2012 US men's Olympic basketball team. In the video, Obama offers what looks like a formal handshake to the white assistant coach of the team, then immediately greets a black player in a very different way—high-fiving him like old friends would do. Whether he was aware of it or not, President Obama was doing what is often referred to as "code-switching"—a strategy in which minorities present themselves one way to each other, another way to the majority.

It can sometimes be insincere and manipulative. But typically code-switching is just a necessary means of survival for minorities: they imitate the majority when it doesn't matter so as not to call unwanted attention to themselves. My guess is that President Obama was not even aware he had greeted the two differently. As a black man, he had probably simply learned that he must treat whites a certain way but can freely be himself around other Black Americans.

Code-switching is one tool in our Christian strategy of subversion. To be wise as a snake and gentle as a dove, we have Jesus' permission not to call attention to ourselves when it's unnecessary. We can lie low in hostile environments like a snake does and bring up our faith only when the time is right. With that metaphor, Jesus acknowledges that we don't have to take on every argument and fight every fight. In fact, we can often find common ground, even with our persecutors. I recommend we take those opportunities when they present themselves.

Taking a vacation day when your corporation is asking all employees to celebrate a sin may be preferable to writing a scathing post on Facebook. Excusing yourself when the conversation at your family reunion begins to denigrate Christian principles may be better than "throwing your pearls before swine," if you can stretch Jesus' metaphor this far (Matthew 7:6). Coyly and indirectly answering questions from hostile bureaucrats about your beliefs may be better than confronting them. In the Hippocratic oath, medical doctors swear to "do no wrong." But they do not swear to heal everyone who is sick.

Being faithful to Jesus *does* require that we never deny him. But it *does not* require that we express every belief we have anytime we hear it discussed.

The reality is that Christians will have to learn how to code-switch. We will have to learn how to be wise as snakes, staying discreet when necessary and exposing ourselves only when it's safe or when we are ready to proclaim the gospel. We will have to learn how to bide our time, knowing when to come out in open faith. When we are with other Christians, we can let down our guard. But when we are with pagans, we may need to wait until God opens the door, knowing that, in the end, the gospel will win.

ALWAYS BE MOVING AWAY FROM COMPROMISE

A couple of years ago, a chain of popular stores, which I'll call "The Marketplace," made a statement celebrating gay marriage and all things LGBTQ+. At the time, I was preaching a series of lessons on living separate from the values of the world. Many of my panicked church members asked, "Are you saying I cannot shop at The Marketplace?"

It is a question that captures the growing difficulties we now face living as exiles in a hostile culture. In today's global market, it is nearly impossible to live in a modern city or suburb and not interact almost daily with organizations who have values that conflict with ours. Where do we draw the line? Should we go to theme parks that have large events celebrating sexual sin? Should we do business with companies that underwrite organizations contrary to our values? Major universities teach all sorts of unchristian positions. Should we attend one of these schools? Sports teams have even begun to take political positions. What do we do if some of these positions conflict with Christian principles?

First-century Christians wrestled with similar questions about the issue of meat sacrificed to idols. The problem emerged because ancient food markets and restaurants sometimes sold food that had first been dedicated to an idol. For example, in Corinth a cow might be offered to the pagan god Apollo, then its meat sold in the markets below the temple. Should Christians buy the meat? When visiting with friends, should one ask where the meat came from?

This question posed a serious challenge to first-century Christians because they believed eating such meat might lead to idolatry. While Romans 14 may also address this question (it is not clear), two other New Testament texts deal with the issue and offer a guide to handling our own disputable matters today.

In 1 Corinthians 8–10, Paul offers a nuanced response to the problem, revealing that he understands the subtleties it poses. Paul begins in chapter 8 by acknowledging that idols are not real gods, so eating meat that has been sacrificed to idols is, in a sense, nothing. "But food does not bring us near to God; we are no worse if we do not eat, and no better if we do" (1 Corinthians 8:8). But then Paul warns that there are some who don't understand this and could easily be led into worshiping an idol if they see us eating idol-meat. "For if someone with a weak conscience sees you, with all your knowledge, eating in an idol's temple, won't that person be emboldened to eat what is sacrificed to idols? So this weak brother or sister, for whom Christ died, is destroyed by your knowledge" (1 Corinthians 8:10–11). Out of love for others, Paul even goes so far as to say that if "what I eat causes my brother or sister to fall into sin, I will never eat meat again, so that I will not cause them to fall" (1 Corinthians 8:13).

In chapter 9, Paul continues with a lengthy discussion about how we should defer our rights whenever our brother or sister's well-being is at stake. Paul uses himself as an illustration, pointing out how he adapts his own exercise of rights to particular circumstances to win people to Christ.

Then, in chapter 10, Paul returns to the subject of idol-meat, issuing a warning: "Flee from idolatry" (1 Corinthians 10:14). The implication is that our own faith may not be as strong as we think it is. After all, the Israelites saw great miracles from God and still fell when they were influenced by paganism. Idols may not be real, but behind the idols are demons at work. Is Paul saying here that, if we eat idol-meat, we ourselves might end up compromising Christ for the lies of demons?

At this point, in 1 Corinthians 10:21, it appears that Paul wants to forbid us from eating meat sacrificed to idols: "I do not want you to be participants with demons. You cannot drink the cup of the Lord and the cup of demons too; you cannot have a part in both the Lord's table and the table of demons" (1 Corinthians 10:20–21). Then, just when you think Paul is about to say, *Christians cannot eat idol-meat*, Paul returns to his earlier point:

> Eat anything sold in the meat market without raising questions of conscience, for, "The earth is the Lord's, and everything in it." If an unbeliever invites you to a meal and you want to go, eat whatever is put before you without raising questions of conscience. But if someone says to you, "This has been offered in sacrifice," then do not eat it, both for the sake of the one who told you and for the sake of conscience. (1 Corinthians 10:25–28)

Paul's nuanced and brilliant answer wisely acknowledges that it may not always be easy to decide certain questionable issues. Yet he gives us four firm principles by which we must judge these matters:

1. You don't have to investigate every questionable situation, but if you discover one, it's best to avoid the situation.
2. Don't do questionable things if doing so would lead others into sin.
3. Don't assume you can bend in questionable areas without breaking; you may be the one who falls.
4. Remember there is a spiritual battle raging behind every circumstance; be careful not to mix Christ with demons.

The subject of eating idol-meat comes up again in the book of Revelation under very different circumstances. Jesus is addressing churches where false teachers are leading Christians to adopt the world's sexual ethics and join in the idol-meat festivities. These churches weren't struggling with ambiguity. They were compromising their faith to accommodate pagans. Thus, in Revelation, eating idol-meat is strongly condemned. God promises to punish churches that promote it. With Revelation in mind then, we can add a fifth principle:

5. If you do questionable things to conform to pagan values, you are rejecting Christ.

Other sub-principles can be discerned from these texts, but all of them can be summarized in a simple formula: *Move away from compromise* (1 Corinthians 10:14 says, "flee"). In a complex pagan world, we are to *always be moving away from compromise, not toward it.*

What does all this have to do with Christians today? A lot.

Some of the issues we face as exiles in a hostile culture are similar to the issue of eating meat sacrificed to idols: they are questionable. But the firm principles from Paul and Revelation can guide us in how we deal with questionable issues: *Always be moving away from compromise, not toward it.* We must remember the evil one is working behind every single challenge we face. We cannot afford to dismiss the danger that Satan poses to us, to the compromised institutions, or to those watching what we do—such as our own children.

In our complex world, we are simply unable to compile a total list of do's and don'ts, such as businesses Christians should not patronize, movies Christians should not watch, or positions Christians should not take. Instead, when it comes to questionable things, we should think in terms of a *direction* rather than of an *approved list.* Some businesses are deeply compromised. You should be moving away from them. Some jobs will require you to violate your faith. You must look for another job. Some entertainment will steadily flaunt sinful conduct. You must avoid these. At some point, compromised institutions will begin to cost you your holiness. Be moving away from compromise before the decisive moment arises.

Be moving away from compromise before the decisive moment arises.

So shop at The Marketplace, but if the store continually announces positions contrary to your Christian faith, begin moving away from it. Find a Christian business and patronize it, even if it costs a little more! Attend that university. But if the university increasingly stands against Christian principles, move away from it. Take that job. But if it increasingly pressures you to personally compromise your faith, move away from it. Send your children to that public school. But if it begins to overwhelm your child with secular messages, consider a solidly Christian school or homeschooling. There are many great homeschool cooperatives that promote Christian values across the nation. And address people by whatever pronoun they first present to you, but because you know the truth, be moving away from mislabeled pronouns.

These same principles apply to questions about gay weddings. On its face, a wedding is a celebration of a marital union, but for the Christian there can be no marital union of gay relationships. And because same-sex behavior is sinful, Christians cannot celebrate it. So as a matter of truth and conviction, I believe Christians should avoid same-sex weddings.

But there may be cases where Christians can, for limited reasons or with clear caveats, attend such weddings. For example, attending the same-sex wedding of a work colleague may be permissible when that colleague knows your biblical position and you make it clear to them (and your church) that you are attending because you want to lead them to Jesus, not because you approve of same-sex activity. It's critical that we make it clear that we are not lending our approval to such ceremonies, even if we are seeking to demonstrate love. After all, we don't want to treat such unions as normal or healthy—if we want to be faithful to Christ.

Assimilation is the greatest threat to exile communities. So we must always be moving away from the compromises we face every day. We must be moving toward holiness. We must be wise, like snakes who lie in the grass, but strike when necessary. And we must be gentle, as doves who spread beauty across the creation.

OVERCOME THE WORLD

Pagan Rome unleashed ten great persecutions against the early church. The last one was the worst. The Roman Emperor Diocletian had divided the empire into four territories and given the region of the Danube to Galerius. Galerius's mother, Romula, was a committed pagan who worshiped the gods of the hills. She frequently held feasts to her idols and soon noticed the Christians would not honor her festivals. Her own Christian slaves helped her organize the feasts to the gods but then refused to bow before her gods. Incensed, in AD 303, she convinced Galerius and Diocletian to terrorize Christians across the empire. Christians were fired, their property confiscated, church buildings destroyed, and civil rights denied. Authorities passed laws designed to entrap Christians. Many Christians were arrested and a number martyred. But the Christians wouldn't back down.

By the year 310, the carnage had become so bad that even the pagans grew tired of it. Galerius revoked the persecution and shortly thereafter fell deathly ill. By now, so impressed by the Christians' resilient faithfulness, Galerius humbled himself and actually asked the Christians to pray for him. In May of that year, he died a grizzly death. Only two years later, a new emperor emerged: Constantine, who converted to the Christian faith and declared Christianity to be a legal religion. Christians had made it through the worst persecution the Empire could put it through. Centuries later, the Roman Empire remains a matter of ancient history, while the church continues on.

The refusal by Christians to assimilate had solved the crisis of persecution so effectively that it actually created a new problem. Now Christians *ruled* the world, and they began to face a different set of temptations.

The world is pushing hard against us, treating us as strangers. But rejoice in your exile status, for one day soon, alongside Jesus, we, too, will rule the world in the new heaven and new earth (2 Timothy 2:12).

Small Group Questions

1. Did you finish reading the chapter? If so, what stood out to you from the readings and why?
2. This chapter gives us four main injunctions:

    a. Refuse to assimilate.
    b. Be a faithful presence.
    c. Practice Christian subversion.
    d. Always be moving away from compromise.

    Which is the most difficult for you and why?

3. Let's take time to review 1 Corinthians 10:25–28. This chapter explains that Paul teaches the following:

    a. You don't have to investigate every questionable situation, but if you discover one, it's best to avoid the situation.
    b. Don't do questionable things if doing so would lead others into sin.
    c. Don't assume you can bend in questionable areas without breaking; you may be the one who falls.
    d. Remember there is a spiritual battle raging behind every circumstance; be careful not to mix Christ with demons.

Which principle stands out most strongly to you from this passage of Scripture and why?

4. Are there any situations that arise in this chapter where it would be helpful to role-play a conversation or a specific situation in order to help each other anticipate what we might face?
5. In light of the conversation we have had over this chapter, how can we pray for each other?

11

CULTIVATE AUTHENTIC CHRISTIAN COMMUNITY

"Though one may be overpowered, two can defend themselves. A cord of three strands is not quickly broken" (Ecclesiastes 4:12).

Rosaria Butterfield was a progressive secular lesbian professor specializing in British literature, feminist studies, and queer theory at Syracuse University. Though she grew up nominally Catholic, by her early adulthood, Butterfield had left Christianity behind and adopted a Marxist view of history, where people such as herself are perennially considered an oppressed class. The oppressors, she decided, were Christians, especially white, evangelical, male Christians—a common trope among many progressives.

As a result, she had developed a deep loathing for Bible-believing Christians. After reading an article about Promise Keepers (PK), a Christian organization that inspires men to be faithful and loving toward their families, Butterfield decided to write a critique of evangelicalism—believing PK was just another oppressive Christian organization. When she posted her harsh criticisms of evangelical

Christianity, however, she received a strange response from a local evangelical pastor.

Rather than attacking her for her beliefs, Pastor Ken Smith of the Syracuse Reformed Presbyterian Church invited Butterfield to his home for dinner. Wanting to know what evangelicals actually believe, Butterfield took Smith up on the invitation. The dinner didn't go as Butterfield had expected. Rather than arguing with and criticizing her, Smith and his wife showed Butterfield warmth and affection, inviting her back every week. Butterfield's heart began to hear the voice of Jesus as week after week the couple shared life with her in their home. When she finally got the courage to sneak into Smith's church, she was warmly greeted and heard messages about the kinds of virtues that she herself knew had value.

Over the course of two years, Butterfield's own convictions began to melt. She read the Bible intensely, sometimes as much as five hours each day. Several Christlike women in the church discipled her, showing her love and grace as she reevaluated her beliefs. They prayed together regularly. They did ministry together and lived life together.

Through the love of this church and its pastor, God convicted the heart of this secular university professor. Then one day, Rosaria Butterfield got out of bed, left her lesbian lover, and professed faith in Jesus Christ. Today Rosaria is married to Kent Butterfield, a Christian pastor, homeschools her children, and brilliantly articulates the Christian faith through speeches, books, articles, and a variety of ministries.

In one of her books, Butterfield describes the role hospitality served in her discovery of the truth and beauty of Jesus. It was the hospitality of Christians that brought her to faith. She then issues a challenge to all Christians:

> Let God use your home, apartment, dorm room, front yard, community gymnasium, or garden for the purpose of making strangers into neighbors and neighbors into family. Because that

> is the point—building the church and living like a family, the family of God.[68]

Now I've worked for churches for more than forty years, so I know no church, including Syracuse Reformed, is perfect. I'm sure nobody at that church would say it is perfect. But one thing can be said of that congregation: their members understood the absolute need for an authentic community where people love each other and live their Christian lives together.

If we are to survive as the people of God in a hostile culture, we must make this kind of commitment to one another. We must move our churches from events and programs to places where we cultivate authentic community, where life is lived together. In times of persecution, churches survive when their members think of themselves as a real family—the family of God. And churches that merely think of themselves as religious vending machines do not survive.

The earliest image of the church presented in Scripture is of a congregation of people devoted to each other, sharing life together, and regarding each other as family:

> They devoted themselves to the apostles' teaching and to fellowship, to the breaking of bread and to prayer. Everyone was filled with awe at the many wonders and signs performed by the apostles. All the believers were together and had everything in common. They sold property and possessions to give to anyone who had need. Every day they continued to meet together in the temple courts. They broke bread in their homes and ate together with glad and sincere hearts, praising God and enjoying the favor of all the people. And the Lord added to their number daily those who were being saved. (Acts 2:42–47)

The Acts 2 church was a shock-and-awe body of believers, filled with miracles, power, praise, love, devotion, commitment, and explosive growth. It forever defines what a church can look like—what your local church can look like. The Acts 2 church is the archetype of all healthy churches. But if you want Acts 2 results, you must make Acts 2 commitments. You must cultivate authentic community.

Unfortunately, many churches in North America are not designed to create authentic community, and many of us are unwilling to make a deep commitment to other believers. Perhaps it is the legacy of "Christian America"—where the assumption was that everybody was already a Christian—so the only need people had was for a good Sunday experience. Perhaps it is the result of consumerism in America—where people shop for what meets their needs and, as a result, think of the church as a religious shop and themselves as customers. In these consumeristic models, the Sunday experience and programs become everything. But these are poor substitutes for an authentic community.

People are facing powerful temptations, strong resistance, the collapse of their families, heresy, doubt, and the constant assault of progressivism. To care for people in a hostile culture, the church will need to become a real family, where we make real, daily commitments to one another, where we support one another, encourage one another, and live life with one another. Nothing short of an authentic community can keep your faith alive in times of hostility.

> The church will need to become a real family.

As the hostility increases against Christians in twenty-first century America, we Christians need the kind of community that, when one of us loses a job because of our faith, our spiritual family will care for us. When one of us loses a child to progressivism's sexual lies, we need a church that can love us like family. When we face threats from our institutions, cancelation, censorship, discrimination, or harassment, we need a place where we are encouraged in our convictions, where we are comforted, consoled, and lifted up.

Rosaria Butterfield probably would not have become a believer if all she had was a Sunday service and a couple of programs. She became a believer because of loving hospitality. In fact, Butterfield insists that much of the power of the LGBTQ+ community she left behind lies in its sense of community. Every night before her conversion to Christ, she gathered with other LGBTQ+ persons in someone's home, where they shared their lives and genuinely cared for each other. This is one reason why she and her husband open their home to others virtually every night of the week. If we think a couple hours on Sunday can take the place of a genuine community, we are deceiving ourselves. Our churches will not survive. Your faith will not survive.

PRACTICE DEEP HOSPITALITY

First, a critical part of living in community is practicing deep hospitality. The Acts 2 church met not only on Sundays, but every day. Luke says, "All the believers were together and had everything in common. *Every day* they continued to meet together . . . they broke bread in their homes and ate together with glad and sincere hearts" (Acts 2:44–46). The Acts 2 church flourished because its members lived their whole lives together in authentic community.

This is necessary in a hostile culture because we need the encouragement and support of other believers. We require community, for "a cord of three strands is not quickly broken" (Ecclesiastes 4:12). Furthermore, our values come to us through the communities where we live and do life. If you associate with other Christians, then Christian values will make sense to you. But if you live your life largely among pagans, eventually Christian values become incomprehensible to you. As the apostle Paul warns, "Bad company corrupts good character" (1 Corinthians 15:33).

We must realize that Bible-believing Christians are no longer the home team in North America. We are the visitors, and the crowds are booing us. Throughout history, minority communities spent their days in the marketplace with the majority culture. When they came home, they found *their* people: people who spoke *their* language, who shared *their* values, who told stories about *their* joys and sorrows, who shared *their* music, art, customs, traditions, holidays, and values. Our children may go to public schools, but when they come home, they bring their Christian friends with them and live life together. Rod Dreher goes so far as to suggest that we even buy our homes near each other so that we can naturally live life together.[69]

Several years ago, I began a set of relationships with Korean Pentecostal churches from Washington, DC, to New York City. Many of these churches' older members are first-generation immigrants. They know they are a minority community but are happy to be Korean Christians. They have church services in Korean (my sermons must be translated from English into Korean). They gather in each other's homes many times per week. They plan trips together, sometimes back to Korea, other times simply on vacations here in the US. They are deliberate about raising their second-generation children to keep their traditions, so their children have after-school programs together nearly every day of the week, hanging out together at church buildings until close to bedtime. They bring meals to church nearly every night for the children—which is not a problem for most, because they also have worship services every evening for the entire church. Every night of the week, they get to be together. These Koreans live in America, and many are prospering financially. But they won't give up their own culture to succeed in the US, and hospitality—time spent with each other—is the primary way they keep their distinctive identity.

My own congregation has both a Spanish and a Chinese church. I can tell you that though they mix with our white and Black members, both the Spanish and the Chinese churches have special relationships among themselves that offer a richness to their faith. They live life together in a way that strengthens and gives them family.

For many of us whose families have been in the US for generations, practicing this level of hospitality is a serious challenge. We've never had to live as minorities or expatriates. We live in an individualistic society obsessed with entertainment, relaxation, and privacy. North Americans now prefer backyard decks surrounded by privacy fences over front yard porches where we can welcome neighbors into conversations. Many of us are simply strung out from dealing with people at work all day, and the thought of opening up our homes in the evenings is exhausting. A lot of us are just introverts, requiring downtime simply to function.

But hospitality is essential for the persecuted church, and it can be achieved if we make some adjustments to our lives. Learn to invite others to join you in the things you already do; this is easier than trying to plan something unique on a regular basis. Invite others to join you when you travel, when you go to sporting events, and when you do ministry. Prepare your meals with a little extra food and invite others to join you. Many people have moved into large homes with great rooms and elaborate kitchens—so use your oversized house for the kingdom! And to make things even more simple, don't try to put on airs at home. Don't require yourself to keep a spotless home. Don't require yourself to be a perfect host. Just be who you are, and let others love you as you are. It's okay to wear your gym shorts for the sake of authentic community.

If we make deep hospitality one of our primary practices, we will give our brothers and sisters the community they need to survive the hostility we face. Truth matters, but love is stronger than truth. Jesus invested in the lives of his disciples, hanging out with them even when he was not doing ministry. The community he built gave the disciples the strength they needed to face the persecution they eventually faced. The same will be true for us.

POUR INTO SMALL GROUPS

Over the course of the twentieth century, Marxist regimes in Europe and Asia persecuted Christians—often ruthlessly. In the Soviet Union, the church took a massive hit, as the number of believers dwindled throughout the persecution. But in China, the church has actually grown through persecution—especially in the last twenty years. Today there are thousands of baptisms (many in secrecy) every week in China, in spite of the harsh treatment Christians are receiving there.

Why would Christianity weaken under one Marxist government but grow under another? One clear difference between the Christianity of the two countries is how they have done church. In the former Soviet Union, the church was rigidly hierarchical, with the clergy leading the members, often using rituals that did not naturally connect with the average person. In China, on the other hand, the church has typically been composed of small groups, with every house church raising up its own leaders. In these house churches, Christians develop intense levels of companionship with a sense of closeness that Marxists can only dream of having. The big difference between the persecuted church in the Soviet Union and the persecuted church in China is small groups. In China, Christianity is a small group phenomenon.[70]

Likewise, if your local church is going to be resilient and survive the hostilities we face in America, it must get small. Small groups are the only means by which people can build the kinds of relationships that will support them when they are struggling, lift them up when they are weak, hold them accountable when they stumble, and love them through the pain of the hostility we face.

Your local church must get small.

Now, many churches have small group ministries—our church has had them for decades. But having a small group ministry is not the same as being a small group church. In the latter, you push virtually everything you do as a church down to the level of small groups. Ministries get done through small groups. Leaders grow in small groups. The "one another" texts of Scripture get practiced in small groups. Discipleship occurs in small groups. Evangelism gets encouraged in small groups. If your small group ministry is merely another Bible study, pie-tasting club, or Super Bowl party, you are not adequately training your people for the work of the church. The healthy small group becomes a *spiritual family*—where everything the Christian faith teaches and everything the Christian church does is cultivated.

This means you need to be in a committed small group where the other members become your spiritual family—as close to you, as transparent with you, and as real to you as your own birth family. There is no other way to survive in a hostile world.

To transform your small group from a series of meetings to a real family will take time, resources, and for many of us, a new way of thinking. We will need to conceive of our groups as sets of relationships, not mere meetings or Bible studies. We will need to train one another to live life together, to become deeply involved in one another's lives, to pastor one another, to vacation with one another, to eat with one another, to help each other raise our children, to do ministry with one another, to make disciples of one another, and to bring others into the kingdom, working with one another. Leaders will need to be trained to do this because the leadership of these groups will determine their success. Those of us who lead small groups must think of ourselves as pastors for our little flocks—as parents in a spiritual family. We must lead our flocks to become more like Christ, not just conduct a meeting once per week. If we don't, very little else we do will have eternal consequence.

If you are an elder or pastor in your local church, I urge you to make small groups the *centerpiece* of your church, and not just another ministry. Most churches think chiefly about two things: (1) programs and (2) the Sunday gatherings. These are both important functions of a church, and I don't want to undervalue them. But we should realize that neither programs nor the Sunday services are sufficient for sustaining people's faith during times of persecution. Programs tend to be impersonal, and people come and go in programs. Sunday services tend to require very little commitment from people. We "attend" our services, but we aren't necessarily transformed by them. And who knows if our Sunday services may one day be so restricted by American authorities that we have to cut them down in ways that render them ineffectual?

This power of investing heavily in your small groups is illustrated by the work of two revivalist preachers in the mid- to late-eighteenth century in America. George Whitefield was the greatest Christian orator of his age, and his sermons brought together thousands of people who wanted to hear him preach. But he didn't build many churches, and his sermons did not create institutions that would perpetuate the message he preached. Conversely, John Wesley also preached in the revivals of the eighteenth century, but Wesley insisted on planting churches built around small groups.

Both Whitefield and Wesley were Methodists, but the former focused on oratory while the latter focused on disciple making through small groups. Where Whitefield preached about prayer, Wesley's small groups prayed. Where Whitefield spoke of forgiveness, Wesley's small groups forgave. Where Whitefield talked about love, Wesley's small groups loved one another. Whitefield may have attracted people to the Christian message, but Wesley's small groups exploded in Christian growth. When the Revolutionary War began, there were only a few dozen Methodist churches in America. By the American Civil War, as many as one out of every three Americans were Methodists. Most came through the small groups that Wesley had established. Small groups give people the spiritual families they need to grow up in Christ. Wesley changed the world through small groups.

Likewise, the largest congregation in the world is the Yoido Full Gospel Church in Seoul, Korea. That one single congregation has had as many as a million members. When Yoido first launched in 1958, they had only seven people in attendance, including one elderly woman who only came in to get out of the rain. How did this tiny church explode into the world's largest Christian congregation? Through small groups and prayer. Prayer seems to be a special gift God gave the Korean people, and so the congregation is now famous for its prayer mountain, where people can spend days simply in prayer.

But the founding pastor, David Cho, understood the power of small groups from the beginning, so the congregation has always done ministry through its small groups. People in the Yoido congregation learn to practice their Christian faith deeply in their lives by spending enormous amounts of time in their small groups, which serve as Christian families. To become big, the Yoido Full Gospel Church became small. They learned what the rest of us must learn.

Start a small group, join a small group, or strengthen your small group. But make it a spiritual family. In a hostile culture, the health of your small group may be the difference between life and death.

OFFER LOVING DISCIPLINE TO ONE ANOTHER

Americans have a very low view of discipline—especially discipline that seeks to constrain our desire to do what we want to do. Americans *hate* rules. Parents side with their unruly children when the school is forced to discipline them. Protestors accuse the police of injustice when the police try to stop them from damaging or destroying property. Restaurants claim they have "no rules." Car ads suggest that buying their vehicles will allow you to "color outside the lines." Even to children, Disney's Elsa sings, "No rules for me!"

This aversion to a healthy respect for rules has infiltrated our churches. According to a 2018 Lifeway Research study, nearly eight in ten senior pastors said their church had not disciplined a member in the past three years, and half of evangelical senior pastors say that, as far as they know, their church has never disciplined a member. But the early church understood that discipline is a necessary part of growth.[71] So we must learn to offer one another loving discipline.

Of course, discipline is hard to do and *very* hard to do well. When I was raising my children, practicing discipline with them was the hardest thing I had to do. It would have been much easier for me to simply allow my children to live how they wanted. But because I love them, I wanted them to become the best version of themselves available. Discipline is necessary for that to happen.

In a world of hostility, discipline is critical for our survival. We Christians are described as "sheep" in the Bible, and sheep need fences to protect them from predators. But sheep also need guidance to ensure they find green pastures and fresh water. Christians who don't practice discipline are leaving one another exposed to predators and are failing to lead one another to spiritual maturity. But how can the ordinary Christian practice church discipline in a way that demonstrates genuine love, honors God, and encourages repentance when necessary? Here are a few thoughts:

First, remember that discipline is not the same as punishment, even though consequences are sometimes necessary to accomplish discipline. Effective discipline starts with encouragement, love, support, grace, and a real relationship. A Christian who wants to practice discipline must focus first on encouraging others without ceasing. If you haven't cultivated a strong atmosphere of encouragement, love, and support, start there. You don't speak to your children only when they do something wrong; rather, you invest in their lives constantly. After all, the goal of any discipline is a healthy life, not a punished life. Create a loving Christian environment around you so that discipline makes sense when it must be done.

Second, live in covenant with each other. Make it clear that our discipline for each other is premised on the truth that, as the apostle Paul says, "we belong to each other" (Romans 12:5). I never attempted to discipline my neighbor's kids, even though I routinely disciplined my own. I had no real relationship with the neighbor's kids. In the same way, if Christians don't live in a covenant relationship with one another, we really haven't earned much of a right to discipline each other. "Disfellowshipping" someone makes no sense in an environment where there is hardly any fellowship in the first place.

So Christian discipline is a graded thing based on a covenant relationship designed to hold up one another to the high standards of our faith. For those who are weaker, show enormous patience. Look for everything good you can find and pour fuel on that. Accountability matters, but let it be graded—gradually increasing it only as believers are able to hear it. For example, when my son was a boy, I didn't expect him to act like a man, although I continually pointed him in that direction. Most of all, I *encourage*d him. I spent enormous amounts of time with him. I loved him. At times, I merely suggested that he consider changing a bad behavior. At other times, I was firmer. I could do all this because I was in a relationship with him and because I cared about him.

And one day, my son grew up. Today, he is a godly man who has made his daddy prouder than I can say. But it took the right kind of love to help him arrive.

If a believer in your circles remains in their sin and refuses to repent—after long and intense loving encouragement, you may need to limit your fellowship with them. Now let me quickly say that I do not believe this principle applies to minors—to our children. You cannot withdraw fellowship with them; they are only children. But if an adult Christian refuses to repent after you've taken a thousand steps to help them, you may need to withhold a level of your fellowship from that person.

The principle is biblical because it is actually a supreme act of love. Jesus says that sinners should be confronted by their victims, and, should the offending person refuse to repent, the church is to treat the offending person as they would treat "a pagan or tax collector" (Matthew 18:15–17). Paul says we should avoid those in the church who cause division (Romans 16:17); that we are to warn those who are lazy or disruptive (1 Thessalonians 5:14); that we are not to associate with those who refuse to obey Paul's teachings (2 Thessalonians 3:13–14); and that we are to have nothing to do with divisive persons who won't respond to warnings (Titus 3:10). Paul's language in 1 Corinthians 5:1–5 is strong: the church should hand over unrepentant immoral people to Satan, even refusing to take meals with them (1 Corinthians 5:11). Jesus praises the church at Ephesus for testing false teachers (Revelation 2:2), and he warns the church at Thyatira not to accept those church members who were teaching immorality and idolatry (Revelation 2:14–16). Though he was speaking of personal disciplines, the twentieth-century German evangelist Dietrich Bonhoeffer's statement applies to church discipline too: "Therefore we have to practice strictest daily discipline; only so can the flesh learn the painful lesson that it has no rights of its own."[72]

Christian discipline is intended to accomplish two things. First, to keep the church pure from sin and false teaching. This is the primary concern of Jesus' warnings in Revelation. Several churches in Asia Minor were at risk of losing their holiness because they wouldn't discipline those who were teaching sexual sin. As Paul says to the church at Corinth: "Don't you know that a little yeast leavens the whole batch of dough?" (1 Corinthians 5:6). When we allow the church to fill with people who are unwilling to correct their ways, make wrongs right, and grow in their faith, we create an unholy people. And an unholy people simply cannot survive as the people of God.

Second, Christian discipline offers people the opportunity to be rescued from sin and to flourish as followers of Jesus. James praises the one who turns away a sinner from sin, saying that the Christian saves the sinner from death (James 5:19–20). Even when withholding fellowship is necessary for the unrepentant sinner, it is done for the sake of the person in bondage to their own sin—"so that his spirit may be saved on the day of the Lord" (1 Corinthians 5:5). The hope of all church discipline is the restoration of the person wandering from God (cf., 2 Corinthians 7:8–9). As God disciplines us out of love, we are to discipline one another out of love (Hebrews 12:6).

I have a friend who was in a university sorority when she was a student. She once told me about the rules of the sorority, as well as how the sorority disciplined its members. The sorority has a written set of standards, and all members must internalize them. For this reason, it takes months to become a member. The sorority has a "VP of standards" who ensures that everyone is following the rules. There are punishments for violating the sorority's standards—for such things as poor academics, mistreating other members, or embarrassing the sorority publicly. When I asked her why anyone would want to join such an organization, she said, "I want a place where people genuinely care about living well, where they work hard but love each other, where laziness is not welcome, where people stay clean and live by high standards. I want a family while at school." If a sorority at a public university understands the value of standards and discipline, shouldn't Christians?

So how do we do this? Well, as with our own children, discipline can look different in each case. Whatever else we do, we must watch our own selves, lest we correct others while falling ourselves (Galatians 6:1). Humility and modesty must govern our actions.

We must watch our own selves.

Second, we must never cut off a person to the point that they cannot come back to us. The goal of any discipline is restoration. When we discipline others, we must do so with open doors, always inviting people back to Jesus. As Paul says, we do not treat erring brothers and sisters as enemies (1 Corinthians 5:11). We treat them as family.

And finally, we should never stop pursuing those who have fallen away. People's moods and commitments change over time. Who knows what God is doing in the hearts of even those who have fallen away? By pursuing these brothers and sisters first, we constantly give them the chance to rediscover the beauty of what they left.

Discipline is essential to growth, and churches facing persecution take discipline seriously, knowing it will strengthen faith. We must stand on the truth. There is no other foundation for the Christian. To survive a hostile world, we must be clear on where we stand, and we must help our churches find that same clarity.

> My brothers and sisters, if one of you should wander from the truth and someone should bring that person back, remember this: Whoever turns a sinner from the error of their way will save them from death and cover over a multitude of sins. (James 5:19–20)

GET REAL ABOUT LOVE

In the early twentieth century, Charlie Chaplin was a huge celebrity. By 1920, there were numerous impersonators of Chaplin throughout the US. For fun, various organizations hosted Chaplin look-alike contests. Though it may only be an urban myth, there is a story that says Chaplin himself—as a joke—entered a Charlie Chaplin look-alike contest under a disguised name. He didn't fare well.

Legend says that in a Chaplin look-alike contest, Charlie Chaplin himself came in twenty-seventh out of forty contestants. That means that there were twenty-six pretenders so well disguised that judges didn't recognize the real person. Of course, when payday came for Chaplin's performances, only the real Charlie got the paycheck.

In his book, *The Insanity of Obedience*, Nik Ripken identifies five different kinds of Christians. There are *census Christians*: those who mark "Christian" on the census. There are *member Christians*: those who identify with a particular congregation. There are *practicing Christians*: those who participate in Christian ministries, programs, events, and the like. And there are *committed Christians*: those who are shaped by Jesus and whose faith in Christ is central to their life.

But Ripken has spent large amounts of time with persecuted Christians around the globe and identifies another kind of Christian. These he calls *hidden* Christians. They are the radical believers who have made a lifelong commitment to Christ and to the people of God; they can withstand any opposition the hostile culture levels against them. This last category is for Christians who make a deep commitment to one another. It is the category defined by an intense love among believers who regard one another as God's eternal family. It is a category where discipline is lovingly practiced to give all of us the encouragement and boldness to rise up to the fullness of the image of Christ.

Such hidden Christians are motivated by a rich love for God and for others—something that can only be learned in authentic community.

Small Group Questions

1. Did you finish reading the chapter? If so, what stood out to you from the readings and why?
2. Read John 13:34–35 and Acts 2:42–47. According to John 13, how did Jesus teach his disciples that they were to love one another? In Acts 2, what stands out to you most about how the earliest Christians lived out Jesus' teachings?
3. Think back to John 13:34–35 and Acts 2:42–47. What part of these teachings/examples do you see this small group practicing best? How do you feel about that? What are some ways this group can practice Jesus' teachings at an even deeper level?
4. What was the historic difference this chapter points out between Whitfield and Wesley? How can our church be more like Wesley?
5. Read Matthew 18:15–17. What does this passage teach, and how can we follow it today?
6. Are there any situations that arise in this chapter in which we are going to need to help each other?
7. In light of the conversation we have had over this chapter, how can we pray for each other?

12

SEIZE THE OFFENSE BY MAKING DISCIPLES

"All authority in heaven and on earth has been given to me. Therefore go and make disciples of all nations, baptizing them in the name of the Father and of the Son and of the Holy Spirit, and teaching them to obey everything I have commanded you. And surely I am with you always, to the very end of the age" (Matthew 28:18–20).

Several years ago, a man I'll call Abdul (not his real name) entered a large church in West Africa. Our congregation partners with this church in making disciples and planting churches across West Africa. Every Sunday, they have as many as four hundred animated worshipers in this one congregation, praising the Father through Christ in the power of the Holy Spirit.

Abdul was raised in a radical Muslim family—part of a Muslim extremist group dedicated to eradicating Christianity among Africans. The man was young, single, and easily radicalized by the leaders of his people.

He visited the church on a Sunday morning, trying to look like an innocent visitor. Unbeknownst to the worshipers, however, he was there to scope out the building. He planned to return wearing a suicide vest to blow up the building with as many Christians in it as he could. He mingled with the crowd, thinking about the best place to detonate his bomb.

But something amazing happened to Abdul.

Little did he know that this church had been praying that God would open doors into the hearts of their sworn enemies so that they could make disciples, even of those who wished to do them harm. They are a people deeply devoted to prayer and to walking in the power of the Holy Spirit. And above all, they are committed to making disciples of all nations—which explains why this movement has helped increase the Christian faith in their nation from around ten percent of the population to nearly forty percent in a mere twenty years. They make disciples, even in hard and hostile circumstances.

They invited Abdul to join one of their circles of Bible study and prayer that precedes the worship service. As he sat there, the Spirit began to move him. He was conflicted inside, angry and confused. Within the hour, someone asked him if he would join the group during the week for prayer and discovery of what God can do through Christ. Fatefully, he said yes.

Within a few weeks, Abdul was had. The Holy Spirit used the Word of God to convict his heart, and he soon found himself claiming Jesus as his Savior and Lord. He was baptized into Christ—even though it meant that he would now have a bounty on his head from his family and tribe who would seek to kill him because they would see his conversion as a betrayal to Islam, their family, and their tribe. Abdul lost everything but counted it as nothing because in Jesus he actually found everything. Soon, Abdul was sneaking back to his people and discipling them. When I met Abdul, he had already planted several churches among his hostile people and was planning to plant even more. When I saw him worship on a Sunday morning, his face had the most glorious look on it.

The disciple making mission of this church in West Africa demonstrates a fundamental truth that we must embrace to survive hostility in North America. We don't play defense. We play offense. We pray for our enemies, target them with the gospel, and seek to make disciples of them for King Jesus.

We make disciples. That's how we fight. And if you have not made disciple making your mission, you will grow weak in the face of opposition, while your enemies grow strong. Prayerfully, in the power of the Spirit, with the strength of Christ, we make disciples—that's how we seize the offensive.

But unfortunately, many of us have lost the desire to make disciple making the mission of our lives. Because disciple making is the only real way to defeat our enemies, losing this mission will cost us. It will cost our children even more. The fewer disciples we make, the more hostility our own children will face in America. If we restore the disciple making mission to our lives today, Scripture tells us that the world will be increasingly and fiercely transformed by the mission of Jesus, and opposition will fade. The best defense is a good offense.

RECOVER YOUR DISCIPLE MAKING MISSION

When Jesus came to earth, he did numerous things. He preached, healed, taught, worked miracles, died to atone for our sins, rose from the dead, and ascended back into heaven. But the daily thing that Jesus did was call twelve ordinary men and invite them into a personal relationship with him for three years while he trained them to change the world. The term for this is disciple making, and everything Jesus did up to his crucifixion centered on this task. Jesus made disciples.

Then just before he ascended back into heaven, Jesus commissioned his disciples to go and make other disciples. The commission appears, in some form, in all four of our Gospels, as well as in the book of Acts. In the longer ending of Mark's Gospel, Jesus says, "Go into all the world and preach the gospel to all creation. Whoever believes and is baptized will be saved, but whoever does not believe will be condemned" (Mark 16:15–16). At the end of Luke, Jesus says, "This is what is written: The Messiah will suffer and rise from the dead on the third day, and repentance for the forgiveness of sins will be preached in his name to all nations, beginning at Jerusalem. You are witnesses of these things" (Luke 24:46–48). At the end of the Gospel of John, Jesus says "Peace be with you! As the Father has sent me, I am sending you" (John 20:21). And Matthew's Gospel ends with the most distinct statement of our commission:

> All authority in heaven and on earth has been given to me. Therefore go and make disciples of all nations, baptizing them in the name of the Father and of the Son and of the Holy Spirit, and teaching them to obey everything I have commanded you. And surely I am with you always, to the very end of the age. (Matthew 28:18–20)

And in the book of Acts, Jesus repeats the commission one final time, just before his ascension: "But you will receive power when the Holy Spirit comes on you; and you will be my witnesses in Jerusalem, and in all Judea and Samaria, and to the ends of the earth" (Acts 1:8).

Just as Jesus made disciples of those who were in his circle, so he teaches us to do the same thing. This is clear in all four Gospels but is even more explicit in Matthew's Gospel. There, Jesus says, "Go make disciples . . . teaching them to obey what I commanded you." And what did Jesus just command them to do? Make disciples! Jesus told his disciples to make other disciples and to teach their disciples to make other disciples, and so on, until the whole world gets the chance to say yes to King Jesus.

The subsequent history of Christianity in the Roman Empire proves that disciple making was the key to winning the world for Christ.

Disciple making was the key to winning the world for Christ.

The book of Acts overflows with the mission of disciple making. It starts in chapter 1 with the commission to be witnesses here (in Jerusalem), near (in Judea and Samaria), and clear to the ends of the earth. This statement in Acts 1:8 becomes the paradigm through which the rest of the book of Acts is to be read, as the book's story starts in Jerusalem, moves to Judea and Samaria, and ends in the imperial city of Rome. Chapter 2 of Acts jumpstarts the church's disciple making mission, as Peter preached a sermon to the thousands who had gathered in Jerusalem for Pentecost and established the first post-resurrection church. This church was marked by disciple making, as they devoted themselves to one another in such a way that God added members to their number every single day (Acts 2:47).

In nearly every chapter after this, various members of the church can be found witnessing to the world: Peter, John, Stephen and Philip, and of course, the apostle Paul. Early on when the church was bunched up in Jerusalem, God allowed persecution to break out, forcing Christians to spread out all over the world "preaching the word" (Acts 8:4). When members of the church weren't traveling to preach, they were sending out others (Acts 13:1–4). The accusation that Jews made against the Christians in Thessalonica illustrates the success and power of preaching the gospel: "These men . . . have turned the world upside down" (Acts 17:6–7, ESV).

Christian history suggests that this style of disciple making became the norm in the church. Older women are to train younger women (Titus 2:3–5). Timothy was to train reliable men who would then be qualified to train other men (2 Timothy 2:2). Paul commends the Thessalonians for imitating him; that is, for being faithful disciples of Jesus through his work. And he invites others to do the same

(1 Thessalonians 1:6; 1 Corinthians 4:16, 11:1; Philippians 3:17). Early church history claims that the apostle John trained Polycarp, a bishop in the church of Smyrna. Polycarp trained Irenaeus, one of the fathers of Christian orthodoxy, who trained Hippolytus. And so forth. Disciple making was so ingrained in the early church that the second-century apologist Tertullian once called Christians "students in God's school."

Throughout the early years of tremendous growth, the church never took its eyes off its singular mission: making disciples of all nations. In his classic work, *Christian Heroes and Martyrs*, William Foster describes how the early church dealt with persecution:

> In that age every Christian was a missionary. The soldier tried to win recruits for the heavenly host; the prisoner sought to bring his jailer to Christ; the slave girl whispered the gospel in the ears of her mistress; the young wife begged her husband to be baptized that their souls might not be parted after death; every one who had experienced the joys of believing tried to bring others to the faith.[73]

Elaborating on a quote from nineteenth-century philosopher Will Durant, Herbert Cane, the historian of Christian missions, described the early church's missionary zeal this way:

> Nearly every convert, with the ardor of a revolutionary, made himself an office of propaganda. With no weapon but the truth and no banner but love, these single-minded, warm-hearted followers of Jesus traveled by land and sea to all parts of the Empire, and wherever they went, they gladly shared their newfound faith with friends and neighbors and strangers. As slaves, traders, and later on soldiers, they used their secular calling to advance the call of Christ. Even as exiles, they carried the contagion of their faith to distant shores and inhospitable regions.[74]

The church's influence changed the world through disciple making. It took three hundred years, but after changing the hearts of millions of people, the church simply woke up one day with critical mass. The world changed because the hearts of so many had been changed. In the same way, we only have one mission today: be a disciple of Jesus who makes disciples of Jesus.

Pastor Steve Murrell has led a disciple making movement of tens of thousands in the Philippines. He states clearly the comprehensive call:

> It is the central underlying idea that every disciple should make disciples. Not many, not most, but every disciple should make disciples. Not just church staff, not just mature Christians, not just evangelistic types. Regardless of travel and work schedule, status, gender, or age, every disciple should make disciples.[75]

Here's the bottom line. The Christian movement faced extreme hostility during the first three centuries of its existence. Early Christians could have responded politically—by marching in the streets, advocating for certain political candidates, and turning their churches into advisors for legislative action. For the most part, they didn't. The movement could have kept quiet about the gospel, simply trying to live their lives for Jesus while avoiding conflict through silence and accommodation to the pagan world around them. They didn't. The movement could have responded defensively, by running to the hills and hiding from the persecution, building their own small communities out in the desert. Some did, which is how the monastic movement started. But most did not. Rather, they lived their disciple making mission smack dab in the middle of a hostile world, knowing they could only change the world if they made disciples of the people of the world.

The apostle Paul says we have no warrant for withdrawing from the world (1 Corinthians 5:10). Rather, we are to engage the world, including those who are hostile toward us, with the gospel. Take that job but use it as access to other people for the sake of discipling them. Go to that school but use it as access to others for the sake of discipling them to follow Jesus. Move into that neighborhood but use it as access to disciple others. Invite those lost people into your home with the intent of ultimately leading them to follow Jesus.

This is critical for Christians living in a hostile world.

Some time back, a member of our congregation asked about working part time at a small business whose owners are open advocates for same-sex activity. "Should I take this job?" he asked. My response: "If you are taking the job simply to make money, reconsider the offer. After all, if your goal is simply to make money, you may end up compromising your beliefs to accommodate the business owners' values. But—and this is the big point here—if your life's mission is to make disciples, then take the job and begin the long and risky business of showing these owners the way of Christ. Love them. And disciple them." This is how we move from defense to offense.

LEARN HOW TO MAKE DISCIPLES

So how do we go about making disciples of people, especially those who vehemently oppose us and our values? Lots of things Christians do aid in disciple making: attending church, preaching, doing good works, loving the poor and marginalized, and the like. But in disciple making, nothing can take the place of building relationships with people for the purpose of "helping Christ be formed in them," as Paul puts it (Galatians 4:19).

Jesus personally shows us how to make disciples. First, he calls the disciples, inviting them to follow him so that he can teach them to bring others to him as well (Matthew 4:18–20). After calling each individual and spending an evening in prayer, Jesus then appoints the Twelve to be with him, to preach to others, and to exert authority over evil spirits (Mark 3:14–15). For the next three years, Jesus lived with the disciples, joined them for meals (Matthew 9:10), gave private lessons to them (Mark 4:33–34), shared ministry with them (Mark 6:37), and then sent them out to preach (Matthew 10:1ff). After his resurrection, he told them to go do with others what he had done with them.

Jesus' style of disciple making was similar to the philosophers of the Hellenistic world, as well as the rabbis of the Jewish world. A teacher would take a group of students under his care and train them to be like him. More than a lecturer, the teacher was a mentor and a coach who would then appoint one or more of his followers to go out and make other disciples. Moses appointed Joshua (Deuteronomy 34:9). Elijah appointed Elisha (2 Kings 2:12–15). Paul mentored Timothy and gave him missionary authority (2 Timothy 3:10–11). Peter evidently mentored Mark to the point that the Gospel of Mark was considered by the early church to be Peter's Gospel (cf., 1 Peter 5:13).

This is how we make disciples too. We invite others into our lives through meals, through hospitality, through friendships, and through openly sharing the gospel at strategic moments. This is how Rosaria Butterfield (see chapter 11) was won to Christ from her enmity toward all things Christian. Pastor Ken Smith and his wife frequently invited Rosaria into their homes. They talked life and shared recipes. They loved each other. And eventually, after two years, Rosaria realized that she loved Jesus and his Bible. She left her sinful life behind, became a Christian, married a pastor, and now makes disciples of others.

Pastor Smith and his wife treated their home as a disciple making venue, and they used their relationships to help Rosaria find Jesus. She had started as an enemy of the faith. Rather than condemn and openly oppose her, they loved Rosaria enough to welcome her into their home and win her to Jesus. When they finally shared the Bible with her, she was ready to hear it.

In another of my books, *King Jesus*, I tell the story of how my son Jonathan lost his faith as a teenager. He was not hostile toward the Christian faith, but he was done with it. Then two older men—one a filmmaker and the other a grand master in Taekwondo—began to invest in Jonathan's life using their professions to build a relationship with him. They gradually showed him Jesus—praying with him, speaking Christ's words into his problems, loving him, and helping Jonathan to overcome his doubts. They did this day after day, for months. After six months, my son not only came back to Jesus, but he is now a church planter in the Northwest who is totally sold out to Jesus. He married a Christian campus minister, and they are now making disciples. This is how the gospel goes on the offensive. We make disciples—even of our enemies. After all, who needs the gospel more than those who oppose the Christian faith?

> Who needs the gospel more than those who oppose the Christian faith?

START WITH YOUR FAMILY

The hostility we face is personal in the US, and it has targeted our families above all. This is one of the most painful parts of trying to live faithfully in a faithless age. Our own family members are tempted to stray. They might begin to compromise and even turn against us. So it is imperative that we begin our offensive by discipling our own families.

The family is the basic building block for civilization, and it is where faith is most commonly passed from generation to generation. Because progressivism is attempting to remake civilization, it attacks the Christian family above all. This movement is trying to steal your children. Its destructive efforts are consistent with those of hostile systems throughout the twentieth century. Both fascism and Marxism threatened to disrupt the work that only the family can do—this was especially true of Marxist governments. From the beginning, Marxism has seen the family as an obstacle to its ambitions because the family offers a rival organization to its collectivist ideals. The old Soviet establishment hated the family, which is why the Soviet Union sought to collectivize the family.

In the same way, as North American progressivism has developed along the lines of Marxist assumptions, the family is increasingly seen as a problem. This explains why progressives seek to redefine marriage and family, and why their policies and ethics undermine the family. The family is just one more obstacle standing in the way of their utopian vision. With secular progressivism undermining our families, the church has become the final bastion for cultivating strong families, and you must place priority on discipling your family.

In this hostile environment, churches must prioritize building strong families. One way is simply to apply many of the efforts—sermons, ministries, pastoring—to marriage and the family. Make it the centerpiece of what you do. But be careful not to define family in a way that leaves out single adults or widows. Everyone should be encouraged to value families, married or not.

Of course, the best way to raise strong families is to disciple them relationally—pairing younger families with older families to be discipled in Christian maturity. Ask older married couples to mentor younger married couples. Enlist older men to disciple teenage boys in small groups. Invite older women to disciple teenage girls in small groups. Encourage older mothers to disciple younger mothers and older fathers to disciple younger fathers. This is not rocket science. Most of us grow best when we grow in loving relationships, guided by more mature believers who invest in our lives. Disciple making is not only evangelizing but also maturing the saved.

When my wife and I were younger, three couples at our church adopted us; the three men were elders at our church. We had meals together several times per week and met to discuss church problems. We did ministry together and vacationed together. When my children were born, all three couples served as grandparents to my children and still love them to this day. From the mentoring these men gave me, I learned how to be a man. I learned how to ask questions about how to do the right thing. I learned courage and how to be generous. I learned when and when not to take a risk. Because I was discipled by mature followers of Jesus, I became much more mature in following Jesus. You can offer this to others too.

But the most important thing you can do for your family is disciple family members personally. This means praying regularly both for and with your family, spending enormous amounts of time with them, showing them what Jesus is doing in your life, and walking the path of faith with them. Show them how to prioritize Jesus over all else by the way you interact with them. Demonstrate Christian truth, conviction, discipline, grace, forgiveness, gentleness, etc. Seeing you walk the walk while you invest heavily in your family members' lives is the purest form of disciple making.

When it comes to your children, learn to mix strong relationships with a handful of basic Christian rules. A lack of a gracious relationship or too many rules can exasperate your children, turning them against the faith. Too few rules can lead your children to spiritual laziness, resulting in the loss of faith.[76] We seek basic Christian principles, applied firmly but graciously in a rich, full, and joyous relationship. This is the best formula for children; it is also the best formula for other family members. Disciple your family members—especially your children—with truth and conviction but also with beauty and joy. Let them see—a hundred times a day—Christ living in you.

And remember that compromising your Christian principles to keep your children may work—at least in the sense that you and your children can stand together for the wrong values. But it will condemn both you and your children to the dystopia that paganism creates, and it will rob your children of the faithful witness they need to see in you.

The world gets the lion's share of your children's attention, so you may not be able to prevent some of your children from abandoning Christ and his truths. But there are some things you can do. Let your Christian principles order your family life. When my children were still living with us, my wife and I didn't let sports, sleepovers, special events, and the like get in the way of going to church. And even when my son lost his faith for a few years in his teenage years, I made it clear to him that he would still live with Christian rhythms as long as he lived in my house—which kept him grounded until he rediscovered his faith and, in his twenties, became a church planter.

Second, you can shield your children from much of the pagan influence in the world in common sense ways. Turn off the television—or at least limit your children's exposure to it to a couple hours per week. Don't give your children smart phones until they are older teens—after all, there is no God-given right to a smart phone. Be very strict in what friends you allow into your children's circles. Humans do, indeed, become like those we associate with and befriend. Consider taking your children out of public schools if those schools are determined to indoctrinate your children in paganism. If you cannot find a good public or private alternative, then homeschool your children. Losing one of your salaries is a small price to pay for keeping your children.

But even if you practice healthy Christian child-rearing principles, you should know that some children will leave their faith. God is the best Father the world has ever seen. And except for Jesus, every single one of his children rebelled (including me). To keep your children, you will inevitably feel pressure to compromise. Don't.

If your teenager or young adult starts to leave biblical faith, make it clear to them that you will never stop loving them—let them feel your love. At the same time, make it clear to them that you will not accept their sinfulness, that you won't bless it, you won't celebrate it, and you will not pay for it. This does not mean cutting off your children; I cannot conceive of a situation where I would cut off my children. Rather, it means standing for the oath you swore to King Jesus in spite of what everyone else around you is doing—including your own children—but doing so with grace. Let your children know that you will never close the invitation for them to re-enter the faith.

Peter advises wives that their good lives may lead an unbelieving husband to Christ (1 Peter 3:1–2). In the same way, your faithfulness to Christ may lead your children back to Jesus. But even if it doesn't, you are mistaken if you think that becoming like a pagan will lead your children to become like Jesus. You will only remove from them any clear path back to Jesus.

BE SHREWD ABOUT POLITICS

Politics matter. The physical, economic, and social well-being of billions of people depend upon politics. Millions of lives have been lost because of bad politics. Paul reminds us that God gives us government, and therefore, politics, for the purpose of rewarding the good and punishing the bad (Romans 13:1–7). So politics matter to Christians, and the world becomes a better place when Christian convictions influence politics.

Having said that, I want to recommend that you be shrewd in your political comments, positions, and involvement. The easiest—and laziest—thing Christians can do in a hostile culture is to posture ourselves politically: to tweet our rage against politicians, to post angry Facebook posts, to rally politically behind this or that politician, etc. As I mentioned before, all the mainline Protestant denominations get heavily involved in politics, taking positions on virtually every political fad passing through America. But evangelical and conservative Christians do it too, especially when we feel our traditional values are being threatened.

Now again, I'm for political engagement by Christians. But I want to say that if we allow ourselves to indulge in excessive political engagement, we will take our eyes off our primary mission, which is not to promote this or that policy or candidate, but to make disciples. Indeed, by making disciples, we will get many of the changes we want politically. Making disciples of Jesus will reduce poverty in America because it will teach men and women to marry before having children, and then to remain faithful to their families through the years. It will reduce crime, because it will teach people to respect others' property. It will reduce drug use, alcoholism, even mental health issues because Christ has tremendous power to heal us from many of these addictions and diseases. It will reduce racial injustice, lead men to treat women rightly, remind us to treat our environment with love and concern, end abortion, and produce a million other good social and political outcomes.

And making disciples will bring about these important changes while at the same time preparing men and women for eternity. It will lead them to Christ so that we have a more just and compassionate world here, and can then together enjoy the perfect world he will bring in the hereafter. If you want to change the world, start by making disciples and don't take your eyes off this goal for mere policy or political reform.

If you want to change the world, start by making disciples.

CHANGE THE WORLD

In early 2021, I was meeting with my team of elders, and we were discussing the opposition that we see being leveled against Christians in twenty-first century America—the very concerns I'm dealing with in this book. We spent a significant amount of time trying to identify some of the threats we see our members facing. We discussed national and local issues and congregational concerns, as well as the concerns of individual believers. Each week when we met about these things, we spent considerable time praying that God would guide us to respond in Christlike ways. Above all, we want to be faithful to Jesus regardless of what the world is doing.

One of our elders works for a company where he feels pressure every single week. We'll call him Tom. In some ways, Tom is on the front lines of the battle because not only does his family face the same pressures that every family faces but he also has to dodge those company policies and politics that openly defy his faith. Dozens of people have been fired from his work for not toeing the line on secular progressivism.

One evening the discussion on our Zoom meeting (due to COVID risks) became particularly pointed as we discussed how sad we were to see the world bullying people into compromising Christian principles. As with other nights, the question again came up: "What are we going to do?" Tom had been in the meeting but with his camera turned off.

Suddenly Tom turned on his camera. His face popped up on the screen, and he spoke with crispness, confidence, and clarity. "Brothers," Tom said, "I know what I'm going to do. I'm going to keep making disciples just like I've been doing."

Tom's answer reflects the centuries-old strategy the church has always used in the face of persecution. We don't play defense. We play offense. We make disciples, regardless of what the world is doing.

Make disciples.

Small Group Questions

1. Did you finish reading the chapter? If so, what stood out to you from the readings and why?
2. Read Matthew 28:18–20. What are the elements of following Jesus described in this passage, and how do they apply to each of us today? Explain.
3. How do you feel about William Foster's statement about the early persecution (see below)? Explain.

   "In that age every Christian was a missionary. The soldier tried to win recruits for the heavenly host; the prisoner sought to bring his jailer to Christ; the slave girl whispered the gospel in the ears of her mistress; the young wife begged her husband to be baptized that their souls might not be parted after death; every one who had experienced the joys of believing tried to bring others to the faith."[77]

4. Read Deuteronomy 6:6–9. What does this passage teach parents? How can we encourage parents to follow this teaching in their homes today?
5. What is your reaction to this chapter's teachings on social media and politics? Explain.
6. Are there any situations that arise in this chapter in which we are going to need to help each other?
7. In light of the conversation we have had over this chapter, how can we pray for each other?

13

LIVE IN FEARLESS HOPE

"Then the end will come, when he hands over the kingdom to God the Father after he has destroyed all dominion, authority and power. For he must reign until he has put all his enemies under his feet" (1 Corinthians 15:24–25).

In AD 410, Alaric the Goth sacked the city of Rome. It was among the greatest shocks the world has ever seen—far more cataclysmic than Pearl Harbor or 9/11. The eternal city had stood undisturbed for eight hundred years. Its fall signaled the end of the world as people had known it for centuries. Even people who hated the Roman Empire were shaken by the disaster, aware that the very foundations of the world they had known had shuddered and collapsed. "The city which had taken the whole world was itself taken," commented St. Jerome.[78]

In response to the catastrophe and the worldwide instability it created, one of the world's most important Christian theologians, Augustine, wrote one of the world's most important books, *The City of God*. He wrote it to offer a Christian interpretation of Rome's collapse, to defend the church against accusations that it was responsible for the disaster, and to encourage Christians to keep their eyes fixed on Jesus.

Augustine offers a high-level view of history, reminding us to measure our lives against eternity rather than against the calamities of the world. He reminds us that only two cities exist: the city of God, composed of those devoted to the one true God; and the city of man, composed of those in rebellion against God. These two cities have opposed each other since the fall of humanity in the Garden of Eden, and they will continue to be at odds until Jesus returns. Only then will the city of God win—with its citizens reigning eternally—while the city of man will suffer eternal punishment with its god, the devil. Augustine says:

> Accordingly, two cities have been formed by two loves: the earthly by the love of self, even to the contempt of God; the heavenly by the love of God, even to the contempt of self. The former, in a word, glories in itself, the latter in the Lord.[79]

As Christians face increasing hostility from the city of man, we must continually remind ourselves that we were never really citizens of this world, anyway. Our citizenship was always in heaven, and it is to heaven's kingdom that we look. The trials we suffer now will one day matter not at all. Here's how the writer of Hebrews puts it:

> You have come to Mount Zion, to the city of the living God, the heavenly Jerusalem. You have come to thousands upon thousands of angels in joyful assembly, to the church of the firstborn, whose names are written in heaven. You have come to God, the Judge of all, to the spirits of the righteous made perfect, to Jesus the mediator of a new covenant, and to the sprinkled blood that speaks a better word than the blood of Abel. . . . Therefore, since we are receiving a kingdom that cannot be shaken, let us be thankful, and so worship God acceptably

> with reverence and awe, for our "God is a consuming fire." (Hebrews 12:22–24 and 28–29)

Because we belong to the city of God, we can face *anything* with confidence and joy. As the people of God, and we know that in the final chapter, we are guaranteed a renewed heaven and earth—a paradise where we will once again walk with our God and all things will be made new.

We are the church of Christ. We are the bride of Christ (Revelation 19:6–9), the body of Christ (Romans 12:3–8), the household of God (1 Timothy 3:15), the temple of the Spirit (1 Corinthians 3:16), the sheep of God's flock (Acts 20:28), and the pillar and ground of the truth (1 Timothy 3:15). And we are these things even when we are far less than perfect. We are these things because God declares us to be these things, despite our failures. We are the church of yesterday, the church of tomorrow, the church of the universe, and the church triumphant.

To strengthen our resolve in the face of hardships, we should look beyond the day-to-day struggles we endure as exiles and fix our eyes on Jesus, the author and perfecter of our faith. We should understand ourselves as belonging to the church eternal. Ancient Rome fell in disaster. Today, you can wander through its haunts and ruins and accurately predict where each one of man's cities will one day find itself—including the United States of America. Standing in the ruins of Rome, I remind you that only two institutions survived its collapse: the synagogue and the church. We have survived because we are the church of Christ.

Rome had lifted itself up against Christ and the people of God, and so it was destroyed. Should America lift itself up against Christ and his people, it will fall, too. But the church can never fall. We have been kicking down the gates of hell since Jesus sat down at the right hand of the throne of God. And we will

> **The church can never fall.**

be storming hell's gates until Jesus personally comes to bring all things under his reign. We are the church victorious.

To survive the rising persecution, we must be sure we live in fearless hope. I suggest four concrete ways you can do this.

1. LIVE IN GOD'S STORY RATHER THAN YOUR OWN.

We humans interpret our lives through stories—it's simply a part of how the brain works. Stories help us organize the millions of bits of data that enter our senses every day, prioritizing these data around our values. We develop characters, find tension and conflict, and search for resolutions. And we do this in every aspect of our lives: we tell ourselves stories about our childhood, careers, health, and relationships—hundreds of stories each day to make sense of where we are, what's happening, and what we should do next. And here's the thing: though we don't fully get to determine what data our senses receive, we do get to choose the story we create about that data. We can tell ourselves stories that discourage, deflate, and even ruin our lives. Alternatively, we can tell ourselves stories that inspire, motivate, strengthen, and comfort.

Thankfully, because we are the city of God, we do not have to invent stories to encourage ourselves. God has already given us *his* story—and it is fantastic beyond all imagination. What's missing for many of us is the simple decision to recognize that story in our lives when it matters most. In hard times, we must daily remind ourselves that we are living in God's story—a story bigger than, better than, and sweeter than the adversarial stories the world throws at us. We will win because God wins.

We must keep the redemptive story fresh in our hearts and minds. Although God created the world to be good, creation became arrogant and rebelled, wanting themselves to become God. This started in the Garden of Eden, but since the day Adam and Eve first ate the forbidden fruit, each of us has also gone to that tree, arrogantly accepting a lie and further corrupting God's good creation. Every one of us has thrown garbage into the water from which we must all drink. All of creation now groans from the weight of our arrogance.

But in his rich mercy, God launched a grand rescue mission to offer creation a second chance. After all, God is not about to let his good creation get away from him. Preparing the world for its own salvation, God worked through such holy men and women as Noah, Abraham, Sarah, Moses, Deborah, Ruth, Hannah, Samuel, David, Amos, Isaiah, Ezekiel, Daniel, Esther, and thousands of others who are fellow citizens in the city of God. It took a long time because God doesn't measure time in the same way that we do. The story of God spans centuries and is much bigger than the small part we play.

So when the time was right, God sent his Son to shine his light into a dark, rebellious world. Jesus' life demonstrates how God intended creation to live and shows what the kingdom of God is like. In his death, Jesus took our guilt upon himself—God punishing himself for our sins so he could demonstrate both his justice and love. In his resurrection, Jesus defeats the most frightening weapon darkness has—death itself. Jesus removes the sting of death and promises us that now *nothing* can separate us from the love of God.

Then in his ascension, Jesus received a crown and a throne. He currently directs the affairs of this world through the battle in which we now find ourselves. He is the only one who can open the seven seals of history. He is the one who announces the plans of God in the seven trumpets. He is the one who can pour out the bowls of wrath. Though his angels are holding off a little longer, he is the one who will soon turn them loose, rolling up this creation like a scroll and ushering in a new heaven, a new earth, a new Jerusalem, and new heavenly bodies for the citizens of the city of God. "'Look, he is coming with the clouds,' and 'every eye will see him, even those who pierced him'; and all peoples on earth 'will mourn because of him.' So shall it be! Amen" (Revelation 1:7).

This, my brothers and sisters, is God's story—long, expansive, and much bigger than our small stories. This matters because in our small part in God's grand narrative, we might forget that God is doing something universal with our sufferings. He is using our temporary pain to accomplish something cosmic. "No discipline seems pleasant at the time, but painful. Later on, however, it produces a harvest of righteousness and peace for those who have been trained by it," the Hebrew writer reminds us (Hebrews 12:11). Through our momentary suffering, we are actually part of a great rebirth of all of creation, to use Paul's metaphor (Romans 8:18–24). Our stories, full of frustration and pain, are actually part of God's grander story of redemption—a redemption that includes us too.

And so in God's story, we learn that even in our persecution, God is at work. He uses our sufferings to refine us, as fire refines gold (1 Peter 1:6–9). He uses our trials to produce character in us (James 1:2–4). He invites us to rejoice when we suffer because our suffering allows us to share in the very nature of Christ, who also suffered (1 Peter 4:13). And if we share the sufferings of Christ, we will also share the glory of Christ (Romans 8:17). The persecutions we face are part of a cosmic war between the forces of good and the forces of evil. And the forces of good led by King Jesus are going to win. The trials facing the people of God across the world are just the birth pains of a new creation about to emerge (Romans 8:19–22).

So tell yourself God's story every day. Sing songs about it. Practice gratitude. When a brother or sister droops from hardship, lift them up with the story of God. When they have forgotten the song of the lamb, sing it back to them. God is still in charge of the world, regardless of how much the pagan rages. Good will win over evil. A new creation will be born in which God will redeem every tear. "Those who sow with tears will reap with songs of joy. Those who go out weeping, carrying seed to sow, will return with songs of joy, carrying sheaves with them" (Psalm 126:5–6).

2. DON'T INTERNALIZE FALSE STORIES.

Muslim nations typically practice a social structure called dhimmitude—the practice of placing Muslim concerns, often enshrined in Sharia Law, over the concerns of all other people. Across the Middle East, Christians are subjected to dhimmitude customs and laws. They are often discriminated against. Some jobs are off limits to them. They are frequently forbidden to build church buildings or even repair their current buildings. They face strict blasphemy laws against saying anything offensive to Muslims or about Islam. And at various times in history, Christians have been forced to pay the *jizya*—a special tax for the privilege of not being persecuted even more than they are by their Muslim governments.

Faced with discrimination and hostility, some Christians in Muslim cultures internalize dhimmitude. They begin to think of themselves as inferior to their Muslim peers. Because they must act as inferiors, they can easily begin to think they are inferior. They begin to believe the narrative their oppressors tell them. Their worldview begins to constrict so that they only think in the categories of their oppressors.

This same tendency could easily overtake Christians in America as we face hostility from a secular culture. With our media only telling a limited narrative, we can easily fail to see the bigger picture. Every day our values are reviled in America by corrupt elites. Frequently now, prominent Christians announce that they are abandoning biblical principles—or Jesus altogether. Some of our own leaders have compromised themselves through moral failure.

The immediate future for Bible-believing Christianity in America is unsure. But the truth and beauty of the Christian way of life is not unsure. We have an agenda that is worthy of Christ himself, and we must discipline our minds and hearts to stay focused on that agenda. This means at least two things.

First, don't allow the world to lead your mind around. Social media now rules the world. Our magnetic attraction to Twitter and

Facebook can easily keep our minds drawn to whatever these mediums are most recently screaming about. But this is a huge distraction for followers of Jesus. Just because a post is making the rounds on Twitter doesn't mean it's urgent, important, or even true. Christians must allow Christ to set our priorities, not what's trending on Twitter. Remember that social media (all media, for that matter) companies make their money by keeping you stirred up. Fear and anger sell. But they also distract and distort.

When my children were younger and played soccer, their coaches assigned them positions: forward, midfielder, goalkeeper, etc. But such positions never held. Instead, as you have likely seen yourself, these underdeveloped athletes simply ran around the field in a crowd, following the cloud of dust kicked up wherever the ball went. Scores were frequently accidental, as the ball sometimes just popped out of the mob into the net.

When we allow the social media mob to tell us what questions are most important and what answers are acceptable, we forsake our positions as followers of Jesus to run with the mob, chasing balls that often have no lasting relevance. We allow other stories—fake ones—to crowd out our one true story: the story of God and the victory of good over evil. We internalize defeat, failure, and doom.

But second, the refusal to internalize dhimmitude is not, at the end of the day, a defensive posture. It is an offensive one—a positive one, a beautiful one, a joyful one, and a courageous one. Because even while we are foreigners and strangers in this world, we offer the world a better vision of itself than it could ever produce. We offer the world a glimpse of the city of God victorious. We offer the world a vision of the paradise we were all designed to enjoy—before we traded it in for our own selfish desires.

Augustine points out that when the Goths entered Rome, they spared the lives of those who had fled to its many churches—including even those pagans who sheltered along with the Christians. In this way, Augustine argues, the church continued its eternal mission of saving the lost. "Whoever does not see that this is to be attributed to the name of Christ, and to the Christian temper, is blind; whoever sees this, and gives no praise, is ungrateful; whoever hinders any one from praising it, is mad," Augustine writes.[80] Even while we live in the city of God, even while the city of man persecutes us, we continue to show the world what God intended when he created us. We offer shelter from the storm. We model love, self-sacrifice, holiness, truth, righteousness, gentleness, and an unbending passion for the things of our God amidst a collapsing world.

And we have been doing this for two thousand years. We will be doing this long after our persecutors are dead and gone. The local church has always been the hope of the world. We are the ones who have shone like a thousand points of light across the world, training the world in ethics, modeling holiness, loving our neighbors, interceding for the oppressed, offering peace and reconciliation, caring for the weak, and pointing toward the coming resurrection. The city of God is the only saving grace that the city of man has. By watching our faithful witness, many will abandon the darkness of evil and choose Jesus, the Savior of the world.

In his book, *The Benedict Option*, Rod Dreher argues that we should evangelize with goodness and beauty.[81] The Christian faith offers real hope for the world, and Christians are not pessimists who should merely hide, hoping to be left alone. We form the army of God with the weapons of the Spirit and a message of grace and truth.

Christians have a message of good news, and even in a hostile culture, we can and must promote our story. This is what I've seen in my many interviews of church leaders in persecuted areas. They are among the happiest people I've known. They are not down or in despair. They really don't talk that much about their oppressive governments—it's not that big a deal to them. Rather than worrying about persecution, these Christians are busy thinking about how to win their persecutors to Jesus. This explains why the gospel is exploding in difficult places even today: in China, India, Iran, and across Muslim Africa. The

Christians in these hostile areas have not conceded the story of God to other stories. Instead, they are joyfully living in God's story.

Christians who thrive in persecution do so by refusing to accept mental or spiritual dhimmitude. Rather, they choose to stand courageously, boldly, joyfully, and confidently in God's story. In the midst of their suffering, they are able to say with the apostle Paul, "I know what it is to be in need, and I know what it is to have plenty. I have learned the secret of being content in any and every situation, whether well fed or hungry, whether living in plenty or in want. I can do all this through him who gives me strength" (Philippians 4:12–13). And they say confidently with Paul: "I know whom I have believed, and am convinced that he is able to guard what I have entrusted to him until that day" (2 Timothy 1:12).

3. HOLD TO THE PROMISES OF GOD.

All of life is lived in response to promises. You work for the promise of a paycheck. You marry for the promise of companionship and faithfulness. You eat for the promise of satisfaction or health. Without promises, our lives would break down. Yet with promises, we are able to plan, predict, and hope.

The world lives by its promises—false as they are. Hedonism promises endless pleasure. Greed promises security. Progressivism promises a utopia. Selfishness promises happiness. In each case, the promises of the world fail because every worldly promise is void of the One who is able to make secure promises that are worth living for: God himself.

As a Christian, you must learn to live not by the promises of the world, but by the promises of God. The world's promises will fail you. People will fail you. Even people who are close to you will let you down. They may betray you. They will almost certainly hurt you. They will judge you, sometimes be harsh to you, and even abandon you. And this is true even of your Christian friends. Even of your church. After all, even the church is only made of people. Live by the world's promises, and you will struggle to stand in the face of hostility, because two plus two will never equal four in the world's math. Something will always come up short.

As Christians, learn to live by the promises of God. Learn both to ask for them and to see them. With God's promises, you can stand with both confidence and full hope, no matter how much the promises of others fail you.

> Learn to live by the promises of God.

Throughout Scripture, we see and hear God's numerous promises. Let me give you seven that will strengthen you in times of hostility.

1. God will never leave you (Deuteronomy 31:8).
2. God will not give you more than you can handle (1 Corinthians 10:13).
3. God will give you what you need (Philippians 4:19).
4. God will give you strength (Isaiah 40:29).
5. God will give you the words you need (Luke 12:11–12).
6. God will work all things together for your good (Romans 8:28).
7. God will take you home with him (John 14:1–3).

You are likely to face difficulties living a faithful life here in the US. But God's promises can keep you strong—they offer hope, comfort, strength, and security. If you look for how God is fulfilling any given promise during a time of testing, you will find it, and you will be encouraged. For example, when one of your family members wanders from the faith, look for how God will give you strength to try to win them back. You will find it. When you find yourself in a hostile conversation about Christ, pray—at least in your heart—asking God for just the right words, and see how he will provide them. When your faithfulness costs you relationships, look for how God will use a closed door to open another. Look for God's promises, and you will find them. And in them, you will find hope and strength.

4. CONNECT TO THE WORLDWIDE CHURCH.

To survive a hostile culture, we must always keep one eye on the big picture. We can do this by networking with the global church—including the church in the hostile areas I just mentioned. These believers typically have far more experience than American Christians do in navigating hostile environments. We can share prayers, heroes, songs, and strategies, as well as, of course, the Spirit of God. And in a world now connected through the internet, this is easier to do than we might have imagined.

Connecting with the worldwide church encourages us because it reminds us we are not alone. In fact, connecting to the worldwide church will show us that though the Christian faith is declining in the West, it has actually never been stronger than it is today worldwide. There are tens of thousands of people being baptized into Christ in the global South every week of the year. The gospel is changing entire villages, flipping people's lives, and rewriting the stories of entire people groups. Many simply open the Bible, obey what it says, and experience the power of God. To hear their stories is thrilling and reassuring. The Word has not lost its power at all.

But connecting with the worldwide church also reminds us that the story of God is for everybody who will accept it. Christianity is not, as one person said to me not long ago, a "white man's religion." There are now nearly half a billion believers on the continent of Africa, and those Africans who know about progressivism merely shake their heads. Today, Christianity is growing faster in Iran than in virtually any other country. *Iran!* Enough Hindus are converting to Christ in India that Prime Minister Modi's government is attempting to pass laws to limit conversions in every state. There are now more

Bible-believing Christians in China than there are in the US. In all of these areas, God is using persecution to grow his church.

The Christian faith has a universal appeal. It demonstrates the power of God's story to unite the races in ways that no public policy could ever do. It is a worldwide religion. It is the city of God—not the city of whites, North Americans, or our fledgling denominations.

Several years ago after our congregation committed to planting churches around the world, God brought us Jerry Trousdale, who has been a catalyst for disciple making movements around the world for two decades. I believe that when the history of Christian missions is finally written, Jerry and his now deceased wife Gayle will get their own chapter for the amazing work they have done with the gospel. A few years after some of their movements spread across West Africa, Jerry wrote his fascinating book *Miraculous Movements*, which tells the story of how hundreds of thousands of Muslims are coming to King Jesus through the work of ordinary people committed to the gospel—in some of the world's most hostile cultures.

I got to meet some of these individuals because our congregation began to partner with some of these movements. I have yet to find the words to describe the joy you get when sitting with a former Muslim cleric who went blind before becoming a Christian and has now planted nine churches. He takes a cab or bus into an unknown village, sits under a tree, and then prays for new growth. It is not possible to describe what it's like to visit with a church planter who has worked among the Islamic extremist and extremely violent group Boko Haram, risking his life with joy on his face because he knows who is going to win. I've met people who specialize in planting churches through their construction business, through their work as a radio deejay, through their dental chair, through their accounting firm, and through their health clinics. I've talked with former Muslims who specialize in planting churches in villages that have no roads; or who plant churches only among pygmies or through farming.

In every case, what I've learned is that the gospel is global, and I stand with the church universal. God is still at work, and what he's doing is amazing. In times of hardship, look to the church universal, and you'll find a family eager to welcome you.

TRUST IN THE CHURCH VICTORIOUS

For twenty-five years, US Pastor Andrew Brunson and his family led a small church in Izmir, Turkey, and had planned to stay in Turkey—until President Recep Erdogan began to crack down on Christians. As part of the pressure, Brunson was falsely arrested and charged with aiding terrorism. He was detained for two years in overcrowded prisons, as the US government sought to negotiate his release. Looking back, Brunson describes his first year in prison as a "breaking year." He says he never felt the presence of God, yet he knew people were praying and he knew God was using his persecution. But as his detention dragged on, God began to strengthen and encourage him. Brunson says that the second year of imprisonment taught him to trust God and practice certain disciplines to keep his head turned to God: "If I had been let out after the first year, I'd have been lying on the floor curled up in a fetal position with PTSD. The second year God started to rebuild me," he writes.[82]

As American Christians, we are going through something of a shock right now as we watch our values be attacked and our people bullied. But like Andrew Brunson, we must now move on from a state of shock to a state of confidence. Like Andrew discovered in those two years, God will use our hardships to strengthen us and make us pure. The church has always been an exiled community—it's just that we often didn't know it in North America. As the late missiologist David Bosch wrote to the American church, "Strictly speaking, one ought to say that the church is always

> Move on from a state of shock to a state of confidence.

in a state of crisis and that its greatest shortcoming is that it is only occasionally aware of it."[83] Now we are aware. So now we must look away from DC, New York City, and Hollywood and turn our eyes upward to heaven and to the victory that Christ has already secured for us.

In February 1991, I traveled with a small team to Novosibirsk, Siberia, to plant a church. We had been invited by a professor at a university there, a man whose family had kept its Christian faith alive throughout the Soviet years with clandestine Bible readings, hymn singing, and prayer. It was one of the most humbling trips of my life—I was planting a church in the atheist nation of the USSR, right under pictures of Marx, Engels, Lenin, and Stalin. At the time, it appeared that the Soviet Union would stand forever.

Upon arriving in the Siberian city, our host showed me one of the letters I had sent him while I was preparing for the trip. To my surprise, it had been opened by the Soviet postal service, which routinely monitored all incoming and outgoing mail, censoring whatever they didn't like. A couple of postal workers had written hostile and insulting messages on my mail before sending it on to the professor. Shocked, I shook my head before expressing a bit of anxiety that the Soviet government was watching my team so closely.

"Of course they're watching you," he explained. "Your apartment is bugged, and they know all about each member of your team. The Soviets have been doing this for years. They are experts at it." But then he said something I'll never forget. "But you and I know that when the Soviet Union is long gone, the Christian faith will still be standing."

Ten months later, the Soviet flag was lowered over the Kremlin for the last time—never to be raised again. On Christmas Day of that same year, the Soviet Union dropped dead, swept into the dustbin of history. But the Christian faith lives on.

You and I belong to the church of Christ, and you can be sure that Christ is going to win the battle against those who bully us. His honor is at stake, and he will not be dishonored for long. Every regime that lifts its head against the people of God starts the clock ticking on its own collapse. It is inevitable. God is going to win.

While we face the day-to-day struggles of living in a hostile world, we must look to the ultimate victory that God will give us. We know the end of our story. God wins. Yes, it will be uncomfortable while we wait. We may lose things we once enjoyed. We will have to learn new habits and new strategies. But weren't we always supposed to be on the move? As theologian Hans Kung once remarked, "The church which pitches its tent without constantly looking out for new horizons and does not continually strike camp is not being true to its calling. We must lay down our craving for certainty, accept what is risky, live by improvisation, and experiment."[84] We have a mission to accomplish before Jesus returns: the making of disciples from among all nations. "And this gospel of the kingdom will be preached in the whole world as a testimony to all nations, and then the end will come," Jesus declares in a sermon about the fall of Jerusalem and the end of time (Matthew 24:14).

The hardships we face as Christians in a post-Christian America are nothing new for the people of God. But because we are the city of God, we can be resilient, rejoicing in our sufferings and carrying out our mission. We are, after all, *the church eternal.*

A Small Group Discussion

1. What are your biggest takeaways from this chapter in particular and this book in general, and why?
2. Read Revelation 21:3–7. How often do you focus on God's promises in eternity? When you do focus on those promises, which ones mean the most to you and why?
3. This chapter closes out the book with the following four exhortations:

a. Live in God's story rather than your own.
b. Don't internalize false stories.
c. Hold to the promises of God.
d. Connect to the worldwide church.

Which of these exhortations is most helpful to you and why?

4. Are there any situations that arise in this chapter (and in the book itself) in which we are going to need to help each other?
5. As we complete our reading and discussion of this book, are there any next steps that you think you should take? Explain.
6. Is there anyone with whom you need to share this book? Explain.
7. Close by praying for each other.

CONCLUSION

"'I am the Alpha and the Omega,' says the Lord God, 'who is, and who was, and who is to come, the Almighty'" (Revelation 1:8).

Several years ago, sociologist George Yancey decided to conduct a survey to determine Americans' attitudes toward Christians. He asked questions of nearly four thousand people—many of whom were highly educated, progressive, and wealthy people—about their views of Christians. He was so surprised at the hatred he discovered toward Christians that he coined the term "Christianophobia" to describe the vitriol.

Some survey respondents expressed their hatred in explicit ways in the open-ended question toward the end of the survey, saying things such as, "Churches and houses of religion should be designated as nuclear test zones." "Kill them all, let their god sort them out." "The only good Christian is a dead Christian." And this one: "So many Christians, so few lions." One can only imagine what these same inclusive and tolerant people would say if they heard people say the same things about, say, gays or African Americans. But these progressives felt both safe and self-righteous enough to pour out their hatred toward believers in Jesus Christ.

It's a bad omen for what Christians are facing, but it's nothing new. What is new is that Christians are now encountering hostility in

America—some of the persecution that Christians around the globe have encountered.

We can prepare for this hostility by using the principles Jesus gives us in the sacred Scriptures. We can decide, once and for all, who we are, and *never* back down. We can learn to fight in the power of the Spirit and commit to living holy lives. We can embrace exile even while living in the city of man and commit to keeping disciple making the mission of the church, building our churches into authentic communities, and making our convictions clear to our own members. We can remember that we belong to the church eternal.

We can say what the Jewish King Jehoshaphat said to God when facing a vastly superior army: "We have no power to face this vast army that is attacking us. We do not know what to do, *but our eyes are on you*" (2 Chronicles 20:12). By keeping our eyes on Jesus, we will be able to stand even if the hostility increases. We can be faithful.

And we will be rewarded for our faithfulness. Persecution purges us of contaminants. It strengthens our resolve. And it brings great reward. As Jesus says, "Blessed are those who are persecuted because of righteousness, for theirs is the kingdom of heaven. Blessed are you when people insult you, persecute you and falsely say all kinds of evil against you because of me. Rejoice and be glad, because great is your reward in heaven, for in the same way they persecuted the prophets who were before you" (Matthew 5:10–12). And this: "Truly I tell you," Jesus replied, "no one who has left home or brothers or sisters or mother or father or children or fields for me and the gospel will fail to receive a hundred times as much in this present age: homes, brothers, sisters, mothers, children and fields—along with persecutions—and in the age to come eternal life" (Mark 10:29–30).

Persecution purges us of contaminants. It strengthens our resolve.

As Augustine reflected on the pain that the church felt when it was blamed for the fall of Rome, he sought to put it all in perspective in his magisterial *City of God*. We follow a persecuted and crucified Jesus. Why would we think that we can escape suffering? It is part of our cleansing process. It is part of being a counter-cultural people. It is the pain that accompanies the birth of a new world. And it is the lot of the city of God in the middle of the city of man. But it will end. Augustine writes:

> In this manner, the church proceeds on its pilgrim way in this world, in these evil days. Its troubled course began not merely in the time of the bodily presence of Christ and the time of his apostles; it started with Abel himself, the first righteous man slain by an ungodly brother; and the pilgrimage goes on from that time right up to the end of history, with the persecutions of the world on one side, and on the other the consolations of God.[85]

The church will never be defeated, and the gates of hell will not prevail against us. We are the people of God. We will win.

In Jesus, we stand invincible, firm, resilient.

APPENDIX A

RESOURCES

Note: By recommending these resources, I'm not implying that I am in full agreement with all of the content included.

BOOKS

Sam Allberry, *Is God Anti-Gay? And Other Questions about Homosexuality, the Bible and Same-Sex Attraction* (Croydon, England: The Good Book Company, 2013).

Ryan T. Anderson, *When Harry Became Sally: Responding to the Transgender Moment* (Washington: Encounter Books, 2018).

Voddie Baucham, *Fault Lines: The Social Justice Movement and Evangelicalism's Looming Catastrophe* (Ipswich, MA: Salem Books, 2021).

Christopher Brooks, *Urban Apologetics: Why the Gospel is Good News for the City* (Grand Rapids: Kregel, 2014).

Alisa Childers, *Another Gospel? A Lifelong Christian Seeks Truth in Response to Progressive Christianity* (Carol Stream, IL: Tyndale, 2020).

Natasha Crain, *Keeping Your Kids on God's Side* (Eugene, OR: Harvest House Publishers, 2016).

Alan Dershowitz, *The Case Against the New Censorship: Protecting Free Speech from Big Tech, Progressives and Universities* (New York: Simon and Schuster, 2021).

Kevin DeYoung, *What Does the Bible Teach about Homosexuality* (Wheaton, IL: Crossway, 2015).

John S. Dickerson, *The Great Evangelical Recession: 6 Factors That Will Crash the American Church . . . and How to Prepare* (Grand Rapids: Baker, 2013).

David S. Dockery and John Stonestreet, eds. *Life, Marriage, and Religious Liberty: What Belongs to God, What Belongs to Caesar* (New York: Fidelis, 2019).

Rod Dreher, *The Benedict Option: A Strategy for Christians in a Post-Christian Nation* (New York: Sentinel, 2017).

Rod Dreher, *Live Not by Lies: A Manual for Christian Dissidents* (New York: Sentinel, 2020).

Hillary Morgan Ferrer, *Mama Bear Apologetics* (Eugene, OR: Harvest House Publishers, 2019).

Robert A. J. Gagnon, *The Bible and Homosexual Practice: Texts and Hermeneutics* (Nashville: Abingdon, 2001).

Luke Goodrich, *Free to Believe: The Battle Over Religious Liberty in America* (Colorado Springs: Multnomah, 2019).

Bobby Harrington and W. Scott Sager, *Disciple Making: The Core Mission of the Church* (Nashville: Renew, 2021).

James and Marti Hefley, *By Their Blood: Christian Martyrs of the Twentieth Century* (Grand Rapids: Baker Books, 1979).

Bill Hull, *The Complete Book of Discipleship: On Being and Making Followers of Christ* (Colorado Springs: NavPress, 2007).

Robert Jeffress, *Courageous: 10 Strategies for Thriving in a Hostile World* (Grand Rapids: Baker Books, 2020).

Paul Kengor, *Take Down: From Communists to Progressives, How the Left has Sabotaged Family and Marriage* (Chicago: WND Books, 2015).

Erwin W. Lutzer, *We Will Not Be Silenced* (Eugene, OR: Harvest House, 2020).

Ashley McGuire, *Sex Scandal: The Drive to Abolish Male and Female* (Washington: Regnery, 2017).

Sarah McLaughlin, *The Secular Creed: Engaging Five Secular Claims* (The Gospel Coalition, 2021).

Joshua Mitchell, *American Awakenings: Identity Politics and Other Afflictions of Our Time* (New York: Encounter, 2020).

R. Albert Mohler Jr., *The Gathering Storm: Secularism, Culture, and the Church* (Nashville: Thomas Nelson, 2020).

Jennifer Roback Morse, *The Sexual State: How Elite Ideologies Are Destroying Lives and Why the Church Was Right All Along* (Charlotte, NC: TAN Books, 2018).

National Association of Evangelicals, *For the Health of the Nation: An Evangelical Call to Civic Responsibility* (2004, 2018).

Jim Putman and Bobby Harrington, *DiscipleShift: Five Steps That Help Your Church to Make Disciples Who Make Disciples* (Grand Rapids: Zondervan, 2013).

Jim Putman, *Church Is a Team Sport: A Championship Strategy for Doing Ministry Together* (Grand Rapids: Baker, 2008).

Nik Ripken, *The Insanity of Obedience: Walking with Jesus in Tough Places* (Nashville: B&H Publishing, 2014).

Abigail Shrier, *Irreversible Damage: The Transgender Craze Seducing Our Daughters* (Washington: Regnery Publishing, 2020).

Chris Smith, *Handing Down the Faith: How Parents Pass Their Religion on to the Next Generation* (Oxford, England: University Press, 2021).

Ken Starr, *Religious Liberty in Crisis: Exercising Your Faith in an Age of Uncertainty* (New York: Encounter Books, 2021).

Owen Strachan, *Christianity and Wokeness: How the Social Justice Movement Is Hijacking the Gospel—and the Way to Stop It* (Washington: Salem Books, 2021).

Carol Swain, *Be the People: A Call to Reclaim America's Faith and Promise* (Nashville: Thomas Nelson, 2011).

Carl R. Trueman, *The Rise and Triumph of the Modern Self: Cultural Amnesia, Expressive Individualism, and the Road to Sexual Revolution* (Wheaton, IL: Crossway, 2020).

Andrew T. Walker, *Liberty for All: Defending Everyone's Religious Freedom in a Pluralistic Age* (Grand Rapids: Brazos Press, 2021).

Andrew T. Walker, *God and the Transgender Debate: What Does the Bible Actually Say About Gender Identity?* (London: The Good Book Company, 2017).

Thaddeus J. Williams, *Confronting Injustice Without Compromising Truth* (Grand Rapids: Zondervan, 2020).

George Yancey, *Hostile Environment: Understanding and Responding to Anti-Christian Bias* (Downer's Grove, IL: IVP, 2015).

George Yancey and David Williamson, *So Many Christians, So Few Lions: Is there Christianophobia in the United States* (Lanham, MD: Rowman & Littlefield, 2014).

David Young, *A Grand Illusion: How Progressive Christianity Undermines Biblical Faith* (Nashville: Renew.org, 2019).

MINISTRIES, PERIODICALS, AND OTHER RESOURCES

Becket Fund for Religious Freedom
Chuck Colson Center for Christian Worldview
Ethics and Religious Liberty Commission
Family Action Council of Tennessee
First Things Journal
The Gospel Coalition
Journal of Christian Legal Thought
The Manhattan Declaration: A Call of Christian Conscience
Renew.org
Strength in Weakness Ministry
Voice of the Martyrs

APPENDIX B

DISCOVERY BIBLE STUDY AS A DISCIPLE MAKING TOOL

Because this book is intended to equip you for being resilient and standing firm in a hostile culture, I want to make just a few comments about a method of disciple making that has been effective in much of the world, even though it is still catching on here in the US. It's typically called "Discovery Bible Study" or "DBS" for short.

In DBS we invite others to listen to the Word of God—even those who may not yet believe it—apply it to some area of their lives, obey a simple teaching, and expect a miracle. Then, when they experience the work of God in their lives, we apply another teaching. In some areas of the world, DBS has near-miraculous results. For example, in the global South, where my congregation has planted hundreds of churches, DBS often results in faithful disciples who become disciple makers within a few months of the first invitation. In the US, the results are more mixed, probably because Americans tend to be averse to obeying the Scriptures, even in the context of DBS.

DBS can use any text of the Bible because the process amounts to little more than asking a specific set of questions designed to invite obedience and the subsequent actions of God in people's lives. It starts with prayer and a few questions of interest in someone's life. Here, we address the actual needs that others have in life with love and compassion. Then, DBS moves to four questions: (1) What does this text say about God? (2) What does this text say about humans? (3) What does this text say to me? (4) How can I specifically apply this text to my life today or this week? As they think about and answer these questions, people—lost or saved, immature or mature, follower or leader—learn to listen to the Word of God, which does all the heavy lifting. As a disciple maker, you don't have to have all the answers. Simply let the Word of God speak. After all, the Word of God is the sword of the Holy Spirit and wields the power of God.

The key to a successful DBS is getting people to obey whatever the text says. For example, if you're reading the story of the prodigal son, convince your friends to forgive someone that day. When they do, they experience a powerful work of God, which whets the appetite for more of the Word of God. In the next session, talk about what God did when they obeyed his Word the last time, then move to another text. Read it, ask the questions, and obey it.

Through DBS, even people who know very little about the Bible can disciple others—if it's done in a loving relationship and if obedience is expected. The goal is to discover the Word of God in life, not to tell others what a text means. Theology is lived, not merely taught. Any text is subject to DBS, which means there is an endless supply of DBS texts that can be shared.

You can find more information about DBS from the website of Final Command Ministries, which perfected the method through many conversions to Christ. Or just search the internet for examples, and you'll find plenty. My own church, the North Boulevard church, contains plenty of DBS units, as well as training videos. Of course, the important thing is that you care enough about lost people to get into their lives for the sake of the gospel. DBS is merely a tool to aid you in helping others find Christ.

NOTES

1. John L. Cooper, *Wimpy, Weak, and Woke*, releasing July 2023.

2. It's become trendy for some to use the word "progressive" to describe anybody to the left of where they happen to be, just as it's trendy to use the word "fundamentalist" to describe anybody who happens to be right of where they are. Throughout this book, I'm using the word "progressive" very strategically to describe an actual worldview fed and formed by discernible philosophical and cultural currents.

3. Denise Laugesen, "American Catholics Are Aware of Christian Persecution but Need Leadership From Clerics," *The Hill,* April 9, 2018, thehill.com/opinion/civil-rights/381945-american-catholics-are-aware-of-christian-persecution-but-need (accessed June 4, 2021).

4. "Religious Freedom Upheld at University of Iowa," *InterVarsity,* June 16, 2021, intervarsity.org/news/religious-freedom-upheld-university-iowa (accessed October 31, 2022).

5. "Nobel Laureate Alexievich: 'We Thought That Communism Was Dead' Voice of America," *VOANews,* June 17, 2016, voanews.com/europe/nobel-laureate-alexievich-we-thought-communism-was-dead (accessed May 25, 2021).

6. Adrienne D. Dixson, Celia K. Rousseau Anderson, and Jamel K. Donnor, eds., *Critical Race Theory in Education: All God's Children Got a Song* (New York: Routledge, 2017), 20.

7. Patricia Hill Collins, *Intersectionality as Critical Social Theory* (Durham and London: Duke University Press, 2019), 51–52.

8. And this, at the very time when math scores in vast numbers of districts in the US are dismally low and when the teaching of math is in desperate need of real reform to increase students' ability to think clearly. See Lauren Camera, "Across the Board, Scores Drop in Math and Reading for US Students," *US News and World Report*, October 30, 2019, usnews.com/news/education-news/articles/2019-10-30/across-the-board-scores-drop-in-math-and-reading-for-us-students (accessed May 29, 2021).

9. Brian Flood, "CNN raises eyebrows by claiming 'there is no consensus criteria for assigning sex at birth' in news report,'" *Fox News*, March 31, 2021, foxnews.com/media/cnn-raises-eyebrows-claiming-consensus-assigning-sex-at-birth-in-news-report (accessed April 2, 2021). This absurd statement by a major news organization is all the more bizarre in light of a promo CNN ran a couple years earlier in response to its disagreements with President Trump. The piece showed an apple, arguing that no matter how many times one might choose to call it a banana, it will always be an apple. CNN doesn't believe its own propaganda.

10. Robin DiAngelo, *White Fragility: Why It's So Hard for White People to Talk About Race* (Boston: Beacon Press, 2018), 149–150.

11. Ibram X. Kendi, *Stamped From the Beginning: The Definitive History of Racist Ideas in America* (New York: Bold Type Books, 2016), 11.

12. Rod Dreher, *The Benedict Option: A Strategy for Christians in a Post-Christian Nation* (New York: Sentinel, 2017) and *Live Not By Lies: A Manuel for Christian Dissidents* (New York: Sentinel, 2020).

13. Sam Dorman, "California proposes curriculum on Aztec god honored by human sacrifice," *The New York Post*, March 11, 2021, nypost.com/2021/03/11/california-proposes-curriculum-on-aztec-gods and cde.ca.gov/ci/cr/cf/esmcthirdfieldreview.asp (both accessed on March 18, 2021).

14. I am aware that secularists and their Christian enablers will argue that the shortcomings of the American penal system and the acceptance of the death penalty already demonstrate a lack of sincerity on the part of Christians about the value of human life, but the argument is dishonest. Whatever the weaknesses of the current American justice system, honest people know there can be no genuine comparison between the sometimes unfair implementations of justice for criminals and the deliberate killing of innocent babies. The deliberate obfuscation of these two systems reveals the depths to which Americans will go to maintain and even enforce a heinous practice when they want it.

15. See Bob Van Voris, "Gay conversion church loses appeal over Vimeo account," *Bloomberg*, March 11, 2021, bloomberg.com/news/articles/2021-03-11/vimeo-legally-deleted-account-of-church-backing-gay-conversion (accessed June 5, 2021).

16. Russell Goldman, "Here's a List of 58 Gender Options for Facebook Users," *ABC News,* February 13, 2014, abcnews.go.com/blogs/headlines/2014/02/heres-a-list-of-58-gender-options-for-facebook-users (accessed May 21, 2021).

17. "Pride Flags," Tripridetn.com. tripridetn.org/pride-flags (accessed March 16, 2021).

18. The problem is becoming a tragic epidemic in America. See the heartbreaking work of Abigail Shrier, *Irreversible Damage: The Transgender Craze Seducing Our Daughters* (Washington: Regnery, 2020). Progressives have made numerous attempts to ban Shrier's book. Indeed, an attorney for none other than the American Civil Liberties Union opposed the sale of this book, declaring that "stopping the circulation of this book and these ideas is 100% a hill I will die on." Quoted in M. K. Fain "The Massive Effort to Censor Irreversible Damage," *4W,* November 29, 2020, 4w.pub/the-massive-effort-to-censor-irreversible-damage (accessed May 21, 2021). Book burning is a time-tested form of propaganda used by secular progressives for a century.

19. Erwin Lutzer, *We Will Not Be Silenced* (Eugene: Harvest House Publishers, 2020), 149.

20. Changing the meaning of terms to keep up with an evolving ideology is nothing new. As N. T. Wright points out, many German dictionaries still have the label "N.S." by certain words, indicating that these words were given new meanings by the Nazis in support of their ideology in the 1930s. In the Soviet Union, whole groups of persons were labeled "former persons," because they disagreed with the Socialist assumptions of the ruling party. Matthew Schmitz, "N. T. Wright on Gay Marriage: Nature and Narrative Point to Complementarity," *First Things*, June 11, 2014, firstthings.com/blogs/firstthoughts/2014/06/n-t-wrights-argument-against-same-sex-marriage (accessed May 31, 2021).

21. Rod Dreher summarizes some of the principles that Solzhenitsyn says will guide a person who refuses to live by lies. That person will not say, write, affirm, or distribute anything that distorts the truth; will not go to a demonstration or participate in a collective action unless they truly believe in the cause; will not take part in a meeting in which the discussion is forced, and no one can speak the truth; will not vote for a candidate or proposal he considers to be dubious or unworthy; will walk out of an "event as soon as he hears the speaker utter a lie, ideological drivel, or shameless propaganda"; and will not support journalism that "distorts or hides the underlying facts." See Dreher, *Live Not by Lies: A Manual for Christian Dissidents* (New York City: Sentinel, 2020), 18.

22. Former professor of English and Women's Studies at Syracuse University, Rosaria Butterfield, states that when she taught, she mandated that "every student is expected to write everything from a feminist worldview or perspective." Further, she instructed the students, "Anything written outside of a feminist perspective will receive an automatic F." *Secret Thoughts of an Unlikely Convert* (Pittsburgh: Crown & Covenant Publications, 2014), 87ff.

23. It is worth noting that none of these books, which were censored for standing against progressive ideals, are mentioned in the annual "Banned Book" list created by the progressive American Library Association.

24. George Yancey, *Hostile Environment: Understanding and Responding to Anti-Christian Bias* (Downer's Grove, IL: IVP, 2015), 12–13.

25. Thomas Oden, *A Change of Heart: A Personal and Theological Memoir* (Downer's Grove, IL: Intervarsity, 2014), 317.

26. Martin Luther King Jr., "Draft of Chapter XIII, 'Our God is Able,'" *Stanford: The Martin Luther King Jr. Research and Education Institute*, kinginstitute.stanford.edu/king-papers/documents/draft-chapter-xiii-our-god-able (accessed May 31, 2021). Such stories of resolve attract even the attention of the unbelieving world. Liu Xiaobo was sentenced to eleven years in prison for standing up for human rights in China. He received the Nobel Prize for his stand. His statement before entering prison is a masterpiece of resistance. See "I Have No Enemies," *The Nobel Prize*, nobelprize.org/prizes/peace/2010/xiaobo/lecture (accessed May 31, 2021).

27. David Young, *The Holy Spirit: Filled, Empowered, and Led* (Nashville: Renew, 2021).

28. You can read about Corey's church in Corey Trimble and Josh Brooker, *Authentic Pursuit: Building a Church from Nothing* (Murfreesboro, TN: The Experience Christian Community, 2015).

29. Marvin Olasky, "Tiny, Powerful Heartbeats," *World Magazine*, August 2015.

30. For Jerry's own telling of some of the story, see Jerry Trousdale, *The Kingdom Unleashed* (DMM Library, 2018), 189ff.

31. The entire narrative of both ChildFund and Compassion International can be found in Peter Greer and Chris Horst, *Mission Drift: The Unspoken Crisis Facing Leaders, Charities, and Churches* (Minneapolis: Bethany House Publishers, 2014), 23–32.

32. Jonathan R. Siegel, "Legal scholarship highlight: Justice Scalia's textualist legacy," *SCOTUS blog*, November 14, 2017, scotusblog.com/2017/11/legal-scholarship-highlight-justice-scalias-textualist-legacy/ (accessed June 9, 2021).

33. *Grand Illusion: How Progressive Christianity Undermines Biblical Faith* (Nashville: Renew, 2019).

34. J. Gresham Machen's comments regarding Scripture are still true: "Let it not be said that dependence upon a book is a dead or an artificial thing. The Reformation of the sixteenth century was founded upon the authority of the Bible, yet it set the world aflame. Dependence upon a word of man would be slavish, but dependence upon God's Word is life. Dark and gloomy would be the world if it were left to our own devices and had no blessed Word of God. The Bible, to the Christian, is not a burdensome law, but the very Magna Charta of Christian liberty. It is no wonder, then, that liberalism is totally different from Christianity, for the foundation is different. Christianity is founded upon the Bible. It bases upon the Bible both its sinking and its life. Liberalism is founded upon the shifting emotions of sinful men." J. Gresham Machen, *Christianity and Liberalism* (Grand Rapids: Wm. B. Eerdmans Publishing, 2009, originally published 1923), 78–79.

35. Luke Timothy Johnson, "Homosexuality and the Church," *Commonweal*, June 11, 2007, commonwealmagazine.org/homosexuality-church-0 (accessed April 28, 2021). Even evangelicals who seek to accommodate same-sex activity eventually end up denying the authority of Scripture. As Christopher Brooks says, "It is my experience that one is hard-pressed to find a pro-homosexual theologian who adheres to an inspired, authoritative view of Scripture. More often than not, those who advocate for homosexuality while trying to maintain their allegiance to Christianity do so by portraying the Bible as a primarily human book that has been deeply flawed by the phobias and personalities of the authors." Eric Mason, *Urban Apologetics: Restoring Black Dignity with the Gospel* (Grand Rapids: Zondervan, 2021), 85.

36. Cf., Steve Chalke and Alan Mann, *The Lost Message of Jesus* (Grand Rapids: Zondervan, 2003), 182–183. Brian McLaren makes the term popular, suggesting that the doctrine of atonement renders God a child abuser. McLaren could only mean this if he didn't believe that Jesus is God.

37. Brian McLaren, The Bleeding Purple Podcast, interviewed by Leif Hansen, January 8, 2006, cited in Roger Oakland, *Faith Undone: The Emerging Church, a New Reformation or an End-time Deception?* (Silverton, OR: Lighthouse Trails Publishing, 2007), 192–193.

38. John Nugent, *Endangered Gospel: How Fixing the World is Killing the Church* (Eugene: Cascade, 2016), 114, points out that the Scriptures never really call Christians to make the world a "better place," but, instead, call us to be a better place for the sake of the gospel.

39. Dawn Hutchings, "'The Great Commission' Birthed White Supremacy! Trinity Sunday Sermon," ProgressiveChristianity.org, June 7, 2020, progressivechristianity.org/resources/the-great-commission-birthed-white-supremacy-trinity-sunday-sermon (accessed April 27, 2021).

40. Quoted in Colin Smothers, "African Methodism will not bow the knee to US progressivism," CBMW.org, February 23, 2019, cbmw.org/2019/02/23/african-methodism-will-not-bow-its-knee-to-us-progressivism (accessed June 7, 2021).

41. "How a Whole Church Vanished," *Christianity Today*, November 25, 1966, 3ff.

42. Quoted in Greer and Horst, *Mission Drift*, 51.

43. Kevin DeYoung, *The Hole in Our Holiness: Filling the Gap Between Gospel Passion and the Pursuit of Godliness* (Wheaton, IL: Crossway, 2014).

44. "Acceptance Address by Mr. Aleksandr Solzhenitsyn, May 10, 1983," *Templeton Prize*, www.templetonprize.org/laureate-sub/solzhenitsyn-acceptance-speech (accessed October 23, 2022).

45. "Fast Facts," *Teen Health and the Media,* depts.washington.edu/thmedia/view.cgi?section=medialiteracy&page=fastfacts (accessed April 9, 2021).

46. Nadia Bolz-Weber, *Shameless: A Sexual Revolution* (New York: Convergent Books, 2019). For an excellent review of Bolz-Weber's book, see Alisa Childers, "Nadia Bolz-Weber and the Sexual Revolution We Need," thegospelcoalition.org/reviews/shameless-sexual-reformation (accessed April 7, 2021).

47. An important study of the rise of the sexual revolution and its cultural and psychological assumptions is that of Carl R. Trueman, *The Rise and Triumph of the Modern Self: Cultural Amnesia, Expressive Individualism and the Road to Sexual Revolution* (Wheaton, IL: Crossway, 2020).

48. The damage that has been been inflicted on people by the demise of traditional marriage has been so well-documented that Harvard University's professor emeritus James Q. Wilson once quipped that "even some sociologists had come to believe it." Quoted in Mary Eberstadt, "The Vindication of The Manhattan Declaration, Then and Now," in David S. Dockery and John Stonestreet, eds. *Life, Marriage, and Religious Liberty: What Belongs to God, What Belongs to Caesar* (New York: Fidelis, 2019), 82. For more information about the social costs of America's sexual ethics, see Eberstadt's *Adam and Eve After the Pill: Paradoxes of the Sexual Revolution* (San Francisco: Ignatius Press, 2012) and Jennifer Roback Morse, *The Sexual State: How Elite Ideologies Are Destroying Lives and Why the Church Was Right All Along* (Charlotte, NC: TAN Books, 2018).

49. Mary Eberstadt, "The Fury of the Fatherless," *First Things,* December 2020, 41–46.

50. Sean McDowell, "What if Everyone Lived the Sexual Ethic of Jesus?" October 6, 2018, seanmcdowell.org/blog/what-if-everyone-lived-the-sexual-ethic-of-jesus (accessed April 19, 2021).

51. J. D. Vance, *Hillbilly Elegy: A Memoir of a Family and Culture in Crisis* (New York: HarperCollins, 2016), 158ff. Similar descriptions

are given in Ericka Andersen's work, *Leaving Cloud Nine: The True Story of a Life Resurrected from the Ashes of Poverty, Trauma, and Mental Illness* (Nashville: Thomas Nelson, 2018). Andersen tells the story of her husband, Rick, who was raised in a dysfunctional family resulting from America's sexual ethics. He and his sister were constantly shuffled from place to place, facing poverty, drugs, alcohol, and rejection each time. Such mistreatment of children creates massive amounts of PTSD, which may remain with these children for the rest of their lives.

52. "Dear Gay Community: Your Kids Are Hurting," *The Federalist*, March 17, 2015, thefederalist.com/2015/03/17/dear-gay-community-your-kids-are-hurting (accessed April 8, 2021).

53. As Michael W. Hannon, "Against Heterosexuality," *First Things*, March 2014, suggests that Christians lost the LGBTQ+ argument when we conceded that there is such a thing as "homosexuality," rather than standing on the obvious: there are merely people with different desires. Hannon finds an unlikely ally in none other than Michel Foucault—the founder of postmodernism, who himself practiced same-sex activity (or as he called it, "sodomy"). Foucault demonstrated that both heterosexuality and homosexuality were mere social constructs invented by Western thinkers searching for a way to bolster the traditional family without appealing to the Christian teachings. Hannon quotes Foucault: "Homosexuality appeared as one of the forms of sexuality, when it was transposed from the practice of sodomy onto a kind of interior androgyny, a hermaphrodism of the soul. The sodomite had been a temporary aberration; the homosexual was now a species." Even Gore Vidal agreed with Foucault, as quoted by Hannon: "Actually, there is no such thing as a homosexual person, any more than there is such a thing as a heterosexual person."

54. United States Supreme Court, Murphy v Ramsey (1885), quoted in John R. Vile, *The First Amendment Encyclopedia*, mtsu.edu/first-amendment/article/492/murphy-v-ramsey (accessed June 1, 2021).

55. "Between Man and Woman: Questions and Answers About Marriage and Same-Sex Unions," United States Conference of Catholic Bishops, usccb.org/committees/promotion-defense-marriage/between-man-and-woman-questions-and-answers-about-marriage (accessed June 1, 2021).

56. Linda Chavez, "Homosexuality and the Moral Order," *First Things*, April 1993, 15.

57. See the studies by Robert A. J. Gagnon, *The Bible and Homosexual Practice: Texts and Hermeneutics* (Nashville: Abingdon, 2001) and Kevin DeYoung, *What Does the Bible Teach about Homosexuality?* (Wheaton, IL: Crossway, 2015). See also the more popular books of Wesley Hill, *Washed and Waiting: Reflections on Christian Faithfulness and Homosexuality* (Grand Rapids: Zondervan, 2010), Sam Allberry, *Is God Anti-Gay? And Other Questions about Homosexuality, the Bible and Same-Sex Attraction* (London: The Good Book Company, 2013), and Jackie Hill Perry, *Gay Girl, Good God: The Story of Who I Was and Who God Has Always Been* (Nashville: B&H Publishing, 2018). An austere assessment of same-sex activity is offered by The Reformed Church in the United States in their book *Promoting a Biblical Sexual Morality* (The Synod of the Reformed Church in the United States, 2013).

58. "Fr. Martin's False Comfort," *First Things*, August 28, 2018, firstthings.com/web-exclusives/2018/08/fr-martins-false-comfort (accessed April 8, 2021). There are other stories of persons leaving LGBTQ+ lifestyles behind for the sake of Christ. See, for example, Rachel Gilson, *Born Again: Coming Out, Coming to Faith, and What Comes Next* (London: The Good Book Company, 2020).

59. Jody L. Herman, Andrew R. Flores, Kathryn K. O'Neill, "How Many Adults and Youth Identify as Transgender in the United States?" *Williams Institute*, June 2022, williamsinstitute.law.ucla.edu/publications/trans-adults-united-states (accessed October 28, 2022).

60. For a Christian view of transgenderism, see Mark Yarhouse, *Understanding Gender Dysphoria: Navigating Transgender Issues in a*

Changing Culture (Downer's Grove, IL: IVP, 2015), Andrew T. Walker, *God and the Transgender Debate: What Does the Bible Actually Say About Gender Identity?* (London: The Good Book Company, 2017) and Preston Sprinkle, *Embodied: Transgender Identities, the Church, and What the Bible Has to Say* (Colorado Springs: David C. Cook, 2021).

61. Nigel Barber, "Gender Differences of Animals," *Psychology Today*, October 1, 2019, psychologytoday.com/us/blog/the-human-beast/201910/gender-differences-animals (accessed May 29, 2021).

62. Paul McHugh, "Transgenderism: A Pathogenic Meme" *The Public Discourse*, June 10, 2015, thepublicdiscourse.com/2015/06/15145 (accessed May 28, 2021).

63. For an excellent discussion of this as it relates to church and family, I recommend Renée Sproles, *On Gender: What the Bible Says About Men and Women and Why It Matters* (Nashville: Renew.org, 2019).

64. Paul McHugh, "Transgender Surgery Isn't the Solution," *Wall Street Journal,* May 13, 2016, wsj.com/articles/paul-mchugh-transgender-surgery-isnt-the-solution-1402615120 (accessed May 28, 2021).

65. Paul McHugh, "Transgenderism."

66. You can hear my acquaintance's story at Brandon Redler, "Transgender in the Church," *International Teaching Ministry of Douglas Jacoby*, douglasjacoby.com/transgender-in-the-church-brandon-redler (accessed May 29, 2021).

67. *The Epistle of Mathetes to Diognetus*, *Ante-Nicene Fathers*: Vol. 1 (Albany: The Ages Digital Library, Version 2.0), 57–58.

68. Rosaria Champagne Butterfield, *The Gospel Comes with a House Key: Practicing Radically Ordinary Hospitality in Our Post-Christian World* (Wheaton, IL: Crossway, 2018), 14.

69. Rod Dreher, *Benedict Option*, 130–34.

70. See Rod Dreher, *Live Not By Lies*, 4–6, 171–74. Dreher describes the power that small groups had in preserving the church in

Eastern Europe during persecution. See also Nik Ripken, *The Insanity of Obedience* (Nashville: B&H Books, 2014), 189–195.

71. "Church Discipline Rarely Occurs, New Research Finds," *Lifeway Research*, April 5, 2018, lifewayresearch.com/2018/04/05/church-discipline-rarely-occurs-new-research-finds (accessed June 1, 2021).

72. Dietrich Bonhoeffer, *The Cost of Discipleship* (New York City: McMillan Publishing Company, 1963), 170.

73. William A. Foster, *Christian Heroes and Martyrs* (Philadelphia: Charles Foster Publishing Co, 1895), 41.

74. From Herbert Cane, *A Concise History of the Christian World Mission*, 20, quoting Will Durant, *Caesar and Christ* (New York: Simon and Schuster, 1944), 602.

75. Steve Murrell, *WikiChurch: Making Discipleship Engaging, Empowering, and Viral* (Lake Mary, FL: Charisma House, 2011), 141–42.

76. Cf., Jason Houser, Bobby Harrington, Chad Harrington, *Dedicated: Training Your Children to Trust and Follow Jesus* (Grand Rapids: Zondervan, 2015).

77. William A. Foster, *Christian Heroes and Martyrs* (Philadelphia: Charles Foster Publishing Co, 1895), 41.

78. St Jerome, Letter 127.12, "To Principia," *Nicene and Post-Nicene Fathers*: Series II, vol. 6 (Albany: The Ages Digital Library, Version 2.0), 575.

79. Augustine, *The City of God*, 14.28, *Nicene and Post-Nicene Fathers*: Series I, vol. 2 (Albany: The Ages Digital Library, Version 2.0), 608

80. *The City of God* 1.7, *Nicene and Post-Nicene Fathers*: Series I, vol. 2 (Albany: The Ages Digital Library, Version 2.0), 28.

81. Rod Dreher, *The Benedict Option*, 117–19.

82. "WORLD Magazine announces 2018 Daniel of the Year," *BizWire.com*, gsabizwire.com/world-magazine-announces-2018-daniel-of-the-year, accessed April 19, 2021.

83. David J. Bosch, *Transforming Mission* (Maryknoll, NY: Orbis Books, 1991), 2–3.

84. *The Church as the People of God*, quoted in Alan Hirsch, *The Forgotten Ways: Reactivating the Missional Church* (Grand Rapids: Brazos Press, 2006), 15.

85. Augustine, *The City of God* 18.51, translated by Henry Bettenson (London: Penguin, 1984), 835.